Beyond the Politics of Disappointment?

Beyond the Politics of Disappointment? American Elections, 1980–1998

Wilson Carey McWilliams
Rutgers University

CHATHAM HOUSE PUBLISHERS

SEVEN BRIDGES PRESS, LLC

NEW YORK • LONDON

Seven Bridges Press, LLC
135 Fifth Avenue
New York, NY 10010-7101

Publisher: Robert J. Gormley
Managing Editor: Katharine Miller
Production Supervisor: Melissa A. Martin
Cover Design: Andrea Barish Design
Composition: ediType
Printing and Binding: Versa Press, Inc.

Library of Congress Cataloging-in-Publication Data
McWilliams, Wilson C.
    Beyond the politics of disappointment? : American elections,
1980-1998 / Wilson Carey McWilliams.
        p. cm.
    Includes bibliographical references (p.) and index.
    ISBN 1-889119-18-0
    1. United States – Politics and government – 1981-1989. 2. United
States – Politics and government – 1989-1993. 3. United
States – Politics and government – 1993- 4. Presidents – United
States – Election. 5. Elections – United States – History – 20th
century. I. Title.
E876.M434   1999
324.973'092 – dc21   99-6789
                                                                      CIP

Manufactured in the United States of America
10   9   8   7   6   5   4   3   2   1

*This book is for two exemplary political educators
who never missed a chance to cast a ballot,
my grandmother, Harriet McWilliams (1874–1958),
a lifelong Republican in a family of Democrats,
and my mother, Dorothy McWilliams (1905–1972),
who voted for every Democrat
from Al Smith to George McGovern.*

Contents

Preface

The accounts in this book appeared before or not too long after the elections they describe. In retrospect, my reflections and interpretations sometimes read pretty well, and sometimes they are very wrong. I have left them all as they were written, adding some notes where hindsight seems to require them, because my errors of judgment say at least as much about the problem of narrating elections as the instances where I get things right. And I may look better because this edition begins with Ronald Reagan's victory in 1980; my analysis of the election of 1976, which opened the first edition, was often off the mark, if not the target. The decision to begin with 1980, however, has justifications beyond saving face and space: Reagan's election symbolized the beginning of an era, post-Vietnam and post-Watergate, but scarred by both, from which America just may be beginning to emerge.

The treatments of the presidential elections of 1980–1996 were originally printed in a series of volumes edited by my matchless colleague, Gerald M. Pomper. The first of these books, *The Election of 1976*, was published by David McKay, Inc.; subsequent volumes were all published by Chatham House; the entire series, along with this book, was guided by the late Edward Artinian, an excellent observer of politics and political science, an invaluable publisher, and an even better friend. The concluding chapter on the election of 1998 and the impeachment crisis draws heavily on essays I wrote at the time for *Commonweal*, to whose editors I owe continually mounting debts.

I first wrote seriously about national elections as a junior coauthor with my teacher, John H. Schaar, whose craft and wisdom and knowledge of things American are so remarkable that they rival his gift for friendship. Among many intellectual and personal debts, I am grateful to Dennis Bathory, Myron Aronoff, Ross K. Baker, and my other colleagues at Rutgers University, to Dennis Hale and Marc Landy at Boston College, Bruce L. Payne at Duke University, and Nancy L. Schwartz at Wesleyan, to Henry Plotkin and Judge Florence Riley, and to two former and two current members of Congress — the late Allard Lowenstein, Don Pease, David Price, and Barney Frank — as well as to Attorney General Bill Lockyer in California, for exemplifying honor in public office. And I owe the most important things — patience and prodding and joy among them — to my wife Nancy and my daughters Helen and Susan, all great observers and grand partisans.

CHAPTER ONE
Introduction

After having believed ourselves capable of transforming ourselves, we now believe ourselves incapable of improving ourselves; after having had an excessive pride, we have fallen into a humility that is just as excessive; we thought that we could do everything, and now we think that we can do nothing.... This, to put it simply, is the great malaise of our age....

— Alexis de Tocqueville,
Letter to Arthur de Gobineau, 20 December 1853

This book chronicles almost two decades of American elections marked by a politics of disappointment. In retrospect, Vietnam and Watergate — those symbols of disillusionment — seem only events in a much longer story. America, in the twenty years after World War II, had pains and oppressions to spare, but compared with our times, it also had a broader sphere of commonality, at least among whites, and a greater assurance that the future held something better. Otherwise very diverse Americans — conservatives like Governor Kirk Fordice of Mississippi and neoliberals like Mickey Kaus of the *New Republic* — treat the 1950s as a kind of standard; millions of others, unexpectedly, found themselves mourning Richard Nixon, a symbol of that decade who had preserved its style and tone like a beetle in amber.[1]

There have been good, even triumphant moments since, but most Americans, looking backward, find it hard not to see a long, slow slide: real wages declining, society deteriorating, gaps widening between old and young and rich and poor, the hopeful integrationism of the civil rights movement turned into a bitter politics of race. Even victory in the Cold War has resulted in international disorder, new threats, and few visible dividends.[2] Briefly, Carter, Bush, and Clinton roused hopes, and Ronald Reagan had a longer, more disastrous run, but all fell short of America's probably unrealizable expectations.

That experience has helped make Americans more distrustful of government, their leaders, and one another — a part of democracy's curriculum, but one that too many citizens are exaggerating into a whole.[3] Politically, there are almost no illusions to be shattered, except for the notion that nothing much can be achieved through politics. The only thing we have left to disappoint, Franklin Roosevelt might have said, is disappointment itself.

Even social conservatives, the most visible political crusaders of recent years, are turning away from the political grail, frustrated by America's easy tolerance and preoccupation with well-being. And the Clinton administration, its dignity in rags, is going out with a bang, in Yugoslavia and Iraq, that seems very much like a whimper.

But when the standard is lowered, it gets easier to get passing grades: Bill Clinton's persistently good job ratings reflect the country's comparative prosperity, but also the fact that the president — and with him, the government — is no longer being held to an heroic measure. If democratic public life meets these lessened expectations, it may start to build its nearly exhausted credit.[4] High time: great numbers of Americans are looking for *someone* to take charge of the issues than rankle, and especially to patch the damage done to the social fabric by the dynamism of economics and technology. The great majority of us — some wistful, some raging — yearn for a renewal of the promise of American life, and reflecting on the recent past may help us mark the new limits and possibilities of that old dream.

•

Elections are central to our kind of democracy and have come to be regarded, almost everywhere, as a sine qua non of any legitimate government: "Every people, big or small," Mikhail Gorbachev told Stephen Cohen, "should have free elections."[5] But according to Aristotle, the ancient Greeks associated elections with oligarchy or aristocracy, since they presume that some are better qualified to rule than others. Democratic principles, by contrast, point toward selection by lot, since among equals, one is as good as another.[6] In that older view, democracy presumes citizens who share in rule, participating in sovereign deliberation if not by holding office. Democratic citizenship demands having a say, not merely a vote.

The American framers, on the other hand, while holding consent to be the foundation of just governance, despised ancient democracy as too weak and too turbulent.[7] Convinced that the mass of citizens were unqualified to rule, they regarded them as capable of calling rulers to account.[8] In the framers' version of democracy, citizens act by choosing representatives; the few speak, the many vote.[9] Yet while their usage allows for our large-scale democratic republic with its much-praised diversities, by emphasizing will at the expense of speech, it also entails a political problem.

Elections, constitutional forms, necessarily afford an "unfinished and distorted picture" of political life.[10] They record the preferences of voters, but ignore their motives and reasons, reducing all voters to identical quantities and awarding victory to the greatest number. Voting totals level the wise and the foolish, the passionate and the indifferent, just as they overlook differences of power. Even the equation of the majority with greater force, Locke argued, holds only in a state of nature where such distinctions, for the most part, have not made themselves felt: in civil society, majority rule is an artifice that depends on the good will — moral or interested — of strong and skilled minorities, and hence on the self-restraint of the many.[11]

Elections are at most the tip of the political iceberg. They simplify and organize opinion and, under ordinary circumstances, they provide an unambiguous outcome, but at the price of obscuring the existential variety of political experience and opinion. In George V. Higgins's novel, *Victories,* a retiring congressman, Henry Briggs, also a former major-league pitcher, remarks that statistically, pitchers — like elected officials — get credit for a "win" that is made up of the efforts of a team:

> So how many victories are there in a game or an election? Probably, I think, as many as there are people who took part. So who knows what victories really are, then? What they mean, if they mean anything?[12]

Higgins's feeling for democratic politics is as sure as his ear for dialogue. The meaning of an election lies in the relation between electoral quantities and human qualities, convention and nature. Elections, in other words, are occasions for narration, and the need to tell their story rightly poses a decisive test for our political life and art.

In recent years, of course, American democracy has been through some rough innings. Startlingly few potential voters make it to the polls, reflecting a long-term drift away from the ballot box; too many citizens pay little attention to politics and seem disposed to dismiss our institutions, cursorily, as inept or dominated by special interests.[13] For a multitude of Americans, the political story barely touches personal drama: elections seem radically separated from the dilemmas and aspirations of everyday life.

Not that this is particularly surprising: citizenship, after all, is an acquired taste or discipline. For the most part, people are drawn to politics by private motives, and only later develop public ones — "first by necessity," runs Tocqueville's axiom, "afterwards by choice."[14] Yet this progression presumes that, in the first place, we see our interests as crucially involved with politics and public policy, and second, that the experience of politics offers us something *beyond* interest — the dignity of being recognized and heard, the warmth of political friendship, and ultimately, the possibility of noble deeds and the good life.[15] Yet all of this rests on the citizen's involvement with community and face-to-face associations, and the scale and complexity of our political life is systematically reducing the importance of local politics and personal participation.[16]

Formally, elections offer self-government; existentially, citizens encounter dependence and vulnerability, an exposure to organized power and technological changes — little understood and less subject to personal control — that are shattering and reshaping communities and relationships.[17] Citizens expect government to address these problems, but to be effective in taking on the forces of the time, government must *mirror* them, becoming caught up in the intricacies of technique and power. The result is a two-tier politics in which the world of the governing elites is increasingly removed from that of ordinary citizens. And it is only to be expected that numbers of those citizens will turn away, if only in a despairing assertion of dignity.

Moreover, that so many Americans rely so much on particular governmental policies encourages efforts to define such programs as "rights," subject to administrative and judicial authority but protected against majority opinion.[18] More and more politics, consequently, becomes extra-electoral, limiting the impact of votes and elections and contributing to frustration and disillusionment with the public aspects of democratic life.[19]

Even when government works, it reminds voters — and not always subtly — of their dependence on it, so that any perceived failure is an invitation to indignation. The anger of Americans at government, however, is a mark of their need for it. Less government would not "empower" citizens: it would only leave them subject to the dominations and powers of the market, technology, and international society. By contrast, the Republican landslide in the election of 1994, displacing Democrats from congressional seats that had seemed impregnable, showed that the public *has* power over government and in politics. But our dependence on government makes it a target for resentment, especially in a liberal society historically suspicious of the public sector.[20] Still, elections are at least a sort of catharsis, and the results in 1994 were an argument — vaguely heard, but so far, not much attended — for reforging the links between government and citizen.

Historically, that chain has been best provided by party, but part of the story in these essays is the on-going dilapidation of local party organizations and the broader but related problem of the parties' weakening hold on the electorate. With the ascendancy of the primary system and the declining ability of party organizations to filter candidates, the nominating process — and hence, electoral choice — is more and more defined and determined by the media and by money.[21] In political calculations, cultivating elites counts for more, and developing personal relationships with ordinary voters for less: American politics, like the American economy, is becoming increasingly capital intensive rather than labor intensive.[22] The centralized, national bureaucracies of the major parties wax as their reserves of loyalty among voters wane. In rising numbers, Americans are wishing a plague on both the houses of party.[23]

This trend toward disaffiliation leaves a growing slice of the electorate politically unmoored, its opinions more volatile and open to influence, yet guarded and self-protective; campaigns are more important, more expensive, and more apt to be cast in essentially private terms.[24] Holding Democrats responsible for their discontents with Congress, the president, and government in general, voters in 1994 made a sort of bow in the direction of party government and accountability, but one that was largely negative, inarticulate, and without commitment. In 1998, the electorate delivered a similar rebuke to congressional Republicans — less significant in terms of the number of seats involved, but sharply felt because it was so unexpected; whether it was a portent remains to be seen.

To many observers — Newt Gingrich was strident back in 1994 — recent elections signal that the "information revolution" is creating a new and vigorous civil society that allows for and demands the transfer of power from government to ordinary citizens. In its broadest form, this argument is simply silly. Advances in technology bring resources, but they do not democratize: new skills and sources of power may unsettle old elites, but they also create new ones, and the mass public gains a fair command of such new techniques only after they have been superseded.[25]

It seems likely that essentially abstract interactions in "virtual reality" will prove as inadequate as "virtual representation" did to Americans in 1776, and as incapable of eliciting deep allegiance. Effective political action calls for the aggregation of mass opinion, and while the new technologies make it possible to gather opinion more quickly and in greater volume, they also make it more transient and reduce the likelihood that any individual opinion will receive serious consideration.[26] So far, moreover, the possibilities for interaction remain largely unrealized: associational "membership" solicited by direct mail or electronic communication comes down, pretty much, to the decision to contribute money, since for the most part, members do not deliberate about policy or even vote for officers. And while the "talk shows," elite managed, can mobilize rage, they cannot offer dignity; the sources of dignity and identity are local, like Tip O'Neill's politics. Any political renewal for American democracy will have to be founded on a "host of little democracies," the revitalization of local parties and civic life.[27] Of course, such a rebirth is a long shot at best; what is certain is the passing of the old order.

A major thread connecting these essays is the emergence of what originally was called the "social issue," a debate over the shape and future of American culture rivaling class and economic policy as the preeminent basis of political conflict.[28] Contemporary writers have been apt to treat this "cultural politics" as something new, and so it has been, in a sense. The election of 1972 was a portent: the great Democratic majority, already shaken by the conflict between "hawks" and "doves" over Vietnam (and foreign policy generally), was further divided by the alliance between George McGovern and the "counterculture," and today's Republicans are as eager to remind voters of that year as Democrats are to forget it.

On a broader view, however, the politics of culture is no new story, but part of an old one. American politics has always been shaped by the question of who and what is American. The relationship between culture and citizenship — like the tension between American ways and America's appeal to natural rights — has always been a quarrel more than a given. (It is worth remembering, in fact, that aliens were once allowed to vote in as many as twenty two states.[29]) And at bottom, it is the argument between insiders and outsiders over the qualifications for full and dignified membership in the American polity that has shaped and reshaped our partisan lines of division.[30]

Economic distinctions are a vital part of that history, of course, since economic inequality — especially the extreme disparity that exists in the United States — is a standing threat to political equality.[31] But in the voting booth, differences of wealth and class are potent to the extent that they are indices of dignity, touchstones of civic rank and membership.[32] Economic interests alone will be decisive only when conditions seem overwhelming, as they did during the Great Depression or, in a much milder way, in 1992.[33] Even then, when we vote, our ideas about the direction of the economy as a whole are apt to outweigh our immediate circumstances. Political life is defined by our attachment to groups and to values more than by self-interest, narrowly defined, so that "politics often resembles the world of religion more closely than the world of economics."[34]

For a century after the Civil War, American party politics was framed by the conflict that ranged a Republican Party that was predominantly Protestant, middle-class, and northern against the Democrats' fractious coalition of outsiders, with its strength in the white South and the ethnic minorities of the North — the G.A.R.'s Main Street defending its America against a party rooted in "rum, Romanism, and rebellion."[35] That cultural divide began to blur with the gradual reassimilation of the South and the slow acceptance of Catholics and other white ethnics, both processes edged along by the fading of memory and the increasing restiveness of African Americans. The signs of strain on the party system were visible in the 1920s, becoming full-blown with the politics of civil rights that succeeded World War II, and by 1960 the election of John Kennedy symbolized — though a lot of battles remained and remain to be fought — the transformation of the old America.[36] And that, pretty much, is where this book begins.

Now, the Solid South is a matter for historians, and among whites, ethnic distinctions — still potent here and there — are collapsing as social barriers. Precipitately, American political memory is becoming "vaguer and more fabulous." With a straight face, Newt Gingrich invoked Franklin Roosevelt, and New York Governor George Pataki (also confusing two Sumners, the radical Charles and the Social Darwinist, William Graham) claimed to find inspiration for his effort to shrink government in Theodore Roosevelt, who — as Mencken saw, closer to first-hand — favored "a paternalism concerning itself with all things, from the regulation of coal-mining and meat-packing to . . . spelling and marital rights."[37] And that rewriting of the past is, pretty much, an epitaph for the old party politics.

Traditionally, the divisions of cultural politics loosely follow those of class; today, the two lines of conflict show some tendency to diverge and often seem to be at odds.[38] In circles, the prevailing vision of cultural combat pits the privileged order against the marginalized perspectives of race, class, and gender. But in emphasis — and certainly, in the media's translation of this teaching — class gets short shrift: white, European males and those who identify with them stand opposed to women, racial minorities, and homosexuals, a distinction that evidently cuts across class lines. And it does not help that contemporary cultural elites, devoted to fairly radical versions of personal liberty, are at least suspicious of the repressive potential of the decencies: they take fewer pains than the economic elite to disguise their contempt for the culture of the many, inviting a resentment that makes the cultural divide unusually potent in shaping political attitudes and affiliations.[39]

Our older cultural debates were conducted, for the most part, in a decisively *public* language; challenges to the dominant culture were cast in terms of the American creed, especially the Declaration's proclamation of human equality.[40] That rhetoric, with its appeal from convention to nature, still echoes in American political speech, but more and more contemporary argument — influenced by relativism and, most fashionably, by postmodernism — is inclined to slight equality and commonality in favor of the view that political identities and ideas reflect the plural perspectives of groups, and particularly, their relationship to power. In an increasingly specialized society, where public spaces are threatened and public life is rare, any unraveling of political speech encourages the fragmentation of associations and parties, and hence the ability of the "individually powerless many" to unite against the few.[41]

Two-party systems offer voters the clearest choice and the easiest means of holding government accountable, but they also presume that public opinion can be organized around some basic antithesis, some issue or concern perceived as sufficiently fundamental to unite those who stand on the same side and to override their differences. In that sense, all two-party politics is a single issue politics that suppresses other divisions, the kind of conflict that sparks analogies between politics and war.[42]

On any given issue, two-party politics is natural, even inevitable, since every policy "implies a choice between two kinds of solution."[43] The broader the scope of politics, however, the more likely it is that it will include sets of antitheses that cut across and challenge the two-party line between political allies and enemies.[44] The long-term expansion of the reach of government, consequently, inherently threatens the kind of simplification that two-party politics presumes and requires. Our growing discontent with the two major parties, in other words, is only to be expected. In fact, given the diverging relationship between economics and culture, American opinion might suggest *four* parties rather than three: the division between Democrats and Republicans, for and against government intervention in the economy, is virtually bisected by the distinction between those who support government intervention in moral and social life and those who oppose it. Republican libertarians sit as uneasily with cultural conservatives as Democratic liberals do with populist egalitarians.[45]

But the winner-take-all form of our electoral system rules out third [and even more, fourth] parties, except in the very short term. With the partial exception of the Socialists early in this century, no American third party has managed to make a good showing in two successive elections; Ross Perot did passably in 1996, but his support did not approach his 1992 total and he was never more than a marginal factor in the election. Voters hate to waste their votes if they see even a hair's-breadth of difference between leading candidates, and the major parties can be counted on to strengthen this logic by incorporating at least some of the appeals of any significant third party. Presuming that the electoral system remains as it is — and there is no serious movement to change it — a successful third party does not end the two-party system: it forces a redefinition of that system, and then passes, more or less gracefully, from the political scene. Still, Governor Jesse Ventura of Minnesota is bound to inspire comparisons to Spartacus, who shook the foundations of Rome.

What is certain is that American party politics is entering a new era. The age of the New Deal and the American century, virtual twins, are ending together — great, flawed times, and worth regretting, but sliding into memory. Bill Clinton's New Democrats are happy with their synthesis of social liberalism, technophilia, and sympathy for business; Republican leaders, sensing discontent among traditional Democrats, are trying out Populist themes. In American political history, the birth of a new party alignment, as Walter Dean Burnham observed, has ordinarily resulted from a "spasm" on the part of those middle-American voters who are "normally content to be traditionalists or passive participants in electoral politics."[46] The election of 1994 showed some of the signs, but it involved too few voters and left too many Americans on the outside, unhappy with both alternatives and waiting for an engaging political story. The future shape of American politics, so far, presents itself to us only in hints and shadows.

It will challenge our crafts of state to ensure that any new narrative is worthy of American democracy. Great stakes are involved: the quality and the very possibility of self-government, the question of whether — or how much — democracy can be anything other than the plaything of titanic forces. Even approaching that question side-on will test our parties and our government; even more fundamentally, it will test us. We can only hope Robert Frost was right:

> Our very life depends on everything's
> Recurring till we answer from within.
> The thousandth time may prove the charm. . . . [47]

CHAPTER TWO

Presidential Leadership and Changing Parties
The Election of 1980

Ronald Reagan's election in 1980 seemed like a revolution to most observers, and so it was in many ways. I was more impressed by the continuities. Watergate, coming on the heels of Vietnam, had shaken confidence in government, and in 1976 Jimmy Carter had been elected as an opponent of "big government" and a champion of deregulation. Moreover, Carter — a moderate social liberal, with a good record on race relations — was a "born-again" Christian, an exemplar of traditional faith and morals. And as a candidate, Carter's strength lay in the South, momentarily returned to Democratic allegiance. His administration had its successes, the most showy being the Camp David accords brokered between Menachem Begin and Anwar Sadat, but it was damaged by "stagflation" and events such as the oil boycott of 1979 and, most hurtfully, the seizure of the American embassy in Teheran. Moreover, Carter never had the grace of rhetoric. His election, however, had itself indicated — just as his administration had deepened — the electorate's uneasy disenchantment.

⇒●((●))●⇐

Stand fast in your enchantments and your many sorceries, with which you have labored from your youth; perhaps you may be able to succeed, perhaps you may inspire terror.
—Isaiah 47:12

It didn't mean much. The election of 1980 did not try our souls; it tried our patience. Matthew Josephson's description of the election of 1880 applied a century later: "the indifference of the public seems as marked as the excitement of the professionals seems feigned."[1]

Reagan had a zealous following and there were some Carter loyalists, but most voters saw little to recommend either. Carter was a humorless bungler and Reagan was an amiable simpleton, "the Ted Baxter of American politics."[2] Even the enthusiasm for John Anderson was negative, deriving from distaste for the major-party nominees. A good many voters marked their ballots in a mood of revulsion, and masses of citizens stayed home. The majority of voters finally decided, probably on the basis of the presidential debate, that Reagan was not so kooky as to keep them from gratifying their desire to be rid of Carter. Reagan will have four years to try his hand, but Americans stopped believing in progress in 1980, and few of them feel any confidence in the new experiment. That is the central meaning of the election of 1980.[3]

The election does have other things to tell us. In the first place, the election of 1980 made it clear that the primary-dominated system of nomination is an unqualified disaster. Second, among Democrats, the old Roosevelt coalition is yielding to something we can call the Kennedy coalition. Third, conservative Republicanism is experiencing its own, analogous change, and conservatism may find victory more painful than defeat. The election may, of course, prove to have far more profound and far-reaching consequences for American politics, but no such portents are visible. We will have to wait and see.

The Failure of the Primaries

In 1980 there were more primaries than ever and a record number of voters participated in choosing the candidates. Yet, in a seeming paradox, the result was radically unpopular. By any standard, the primaries failed as a method of choosing presidential candidates.

Primaries have been around since the Progressive era; but until the last decade, nominations resulted from a mixed system in which most delegates were chosen by state conventions and candidates tried to show popular appeal in a few, carefully selected contests. In 1948, for example, Thomas E. Dewey was able to offset Harold Stassen's string of primary victories by defeating him in Oregon after a debate, heard nationwide, in which Dewey opposed and Stassen advocated outlawing the Communist Party.[4] Similarly, when John F. Kennedy defeated Hubert H. Humphrey in West Virginia in 1960, he dispelled the fear that his Catholicism would be a fatal liability in Protestant areas, or at least lessened such anxieties enough to let him win the nomination. But primaries, if often decisive, were only one part of the nominating process. Adlai Stevenson was drafted at the 1952 Democratic convention, and as late as 1968, Humphrey was nominated without seriously contesting, let alone winning, any primaries. Humphrey's victory, however, was *finis:* the disastrous Chicago convention of 1968 set in motion the torrent of reform. Since 1968, the number of primaries has roughly doubled, and about three-fourths of the delegates are now chosen in primary elections.

The record of the new, primary-dominated system is not impressive. Since the election of 1968, not one first-rate person has been nominated for president. It could easily be argued that Richard Nixon was the most able of the major-party nominees. Of course, the old system sometimes selected mediocrities. The choice between Harding and Cox in 1920 was at least as limited as our options in 1980. Yet in the eighteen presidential elections between 1900 and 1968, only ten nominations went to candidates who are even arguably second-rate.[5] Twenty-six major-party nominations went to evidently first-rate people. For the "smoke-filled room," mediocrity was the *exception*; for the primary-dominated system, it has been the *rule*.

The primaries fail because they are based on the assumption that voting in elections is the essence of democracy. At most, however, voting is the *final* act of the democratic process, deciding between alternatives that have been defined by some sort of deliberation.

Voting forces a decision. Our choices are limited, and *the more limited they are*, the more clearly we know the consequences of our choice. If there are two candidates, by voting for one I am voting against the other. But if there are three serious candidates (as it briefly seemed there might be in 1980), if I vote for Anderson, it is not at all clear that I am voting against Reagan and Carter. If I hate Carter and would prefer Reagan, then I am helping Carter by voting for Anderson. Added alternatives make voting complicated and confusing.

This is especially true since my vote is *irrevocable*. I cannot take it back once I see which way the wind is blowing or after I have second thoughts. If I could change my vote, third candidates would not be so confusing; I could vote for a third-party candidate and wait to see if he or she could make a race of it. If not, I could fall back on one of the front-runners. As it is, however, voting encourages us to narrow our alternatives, concentrating on the two leading candidates so that the meaning of our vote is clear: for *A*, against *B*. Even with a more or less proportional distribution of delegates, so that one does not "throw away" a vote for a third candidate, this narrowing tendency is evident in the primaries. In the last stages of this year's campaign, only two candidates remained in each party. An election aims at a clear and irrevocable decision and encourages voters to limit their alternatives.

Deliberation, by contrast, attempts to define the terms of choice rather than to decide between them. In deliberating, we value all the complications and flexibilities that elections aim to rule out. We want to avoid limiting our choices prematurely. We want to consider all possible alternatives — all the candidates who might run, for example, not merely those who have announced so far. Similarly, deliberation encourages the exchange of views; it values second thoughts, changed minds, and modified opinions. It is not enough to express our opinions; we need a chance to respond to other opinions. This response is more than "compromise"; it involves the chance for considered judgment, rendered after weighing (and counting) the opinions of others. We want the best chance to refine our thinking before decision; hence, *Robert's Rules of Order* allows a minority to keep debate open. And even after we decide, *Robert's Rules* allows us, with appropriate constraints, the chance to reconsider. Finally, deliberation aims at agreement or broad consensus, hoping that discussion will obviate the need for decision. Deliberation, then, puts off decisions, multiplies alternatives, permits considered judgment, and strives for consensus.

In nominating a candidate for president, only one vote is *necessary,* the final ballot of the party's convention. All the rest of the process, although it involves decisions to select delegates in the several states, is or ought to be deliberative. Evidently, the party's most authoritative decision only establishes an alternative for the voters in the general election. The nomination is the last step in a process of deliberation and the first step of a contest leading to an electoral decision.

The primary-dominated system, by contrast, all but displaces deliberation. In the first place, primary elections limit us because they demand *early* decisions by candidates. It is quite possible that a majority of Democrats in 1980 would have preferred some candidate other than President Carter or Senator Kennedy. "The voters don't want us," a Carter loyalist told me on the eve of the Florida primary, "but they don't want *them* even more." A great many Republican voters would have preferred President Ford to Ronald Reagan, including a great many who preferred Reagan to George Bush. Ford himself was eager to prevent Reagan's nomination, and when it became likely, Ford offered to run himself. Ford, however, had delayed too long; he would not have been able to enter enough primaries to change the result. Possibly Ford was genuinely unwilling to run unless a Reagan nomination threatened; possibly he secretly hoped, all along, that the party would turn to him. In either case, Ford's experience in 1980 (and Senator Humphrey's in 1976) indicates that our primaries demand that candidates decide early. They cannot respond to events or change their minds.

The primaries thus deprive us of the most powerful argument for persuading excellent people to seek office: the fear that they will otherwise be ruled by second-raters or worse.[6] By the time that such a threat has become credible, it is likely to be too advanced to be evitable.

Similarly, early support matters much more than considered support. Since voters tend to choose between candidates they feel have a "real chance" of winning, a tide runs in favor of candidates who establish themselves as front-runners. Voters in early primaries have a disproportionate influence on events. Several big states (with about 20 percent of the convention delegates) voted on "Super Tuesday," 3 June, after the nominations were effectively decided. It would take away this advantage, of course, if we all voted on the same day, but then *only* early support would matter because voters would have no chance to react to or learn from the elections in other states.

In becoming a front-runner, established celebrities have an edge. Carter won as a dark horse in 1976, but he ran against a field of unknowns. It also helps to have an enthusiastic, ideological following. Even if you don't win, your zealots may keep you among the leaders. And you will have a good chance to win; primary voters are not representative of the party as a whole, and highly committed voters are likely to have disproportionate influence.[7] In the early primaries, moreover, against a fragmented opposition, an ideological following may enable a candidate to win with less than a majority, as Ronald Reagan often did in 1980. Senator George McGovern in 1972 won a similar victory by establishing himself as the candidate of the Democratic left. Senator Edmund Muskie, an acceptable second choice for almost all factions, was driven from the race. The primaries have small place for second choices, even though, like second thoughts, such selections are more likely to reflect a concern for the good of the whole.

The media, of course, play an enormous role in selecting front-runners. In the first place, media predictions tell voters where their "real choice" lies. More important, the media can create an important candidacy by coverage alone, as they certainly did with Congressman Anderson in 1980. The problem does not lie with the supposed ideological biases of the media; the worst distortions result from the desire to make political news exciting. Anderson was noteworthy in early Republican gatherings because he said strikingly different things. In 1972, by contrast, the press severely damaged Senator Muskie by focusing on his crying during a speech in Manchester, New Hampshire. Moreover, while it is important to win primaries, a victor must do "as well as expected" by the media, and a losing candidate who fares better than the polls predict may establish himself as a serious contender. A "good" loss inspires supporters in subsequent states, just as a "bad" victory dispirits them. Muskie lost ground by winning New Hampshire in 1972, and Senator Henry Jackson's candidacy could not survive his victory in New York in 1976. As James Ceaser writes, "the media love the story, which is to say that they tend to look for, and overplay, new and unexpected developments. Thus they turn politics into drama, rather than reporting on the drama of politics."[8] At their best, the media encourage us to react to more or less accurate images, which we have no means of checking.

In short, the primaries give special weight to initial support for candidates who enter early, they advantage ideological followings, and they emphasize media images. They discourage considered judgment and place no particular value on party coalitions. They violate all the requirements of deliberation in precisely that aspect of our electoral process — the choosing of nominees — where deliberateness is most needed.

The older system of precinct and ward caucuses, leading to county and state conventions, was, even at its worst, based on discussion and personal knowledge of the candidates. The deliberation that occurred was often crass, ungrammatical, and parochial, but it *was* deliberation for all that. It was based on local, face-to-face groups where real discussion and participation was possible and where people could select representatives who reflected the gamut of their views. The fault of the old system was simple: it shut people out. Party organizations were too often closed and unresponsive, denying citizens (and partisans) a role in an essential democratic process. But this shortcoming did not reflect on the convention system; it militated against excluding people *from* that system.

The logical reform would have been a more or less open caucus, similar to the present system in Iowa. Instead, the reform tradition insisted on a mass election where citizens cannot deliberate and in which control of such discussion as there is passes to the mass media.[9] Local party organizations and elites may have been discomfited, but at the cost of increasing the sway of far more powerful and less accessible elites, as Henry Jones Ford forecast long ago.[10] More of us vote in primaries, but our voices are not heard, and our vote says little about what we think, feel, and revere. Adding insult to injury, the primary system produces candidates who are unworthy. In 1980 voters made clear their distaste for the result; it is now up to their leaders to scrap the process.

Unfortunately, the primaries are probably here to stay. They are suited to liberal political theory, the "irrational Lockeanism" that dominates our thinking about public matters.[11] In liberal theory, human beings are not naturally political animals. They are isolated individuals, concerned to protect themselves and advance their essentially private interests. In this view, we have an interest in deciding who rules us, but no interest in ruling, since rule requires that we take time away from our private concerns. Self-government becomes government we *choose* rather than government in which we *participate,* and democracy is defined by elections, not deliberation. The primary system, which derives from liberal individualism, is compatible with all the forces that are fragmenting our communities, our political parties, and our public life. At best, we will try to "improve" the primaries, an endeavor that can inspire no confidence. These sadly limited efforts ignore the signs, evident in 1980, of a demand for politics and party government.

The Democrats: The Necessity of Party

For the Democrats, the election of 1980 was their worst defeat in a quarter century. The returns seem unambiguous; the Democratic Party was repudiated by an electorate that decided to "Vote Republican, For a Change." Yet even that statement must be qualified, given the peculiarities of the election.

Toward the end of his campaign, Jimmy Carter appealed more and more to party loyalties and the Democratic pantheon. A Democratic advertisement featured clips of Franklin Roosevelt, Harry Truman, and Jack Kennedy; Lady Bird Johnson and Muriel Humphrey said a few words. It was a celebration of tradition and an appeal to allegiance — and it came entirely too late.

For four years, Carter disdained the party and its organizations. He recognized that party loyalties — and especially, loyalties to party organizations — seemed to be attenuating, and he had no interest in reversing the decline. As Carter apparently saw it, the Democratic Party apparatus was simply a collection of more or less parochial interest groups, committed to inflationary policies and the expansion of the federal bureaucracy and tied to outdated patronage politics. It was part of the "establishment" Carter had opposed in 1976, which for the most part had opposed his nomination. He saw little to hope for from it, and he preferred to build a personal coalition devoted to policies deemed in the public interest, especially as defined by "good management" rather than politics. The personal note was ubiquitous; even the membership organization of the Democratic National Committee called itself "The President's Club."

In the first few months of his administration, Carter initiated a number of highly publicized ventures in direct contact with citizens designed to end the isolation of the Nixon years. He attended a "town meeting"; he answered telephone calls from voters, took notes on their questions, and called back with answers. It was undeniably good politics; the programs were popular, and they enlisted support. Yet they were allowed to lapse. The president evidently thought of them as symbolic gestures, a sort of political fluff to be sacrificed to the real, administrative demands of the presidency. He did not return to the town meeting, for example, until late in his administration.

The president thus scorned party, the traditional basis of support in Congress and the country, but he did not appeal to voters directly in any way sufficiently consistent and compelling to move reluctant members of Congress to his side. Rather half-heartedly, he did invoke the public on behalf of the "windfall profits tax" against the oil lobby, and even that lukewarm appeal contributed to one of the infrequent cases in which his program succeeded. Carter seemed to realize that one cannot successfully appeal to the public very often. He did not recognize, as great presidents always did, that this implies that recourse to the general public is most effective as the exception to a strategy of party government. Party, for all its faults, sometimes *may* move a member of Congress beyond immediate self-interest, which alone is enough to make it invaluable.

We need no encouragement, after all, to be self-interested and parochial. In a country as vast and diverse as the United States, the public interest is a distant abstraction. It may be that it is in my interest to help workers in Youngstown, but the connections that tie my interest to theirs are indirect, impalpable, and subtle. I know, by contrast, that it helps me to pay lower taxes.[12] If you tell me that it is in my interest to pay taxes to support those Ohio workers, I will need persuading. I know, too, that America is a changing, complexly interdependent society that no one fully understands. Even if your reasoning is ingenious, you might be wrong; it might make matters worse to try to help the workers in Youngstown. Moreover, you may not have my best interests at heart. Even presuming that you mean well, you may not understand or care about what matters to me.[13] Surely, I have done all I can be asked to do if I take care of my own. That, at least, is the way all of us are tempted to reason, and many of us submit. Allegiance, public spirit, and support for the common good are in perennial short supply.

Politics — participation and partisanship — are indispensable means for developing civic spirit. My participation in deliberation enlists my support because it makes me feel less helpless: I contribute to the shaping of decisions instead of simply reacting to events. Political participation involves us in, and teaches us to see, the life of a larger society. For most of us, participation can only be local. But even close to home, we can come to know — and possibly, to trust — the local leaders who carry our voice to larger tribunals. These days, of course, even local participation is the exception, although it could be encouraged, and local party organizations are in disarray. But, for most of us, party still gives us some sort of political identity and defines leaders we can trust, "men like ourselves," who can at least be relied on to share more of our basic values than their opponents. Party is still the safest source of trust between rulers and ruled.[14]

Jimmy Carter did more than spurn party; he seemed to violate that trust. Historically, the Democratic Party has stood for compassion and sympathy, for the refusal to allow human relations to be governed by the requirements of "efficiency" or "sound currency." The party's great rhetoric speaks to that commitment, from Bryan's "Cross of Gold" to Roosevelt's credo that "divine justice weighs the sins of the cold-blooded and the sins of the warm-hearted in different scales."[15] Carter's emphasis on management and quasi-monetarist fiscal policies was, at least, a new departure. In 1976, William Shannon wrote, Carter was "saying that government can be compassionate but also skeptical."[16] By 1980 the compassion seemed to have vanished. On the face of it, Carter had broken with Democratic tradition, and he needed politics and party in the *conduct of government*, not merely in campaigns, to persuade voters that he acted out of necessity and with fidelity to the party's heritage. By campaign time, it was too late, especially since Ronald Reagan was clearly a man of warm sympathies. Thomas Jefferson taught that "sentiment, not science" was the source of justice, and whatever else may be said about his argument, it speaks to democratic politics in general and the politics of the Democratic Party in particular.[17] Carter, neglecting Jefferson's maxim, helped seal his political doom.

For its part, Congress magnified all of Carter's faults. The horde of neophytes swept into office by Watergate were not elected by party organization, and most of them had run ahead of Carter in 1976. They owed the party little, and the president less. Carter's failures as a party and a legislative leader left all too many members of Congress disposed to play a lone hand, insisting — with fervor greater than that of the Moral Majority — on pure liberal ideology or following their favorite interest groups. It was an exceptionally unproductive Congress, especially given the energy crisis and our economic troubles. Of course, politically, it is easier to give than to take away, and social justice is a difficult goal in times of relative scarcity.[18] Even if we are generous on that account, however, Congress's record was barren.

A great many voters detested this Congress, not so much because it was liberal as because it was obstructive. If only the Congress had been Republican, Jimmy Carter could have tried to repeat Harry Truman's campaign against the "obstructionists" of the "do-nothing" 80th Congress.[19] In this, at least, Carter and the congressional Democrats were united: Carter could not denounce them effectively. What the voters rejected, however, was not the Democratic Party. It was *government without party*, the combination of Carter's managerialism and Congress's indiscipline. That makes it harder than it ought to be to read the party currents in 1980.

The New Deal Coalition and the New Deal Family

Political parties are not ad hoc coalitions of interest groups for and against particular policies, going out of being as quickly as they appear. Parties make deeper claims on our memories, our identities, and our hopes. In many ways, a party is like a family. New members are added; some old members are lost to new connections; some kinsmen become distant, while others, who have been out of touch, come back into the family circle. With those rare exceptions called "critical elections," parties undergo "slow, all but unconscious transformation."[20] The election of 1980 suggests that the New Deal coalition is no longer with us; but, to this moment at least, the New Deal family is still alive, its relationships strained and altered but still intact.

In 1932 Franklin Roosevelt inherited a political party in which the southern (and western) wing, Protestant and rural, had lost control to an urban, industrial wing, heavily Catholic and rooted in the Northeast.[21] The change was formally ratified in 1936 with the repeal of the "two-thirds" rule that had allowed the South to block any unacceptable candidate. The New Deal coalition picked up support as it went along — notably from Jews and blacks — but its center of gravity continued to lie with the northern white working class, increasingly unionized and composed of predominantly Catholic ethnic communities. John Kennedy's nomination and victory in 1960 relied on those voters, and it reaffirmed their Democratic allegiance.

Nevertheless, two gradual processes were changing the Democratic coalition. The first was obvious: Those who profited from the New Deal developed new economic interests. Protected by trade unions, contracts, seniority, and pension rights, established workers had less to fear from unemployment and more to fear from inflation. Given the entitlements of this expanding "contract society," old anxieties were pushed into the background. Established workers became homeowners worried about property taxes and parents concerned with the costs of higher education. Moving into middle-class styles of life, sometimes at great cost, they felt menaced by affirmative action programs that seemed to threaten their own — and even more, their children's — ascent and that undermined the neighborhood school. A variety of new economic and social interests strained the old ties of established workers to the Democratic Party.

On the whole, however, white ethnic workers remained loyal to the party. Their memories of the past ran too strong, and Republican hostility to their gains was too apparent. The "right to work" crusade by Republican hard-liners in 1958, for example, revitalized Democratic loyalties that had begun to waver in the 1950s. The white working-class communities stayed in the Democratic coalition, but they became increasingly exposed to cross-pressures, propertied proletarians who were vulnerable to issues such as "communism in government" or, more recently, the "social issue."[22]

These ethnic working-class communities, the backbone of "regular" Democratic Party organizations, became increasingly unreliable. The regulars became irregular, undependable voters; "safe" districts, in state or national elections, changed into the arenas of interparty competition. It has been years since the Democratic Party could take these voters for granted, and holding them in the coalition requires increasing attention to their dignity, their particular concerns, and their sense of neglect.[23]

As white working-class Democrats ceased to be the core of the party's support, blacks replaced them. Increasingly, blacks are the "new Irish," the party regulars and the heart of Democratic straight-ticket support. Carter held black voters in 1980 and may even have increased his support marginally. In fact, Carter's achievement in 1976, in bringing the South back into the Democratic fold was possible only because of monolithic support from southern blacks. The relatively high Democratic totals in the South in 1980 reflect Carter's own residual regional popularity, but they also reflect the comparatively large number of black voters. It is not merely a quixotic passion that made Senator Strom Thurmond speak, in the aftermath of Reagan's victory, of "reexamining" the Voting Rights Act of 1965. As long as that act remains in effect, a Democratic South is likely whenever the region's interests and feelings are reasonably reflected in the Democratic platform and nominee.[24]

The fact that blacks have displaced the white working class as the party's regulars, however, is an indication of shifts that have taken place in the Democratic coalition. The blacks have moved to the core; the white ethnics have moved to the periphery; the pattern of urban residence is replicated in party loyalty. This, by any standard, is a change from the old relationships of the New Deal.

In that sense, the Roosevelt coalition has come to an end, as it was bound to. There are middle-aged voters today who were not born when Franklin Roosevelt died, and the youngest voters in 1980 were only a year old when John Kennedy was shot. We will remember Roosevelt and the Great Depression less and less, and — just as Truman has suddenly acquired cachet — Kennedy will increasingly be the symbol whose memory excites Democratic partisans.

There are strong tactical reasons for that change of symbols. Democrats need to give unmistakable evidence, as Kennedy's campaign did in 1960, of their concern for white workers and ethnic Americans. Notably, no Catholic has received the Democratic nomination since Kennedy, despite a sharp rise in ethnic consciousness. Senator Edward Kennedy might have won the nomination in 1980, in fact, if he had been less identified with liberalism and more identified with his ethnic heritage. Attending to the dignity and the concerns of working-class, ethnic audiences must be a Democratic priority. In 1976 William Shannon thought that Carter was "tacitly repositioning his party" to achieve that goal, especially through his concern for "patriotism, a strengthening of families and neighborhoods, and the work ethic."[25] Carter's failure to develop these themes ranks high among the political failures of his administration.

Certainly, Democrats need to be concerned that working-class America be better represented in party councils and that the party give less attention, by contrast, to advocates of abortion rights, gay liberation, and similar movements, who have — given the logic of American politics — nowhere else to go except into third-party impotence. The Democrats have one tactical advantage. When they lose an election, the defeated candidates tend to be drawn from the party's extreme liberal wing, as were so many of this year's losers. Defeat can contain its own corrective, driving the party back to more pragmatic bastions. But that remains to be seen.

A final note is needed. Foreign policy strained the Democratic coalition as severely in 1980 as the tensions inherent in the "contract society." Even among those voters who remember FDR, memories of World War II, the common experience of older and middle-aged voters, have grown more important as recollections of the depression wane. The war years created a deep sense of American power, and everything in the early postwar years strengthened that impression. For all but the youngest voters, American power and independence are basic expectations and fundamental assumptions rooted deep in the emotions. The "decline" of American power has, correspondingly, been both painful and fundamentally incomprehensible.

Since American postwar power depended, in part, on the prostrate condition of Europe and Japan, the decline of our position was predictable. Moreover, declining or no, America is still a colossus. Nevertheless, one does not "reason" with basic feelings. We grew up with the sense that America did not depend on anyone. We were genuinely independent, an "arsenal of democracy" capable, if the need arose, of going it alone. In large measure, these feelings were justified at the time: our only major shortage during World War II was rubber, and we rationed gasoline to save tires. Even during the Arab oil boycott of 1973, we were relatively unaffected and could have taken a high tone if we wished. In recent years, by contrast, we have been forced to deal with the reality of our dependence on others. We need the Saudis to keep the oil flowing at premium prices; we need the Germans to support the dollar; we must listen to both hector us about the need to control inflation. And so on. It does not help much to remind ourselves that other countries need us as much as we need them. The experience of dependence is painful, even if it is shared. In 1980, Steven Roberts observed, we were brought face-to-face with "America, the vulnerable."[26]

The prolonged conflict of America and Iran over the hostages reminded us of all the things we could *not* do, all the constraints and reasons for inaction. Reagan touched a deep chord when he said that, if elected, he would not "do nothing," as Carter had done. Raised in an activist culture, we believe that people can master nature and that civilization can rise above barbarism. Yet our helicopters broke down in the Iranian desert, and there was the Ayatollah, barbarism incarnate, and the crowds chanting, "Khomeini fights, Carter trembles." We *felt* it as a "humiliation," the word Reagan used, and Iran, along with any number of slights and setbacks, readied us for heroic measures in foreign policy. As Richard Betts wrote:

> In the 1970s ... "No more Vietnams" became as misleading and confining a principle as "no more Munichs...." Today, the pendulum is swinging back. Soviet advances in Ethiopia, Afghanistan and Yemen and the collapse of the regime in Teheran, raise the specter of falling dominos. Hysterical reaffirmation of containment by large-scale intervention will be no improvement over adamant abstention.[27]

Betts is probably right, but the mood is unmistakable.

I suspect that we are ready for similarly drastic remedies in domestic affairs, where they may be more clearly needed. The voters do not want a nine-to-five regime that leaves them alone. They selected Reagan partly in the hope that he would prove a "strong leader," and a majority would probably welcome declaration of an "economic state of emergency." Of course, Americans are not eager for constraint and sacrifice. They may be ready for policies that suggest strong action and to which citizens can *contribute*.

President Carter's policies relied on indirect government controls, such as the effort to curb inflation through rising interest rates or the more successful attempt to limit gasoline consumption by allowing prices to rise. Such policies, however, make citizens feel helpless, whether or not they are successful. We are allowed only to react to events. Even when such policies work, we feel we are being manipulated, and all too often we suspect that these policies distribute sacrifice unfairly. Direct controls — gas rationing, for example — are more compatible with our dignity and with our concern for justice. They ask for conscious sacrifice for a public purpose, with the burden distributed on the basis of public criteria. And whatever their other problems, direct controls are more likely to make us feel that our problems can be solved by political action.

Certainly, there is no need for the Democrats to retreat from their commitment to "big government." They should, of course, suggest that they would manage government efficiently, and they need to demonstrate an increased concern for local community. But there is a good deal of reason to believe that, in foreign and domestic policy, many voters who defected to Reagan wanted *more* government, not less, and that they chose him hoping for a regime that would be less hesitant and ambivalent about the use of power. The Roosevelt coalition is passing, and the Kennedy coalition may be succeeding it within the New Deal family. That ought to hint, at least, at nostalgia for Camelot; imperial government may be on the verge of a new wave of popularity.

The Republicans and the New Conservatives

It was surely a sign of the times that the Republican candidate, by his own admission, voted for Roosevelt all four times he ran.[28]

One of Reagan's undoubted advantages was his freedom from the baggage of old-line Republicanism. He quoted Roosevelt happily; he paraded his admittedly peculiar trade-union past and his lifetime membership in the Screen Actors Guild. Even his attacks on the cherished gains of labor — his criticism of the minimum wage, for example — were couched in language designed to make them acceptable. Reagan argued for a "two-tier" wage system, with a lower minimum wage for teenagers and the hard-core unemployed. Whatever else may be said of this proposal, it was tailored to allay the fears of established white workers. Reagan preferred to run as a New Dealer grown conservative, and that stance persuaded millions of voters that he was safe enough to afford them the luxury of dumping Carter.

Reagan's campaign, in other words, signals changes in conservatism more striking than any change in the Democratic majority. Not so long ago, Reagan's rhetorical fondness for organized labor would have been high treason in Republican circles. The "supply-side" economics symbolized by the Kemp-Roth tax proposal, moreover, indicates the change even more clearly. Traditional Republican doctrine always worried about inflation. True to laissez-faire, it wanted to let the market alone and relied heavily on the "bourgeois virtues" of the independent middle class. The cure for inflation, in this doctrine, was less consumption and more saving, self-discipline, and frugality. Asked the cure for rising food prices in 1947, Senator Robert A. Taft responded, "We should eat less."[29] Nothing could have been more alien to the style and substance of Reagan's campaign, and Reagan made much, scornfully, of Carter's suggestion that inflation resulted from the fact that we have lived "too well." Rectitude and self-denial were themes of Congressman Anderson's campaign, but Anderson's old-style, middle-class individualism is now peripheral in Republican politics.

Reagan's proposals turn on the notion that less restraint — a massive tax cut — can stimulate investment and productivity enough to offset inflation. Self-indulgence takes the place of self-denial. After years of learning that "you don't shoot Santa Claus," the Republicans decided to nominate him. Even if Reagan's proposals work as well as he hopes, they make a mockery of middle-class virtues. Ants are only grim, ill-humored folks who eat badly; grasshoppers are good citizens who fight inflation too. Supply-side economics is self-consciously modeled on the Kennedy tax cut of 1963, and it clearly involves government planning, though planning of a decidedly conservative sort.

In fact, a good many of Reagan's promises suggest more government intervention, not less. During the campaign, for example, he argued for "enterprise zones" to stimulate growth in the industrial cities, and his transition team circulated a paper that would deny federal aid to any locality that persisted in rent control. These are conservative plans, but they call for a good deal of government involvement on behalf of the "private sector." And all this says nothing about Reagan's proposals for stronger defense and federal policies to defend the family.

In fact, the term "private sector" is a talisman. In the first place, it suggests that there is a legitimate *public* sector, an inescapable component of government input into and regulation of our economic life. In the second place, referring to the "private sector" allows Reagan to scrap "free enterprise" with its laissez-faire connotations. Like quoting Roosevelt, referring to the "private sector" is a way of disowning the past, abandoning the world of the independent, small-town bourgeoisie for the new world of tax shelters, multinationals, and computer programs, where planning is the rule.

Reagan suggests that the private sector, assisted by a sympathetic government, can make sacrifice unnecessary. We are an "energy-rich" country, and the energy companies will prove it. Taxing ourselves less will still enable us to balance the budget and provide for a bigger military, and at the same time interest rates will come down. Reagan, in other words, presents himself as the defender of the American "fifth freedom," the *right to consume,* and he assures us that we will enjoy that liberty in his term of office.

It is hard to say how much of this the voters believed. Carter took a more somber tone, but he also shied away from any call for self-denial, promising "careful" and "balanced" tax cuts and the like. Voters, in other words, were neither asked nor permitted to choose between austerity and extravagance. Anderson's "new realism" seems the exception to this rule, since he did not hesitate to call for restraint. With few exceptions, however, Anderson's supporters knew he would not win; they knew, in other words, that in practice they would not be required to *make* the sacrifices he urged. His candidacy, therefore, had a secret attraction for well-to-do liberals. Since in practice, a vote for Anderson helped elect Reagan, his supporters could affirm their anti-inflationary *principles* at the same time that they forwarded their inflationary *desires*. In any case, it seems likely that a great many of Reagan's supporters took their candidate's economics with a grain of salt.

It is hard to believe, for example, that a great many voters did not notice that Reagan's faith in the private sector was contradicted by Detroit's dramatic, dismal failure to anticipate the demand for small, fuel-economical cars. In reality, the auto industry showed all the rigidity and lack of imagination that, in conservative doctrine, is supposed to characterize government. The auto industry underrated the need to economize and our willingness to do so; the federal government, by contrast, had been urging the change on a recalcitrant Detroit for some time. The example of the auto industry does not augur well for a policy of "getting the government off the backs of the American people." Detroit will need more help, not less, and the new conservatives will probably provide it. The private sector does not want to be let alone; it wants government to help it and, where necessary, to pick up the tab. In economics, that is likely to be the direction of the new regime.

A good many Democrats who defected to Reagan ignored his economics. They voted for him in the hope that he will do something about the "social issue," introducing government into the world of the family and the other traditional refuges of private life. Clearly, this calls for "big government" with a vengeance, and while the social issue was bound to hurt any Democratic regime, the new Republican administration is not likely to find it much more congenial.

Americans continued to feel society crumbling around them in 1980. Carter had promised to make the American family a major concern of his administration, but the Democrats only damaged themselves when they tried to address the issue. Civil libertarians and partisans of new, "liberated" arrangements protested against making the traditional family the norm of policy, and the administration yielded, although it ought to have been possible to advocate stronger and more stable relationships whether or not these are "traditional." Fundamentalists expected more from Carter than Sunday pieties, and they did not get it. And while Carter himself was against providing federal funds for abortion — little enough to ask, as "right-to-lifers" saw it — the Democratic convention in New York decidedly did not share the president's view.

Reagan made every effort to appeal to social conservatives, especially since the social issue lies at the hiatus between the liberals and working-class Democrats. There is little doubt that Reagan's administration will continue this strategy, and the new president can be relied on to oppose the ERA and abortion, to look for ways to permit prayer in the schools, and possibly to support aid to denominational education.

There is every reason, however, to think that Reagan's social conservatism, though sincere, is also superficial. The forces that are weakening local communities and families are bound up with our individualism, mobility, and commitment to growth. Change, "unsteady, irregular and hard to predict" makes yesterday's certainties into today's follies.[30] We cannot commit ourselves very deeply to the institutions that are so prone to change; and people, like everything else, are only too likely to be different tomorrow.[31] Children, uprooted from homes and neighborhoods, learn through loss to be more reserved in making their commitments. People who are left behind — so often the old — frequently suffer even more than those who leave, and become still more guarded in consequence. Long-distance may be "the next best thing to being there," but AT&T is only reminding us that we will probably *not* live close to our families or old friends. Our communities, as Scott Greer wrote years ago, are "limited liability communities" where we learn to commit ourselves only superficially, retaining the freedom to cut our losses or move up as the social market dictates.[32]

Family relationships are bound to reflect these currents. We have learned more and more to regard divorce as a normal event of life. The election of Reagan, the first divorced person to become president, will probably do more to legitimate divorce than his conservatism will do to stabilize families. Yet the more normal divorce seems, the more we are reminded that we can and do make mistakes in judging others, even in our most important commitments and in our strongest feelings. And thus the more we are likely to limit our subsequent commitments. Herbert Hendin writes that affection and harmony are growing scarcer, "in and out of families." We are drawing more and more into ourselves and away from family, country, and community.[33]

Reagan is not likely to lend federal power to the quest for stability in personal relationships. To do so, however indirectly, would require a willingness to curb individual freedom, change, and economic growth; but both Republican ideology and the corporate economy regard such restraint as anathema. To make family, community, and morality the goals of public policy would require that we subordinate private liberty to civil order, something neither Reagan nor his party is likely to consider. As Reagan's ambassador to the United Nations, Jeane Kirkpatrick, wrote in 1979,

> Republican spokesmen have consistently emphasized private concerns such as profit and taxes, and private virtues such as self-discipline and self-reliance and either have not had, or have not communicated, a persuasive conception of the public good.[34]

The reason is simple: the tradition of liberal individualism, which shapes Republican ideology, acknowledges no public good that is not simply an aggregate of private goods and liberties. Reagan will give social conservatives the symbols, but he will leave the substance to the forces that are making for privatism and social disintegration. If there is light and hope in the future of the Republic, it is not visible in the election of 1980.

CHAPTER THREE

Old Virtues, New Magic
The Election of 1984

Ronald Reagan's administration had its hard days — his first two years were marked by a deep recession and the shattering of industrial America — but by 1984 times seemed better and Reagan had made himself the symbol of a confident, unapologetic America, proof against tragedy and sure of happy endings. If Americans sensed that Reagan's politics were cinematic, most of them were at least happy to be watching a good show. From the beginning, it was clear that Walter Mondale, the eventual Democratic nominee, never stood a chance.

==»(())«==

> *I am giddy, expectation whirls me round*
> *The imaginary relish is so sweet*
> *That it enchants my sense.*
>   — *Troilus and Cressida* (III, ii)

The election of 1984 was not a season for heroes; it was won by summer soldiers and sunshine patriots. Mr. Reagan was pleased to have it so; repeatedly, his campaign assured Americans that the long night of crisis was over, giving way to a new morning. Reagan proclaimed that America is "back," the Republic of our fonder memories, affluent and powerful, a "shining city" and an Opportunity Society, built of alabaster and free from tears.

American voters recognized the hyperbole in the president's rhetoric. They knew that some Americans are poor — in fact, there are more poor people in every section of the country than there were when Ronald Reagan took office — and a good many Americans worried, fitfully, about the "fairness" of the president's policies, but the great majority did not allow such concerns to be decisive. Unemployment, the great Democratic issue, worried voters more than inflation, but relatively few Americans were disturbed about either. Ronald Reagan was credited with curing inflation and restoring a modest economic confidence, allowing Americans to anticipate well-being even if they did not enjoy it. For many voters, foreign affairs were the area of greatest concern, but the country was at peace, and the things Americans feared, however troubling in prospect, were at least not at hand.[1]

Most Americans knew, or suspected, that the good times would not always be with us.[2] For a considerable number, in fact, the Reagan recovery probably represented not springtime but Indian summer. Nevertheless, the Americans who gave Ronald Reagan his great victory wanted at least a respite from the politics of crisis and thought they could expect it. Immediately after the election, when the president's forecasts turned bleak and the administration began to speak of tightening belts, Congressman Newt Gingrich (R-Georgia), a leader of the New Right, observed that "the American people have to feel a little like they thought they were walking into the office of a cruise ship and found out they were in a cancer clinic." Conservative Senator James McClure (R-Idaho), summed it up: "There is nothing you can read in the election that says the American people are ready for sacrifice."[3]

There is more than self-interest in the mood of the majority. Tocqueville wrote that American democracy could endure political conflict and the ordeal of change because of the security Americans found in social and moral life. The health of democracy presumes, Tocqueville declared, that moral ties grow stronger as political bonds are relaxed; in America, the political world was "agitated, uncertain and disputed," but the moral world was "classed, adapted, directed and foreseen."[4] The America Tocqueville was describing, of course, was simpler and more uniform, a republic by, if not only for, Protestant white Anglo-Saxons. Uneasily, the United States has been growing more pluralistic ever since. Nevertheless, Americans could rely, until recently, on certain social and moral decencies as stable standards of right, the sources of direction and meaning. "Our common difficulties," Franklin Roosevelt declared in 1933, "concern, thank God, only material things."[5]

No more: Americans are troubled by social disorganization and moral *dissensus*. The spiritual foundations of the New Deal are at least as eroded as its politics. In 1984 Americans embraced material prosperity, hoping that *it* would provide the basis for social and moral renewal. Like every presidential contest since 1972, the election of 1984 involved a modest mandate to rebuild the private foundations of public life. Some of Reagan's militant supporters favored an outright counterrevolution to overthrow the legacy of the 1960s, if not the New Deal. More generally, however, Americans were concerned to recover some sense of social and moral order without surrendering any of their material gains or their individual liberties. The majority of Americans are ambivalent, unready to make great social and moral commitments. In the moral and social as well as in the economic world, Americans wanted a moment of relaxation, and Ronald Reagan, campaigning as "Dr. Feelgood," knew better than to prescribe any bitter medicine.

Reagan's victory was so one-sided as to suggest a shift in the balance and composition of American political parties, but here, too, Americans were hesitant. The Republican presidential coalition does seem to have acquired considerable stability, and in some locales — especially in the South and among younger voters — there were shifts away from the Democrats. But the Democrats held the House and gained in the Senate. The theory of critical elections presumes that our party loyalties and our political identities are reasonably coherent, consistent, and stable; in this respect, the theory may have become obsolete.[6] The election of 1984 does not indicate a stable change of allegiance so much as the unsettling, for a considerable number of Americans, of *all* political allegiances, a weakening of the bonds between voters and the political system. A new political era is coming to birth, but not necessarily an attractive or a happy one.[7]

Reagan and the Politics of the Electronic Age

The personality and presidency of Ronald Reagan dominate the politics of the 1980s. Reagan has been a more skillful and successful president than most of us expected. In the role of chief of state, Reagan has been the ablest president since Kennedy, carrying out the ceremonial functions of the presidency with considerable grace. He has proved, as we are often reminded, to be a "great communicator," a master of the public presidency in the media age.

From the standpoint of popularity, the Reagan administration had matchless timing. Its worst years were its first, and the very depth of the early recession made the recovery seem even brighter. Jimmy Carter probably finished off his chances for reelection by setting out, in an election year, to cure inflation by means of draconian monetarism; Reagan's administration avoided hard decisions in 1984 until the election was over. He offered us the easy life, not blood and toil, and the results speak for themselves.

Yet Reagan's landslide victory was a mixed blessing for his party. Reagan ran as a moderate candidate, a fact that helped to move the Republicans — in popular perception — closer to the center of American politics. But Reagan virtually portrayed himself as a mainstream Democrat: at the Republican convention, the band played the New Deal anthem, "Happy Days Are Here Again"; Reagan quoted Roosevelt, Truman, and Kennedy to the exclusion of Republicans; his campaign even traveled on Truman's whistle-stop train. Reagan went beyond simple symbols: he embraced programs and policies that, until recently, were considered left of center; he justified mountainous deficits, pledged not to cut present or future entitlements to Social Security, and voiced support for Medicare.[8] It helped that Walter Mondale, encumbered by honor and honesty, was forced to the fiscal right. Mondale felt compelled to offer a plan for reducing the deficit, and even with a tax increase, he was barely able to hold the line on social programs. Mondale had no room for exciting new programs and policies; the deficit, and his attempts to combat it, would have made Mondale seem uninspiring even if he had the tongue of angels.[9]

Moreover, it fell to Mondale to emphasize the limits of federal power on social issues and in foreign policy. The combination of fiscal responsibility and political restraint made Mondale sound vaguely like an old-line Taft Republican.[10] That fact probably enhanced Mondale's appeal to Anderson Republicans, but those voters are too few in number to add more than moral tone. With Walter Mondale's assistance, Ronald Reagan blurred the old lines.

At the same time, the Republican Party became even more dominated by its conservative wing. At the Republican convention, the key victories were won by the right; during the campaign, Republican moderates suffered notable defeats — Elliot Richardson, for example, lost a senatorial primary in Massachusetts, and Charles Percy was denied reelection — while the most visible champion of the right, Jesse Helms, survived. The Republicans, as a party, were bent on drawing the line between left and right, though, admittedly, a line of a new sort.

The president's strategists smoothly ditched his party. Reagan made campaign appearances to support Republican candidates, especially at the end, but this formal support could not eliminate the disparity between the style of the president's campaign and the stance of Republican candidates. Ronald Reagan, in other words, gave the voters no real reason — much less a sense of urgency — to defeat Democratic candidates for Congress. "Why would somebody vote for President Reagan and then vote for John Kerry?" asked Ray Shamie, the defeated Republican nominee for the Senate in Massachusetts. "It doesn't make any sense."[11] But a great deal of Mr. Reagan's campaign was devoted to telling voters, implicitly, that it did make *sense,* even if it was not the choice the president would *prefer.* Had his strategists charted a more partisan campaign, Reagan might have lost another half dozen states, but he might also have won a working majority in Congress. In the end, the public voted for Ronald Reagan for the same reason that it voted the Democrats back into control of the House and strengthened their position in the Senate: it desires no great change.[12]

All through the campaign, the Democrats were daunted by Reagan's mastery of television, as they had been ever since he took office. The president reads a speech extremely well, and his humor — especially, his gift for goodspirited self-deprecation — covers many faults. Even the president's intellectual limitations help: Nixon was too shrewd not to *know* when he was being evasive, distorting the facts or contradicting some earlier position, and it showed; Reagan reads his lines innocently and with evident sincerity. The Democratic candidates were not in Reagan's league; only Jesse Jackson had forensic talent, and Jackson's rhetoric is suited more to the pulpit than to the screen.

The Democrats' disadvantage, however, was due only in part to the idiosyncrasies of their candidates; it has something to do with their party. The Democratic Party in 1984 was still rooted in an older political science and political practice, the pluralistic doctrine that formed the basis of "interest group liberalism."[13] Too many of the leaders of the party — and most notably, its intellectual leaders — failed to recognize the new shape of political society. In 1984, the Democrats were brought face to face with the inadequacy of the public philosophy that succeeded the era of the New Deal.

Pluralistic doctrine plays down the importance of public speech. In line with the traditional assumptions of American political practice, pluralistic political science assumes that speech is *mediated* — that what candidates say passes to voters through "gatekeepers" such as interest groups, local party organizations, and the press in a "two-step flow of communication."[14] In this view, the public is insulated against the media and against public speech, trusting its gatekeepers enough to let them interpret words and events.

What matters, in this view, is not eloquence but the ability to *do,* and especially the ability to persuade the gatekeepers of one's ability, competence, and force. Adlai Stevenson, consequently, was damned as a "talker," too inclined to play Hamlet, and Hubert Humphrey tried vainly to live down his reputation for being "gabby." One's public qualities as a leader, Patrick Caddell observes, are "discounted in Washington, where conviction is less important than the ability to get results."[15] As Caddell implies, Washington insiders are especially likely to esteem leaders who show a mastery of fact, persuasiveness in small and expert groups, and skill in hammering out agreements. Lyndon Johnson and Walter Mondale passed those tests with high marks, and Jimmy Carter — though he failed in many respects — at least aspired to do well.

Ronald Reagan, on the other hand, is not highly regarded — to put it mildly — by the insiders, who tend to be contemptuous of Reagan's superficiality, his administrative weakness, and his too frequent ignorance.[16] Yet the antipathy of the insiders has failed to shake Reagan's appeal to ordinary voters.

In fact, the contemporary public is increasingly without gatekeepers. Local party organizations are in disarray. Even when voters are members of interest groups, they are apt to feel distant and disaffected, as so many trade unionists do. The print media, the citadel of interpretation, have declined in favor of television and other forms of direct access to the public. The shattering of the old structures of mediation confronts the Democrats — and political scientists — with a truth they should not have forgotten: politics is fundamentally a matter of speech, and in democracies, of public speech. But it also confronts America with a public that more and more lacks both the arts of listening and the friendship of critics and guides.

Reagan's staff knows the secrets of campaigning in our mass society. It recognizes, in the first place, that there are no terrors in the press. Reagan's campaign provided good "logistical support" for reporters, but it denied them any real access to the candidate, just as the White House staff kept news conferences to a minimum. Mondale, by contrast, appeared to enjoy give-and-take with reporters, holding a news conference almost every day.[17]

Despite his age, Ronald Reagan is more contemporary than his rivals because he was shaped by movies and by his career as host of *Death Valley Days*: Reagan, in fact, is the first candidate who is genuinely the product of the era of the visual media. All previous candidates — and certainly Walter Mondale — grew up and were formed in the years before television dominated the American scene. Ronald Reagan is part of a *New* Right in precisely this sense. The Old Right was tied to a structure of mediation, the business and professional leaders, the editors, and the Republican officials of small-city, small-town America; the New Right relies on television, as Jerry Falwell does, or on direct mail.

Moreover, Reagan's staff realizes that television can be *dominated*. Since what matters in politics is so often invisible, subtle, and substantive, it will never be well covered by a medium whose hallmarks are visibility, simplification, and a concern with style.[18] Television can be managed because of its limitations: reporters can comment only in the context of a picture; the medium is impotent without "photo opportunities" and cannot easily resist a story with good visual possibilities. Reagan's strategists exploited those weaknesses with few scruples and great skill. The president's campaign assertions went largely untested and unchallenged; and the candidate was portrayed, pretty much, in the way his managers desired.

In one respect, the election of 1984 approximated George Orwell's imagined totalitarianism. Orwell feared that in the future, political regimes would find it possible to manipulate our memory of the past and thereby control the future. Things have not reached that pass, but the possibility is frighteningly foreseeable.[19] Reagan and his advisers recognize, intuitively at least, that the public has less and less memory, less ability to organize and to recall the past. The old, organic sources of political remembrance in families and communities are breaking up and are being replaced by television's presentation of time as a series of disjointed moments, each a discrete unit, available for reordering at will.[20]

Illustratively, Reagan maintained that, in 1981, he inherited a "mess" that was the work, over many years, of his Democratic opponents. Yet Republican presidents held office from 1969 to 1977; just as Reagan attempted to enlist Roosevelt, Truman, and Kennedy, he created the sense that Nixon and Ford somehow counted among the Democrats.[21] One might pass this off as campaign cunning were it not clear that Reagan's own version of history is strikingly disordered; his memories are intertwined with odd fantasies and with bits drawn from old movies, all recalled and related as *fact*. This is an old pattern with Reagan, not a sign of age. He is, in this as in other things, a very modern man, one for whom history is not an objective past but an existential creation, the product of will.[22]

Leadership: Old Values and New America

Ronald Reagan's reputation as a "strong leader" is his greatest political asset, and the quality of his leadership — so generally admired by the electorate — reveals a good deal about the state of America as a political society.

In speech, Reagan is almost invariably firm and decisive, certain of his values and his direction, and inclined to strong language and striking expression. In action, Reagan often wavers and vacillates. In relation to Lebanon, for example, Reagan denounced those who were ready to "cut and run" and proclaimed his own unwillingness to "surrender," only to order the withdrawal of American forces. William V. Shannon was led to write that, in foreign affairs, there is "no knowledge, no understanding and no commitment in anything that Reagan does."[23] Yet at each muddled stage of the imbroglio in Lebanon, including our eventual retreat — the president called it a "redeployment" — Reagan exuded confidence and proclaimed success. In domestic affairs, the president's defeats have been less dramatic and less frequent, but his pragmatic flexibility has been just as evident.

Reagan suits our mood. Americans, for the most part, want a leader who gives us a sense of direction and moral purpose, but not one who really *does* dangerous or demanding things. It is significant that Reagan flatters us outrageously; in his rhetoric, the American people are sinned against but never sinners. Following Reagan's lead, George Bush denounced Jimmy Carter's famous reference to a national "crisis of confidence" because Carter had "blamed the American people." In 1984, at least, Reagan's leadership combined the language of moral purpose with the practice of social and moral complacency.

The president's vulnerabilities, which his critics expect to bring disaster, only endear him to his audience. Americans know that Reagan is not brilliant, that his command of facts is uncertain, and that he is prone to "gaffes," but they excuse and indulge such evidences of fallibility. As Philip Rieff pointed out, in the symbolism of modern politics, political leaders — especially in mass democratic states — cannot afford to be too superior to their constituents. A leader must be one of us, an ordinary citizen glorified, and consequently must have faults. Reagan's mistakes, in fact, enable citizens to feel protective toward the president.[24]

Reagan's particular weaknesses, however, say something about our times. Franklin Roosevelt's weaknesses were physical, like the material problems of the country he governed. Spiritually, Roosevelt seemed to tower; even those, like Justice Holmes, who found his intellect second-rate, conceded that FDR had a first-class temperament. Roosevelt was great-spirited in a way that Ronald Reagan is not. Reagan, on the other hand, vaunts his physical vitalities; in 1984, he delighted in his prowess at arm wrestling. By contrast, he shies away from the political "brain wrestling" with the press at which Roosevelt was a past master. Reagan's vulnerabilities, as the voters have every reason to know, are defects of mind and spirit, suited to a country that is troubled in its soul.

The president celebrates traditional values and symbols, but he understands American ambivalence. As a people, Americans suffer from moral uncertainty and spiritual hunger, and they feel and show considerable nostalgia for the old verities and social landmarks. But most Americans do not want to return to the old order; they prefer life in the cities or suburbs, they have grown accustomed to a second income in the family, and they enjoy a certain amount of liberation and latitude in their personal lives. The public has its moments of guilt and regret, but it is unwilling to live by the old ways.

A television commercial portrays a young man returning for a celebration at the family farm, intoning that "America's coming home to the good taste of butter," but we know that whatever eating habits the young man takes away, he will not *stay* on the farm. A second commercial shows a farm mother gratified because a son who did *not* return for the family get-together sent a van full of appliances in his stead. These and similar commercials almost exactly parallel the "upbeat" advertising of Reagan's campaign, with its suggestion that economic growth is sufficient homage to the old virtues.

Reagan recognizes that Americans want standards set and meanings affirmed, and that they expect traditional beliefs to be shown respect. At the same time, the president realizes that this creed, like his own, is a *civil* religion, devoted to America as a political society rather than to the God of judgment.[25] Reagan gave his evangelical and socially conservative allies little more than symbolic support during his first term, allowing their legislative program to languish, and he is not apt to do more in his second four years.

In relation to moral values and social institutions, Walter Mondale was again the victim of his own virtues. Mondale is visibly a man of the old order. His ideas and programs may look to the future — and a surprisingly large number of voters saw Mondale as a man of vision — but his relationships and affects seem to point to the past. His marriage, for example, is apparently stable and happy and, hence, is one with which few contemporary Americans can identify. Gary Hart's marriage, by contrast, amounted to a contemporary soap opera, full of storm, stress, and separation leading to a happy ending. Similarly, Ronald Reagan's family troubles — his divorce and remarriage, his estrangement from his older son, even his failure to meet his infant grandchild — all make him someone we imagine to be like ourselves, able to understand our hopes and pains. Mondale's undisturbed monogamy was, symbolically, at least as out of date as the brand of politics Tip O'Neill seemed to personify. And to make matters worse, Mondale told us that we had to choose between our decencies and our comforts; most Americans preferred the president's happy discovery that it is possible, after all, to serve both God and mammon.

Reagan also understands the ordinary citizen's sense of grievance against the federal government, the conviction that complex government works to the advantage of the powerful and clever, who understand the loopholes of law and the workings of power. Reagan has usurped the Democrats' role as spokesman for many of America's outsiders. In an important sense, Reagan has reaped where the liberals and the New Left sowed.[26] The critique of American policy in Vietnam and the exposures surrounding Watergate worked, for a time, to the advantage of the liberals and the left, discomfiting their immediate enemies. But the attack on public authority also had the effect of undermining confidence in the federal government as a whole, calling its benevolence into question as much as its competence.

The mood to which Reagan appeals is alienated rather than conservative, more suspicious than committed. A great many voters, obviously, have responded to Reagan's pledge to "get the government off the backs of the American people." That response, however, is not born out of confidence in one's ability to go it alone — Americans know their private indignities too well for that — but out of distrust of the federal government as a champion.

In 1984 Ronald Reagan claimed to have restored America's belief in progress, her secular faith in the future. For Reagan, the old sense of possibility is very much alive, and he speaks of extending prosperity to the poor and developing a "Star Wars" defense against nuclear attack. Reagan remains convinced that human beings can master nature and that, in the president's favorite quotation from Tom Paine, "We have it in our power to begin the world over again."[27]

The public's response was overwhelmingly positive, but it was also cautious and restrained. Despite the vogue of optimism, only 23 percent of Reagan's voters cited his "vision of the future" as a reason for their support.[28] The public seems wary of high hopes; Reagan received a vote of thanks for the present more than a mandate for the future. The great majority of Americans voted for Reagan because, with the country at peace, they were ready to answer "Yes" to the question, "Are you better off now than you were four years ago?"

Most Americans appear to be moved by the president's words, but they are content in practice with a scaled-down prosperity and patriotism, tailored to an age of lowered expectations. The experience of the 1970s taught us something about America's limitations and vulnerabilities. In 1984 the majority of Americans were content to overlook the poor and happy to settle for Grenada — a small-scale victory won at low cost. The prevailing opinion is satisfied with an America that is neither heroic nor beautiful, but one that preserves — for most of us — our private comforts and decencies. Reagan has not drawn us together; he has assured us that public life is unnecessary and that we can, safely and in good conscience, confine ourselves to our separate private interests and existences.

Reagan and America are likely to need less anemic loyalties. Looming economic problems are all around us. The federal deficit is now growing faster than the rate of growth in the gross national product, and the increased interest on the federal debt exceeds all of the cuts in domestic spending effected during Reagan's first term. Even that well-publicized public indebtedness pales when compared with our *private* debt, now growing at about $300 billion a year.[29] Debt has become an economic way of life. When, during his debate with Geraldine Ferraro, Vice-President Bush sought to dramatize inflation under Carter, he did not refer to the high price of goods but to the high cost of *borrowing* ("21 percent interest rates!"). In fact, Americans are outspending their earnings at the rate of about 10 percent a year, an inflationary pressure held in check so far only by an overvalued dollar and cheap imported goods. In the 1960s, the United States borrowed abroad to finance investment; in the 1980s, we have been borrowing to finance consumption.[30]

In the workplace, Americans who were reemployed after the recession now work, on the whole, for smaller paychecks. Moreover, the growing sector of the job market offers only low-status work, often temporary, requiring little skill and offering low pay and benefits.[31]

Economically, the administration and the country have been living on borrowed time as well as borrowed money. Threats in foreign policy and the erosion of our social institutions only reinforce the moral that a government devoted to private comforts and dedicated to leaving us alone is not adequate to the problems we face. In that truth, the Democrats may find their opportunity, if they are equal to it.

The Democratic Prospect

For the Democrats in 1984, the primary process — as usual — was divisive, exhausting, and inclined to emphasize the role of ideological activists, organized interests, and, in states with open primaries, voters from outside the party's ranks. Mondale, the winner, was as disgusted as the losers. Nevertheless, the Democrats are not likely to make any major changes for the better; the "Fairness Commission," promised to placate Senator Hart, Jesse Jackson, and their supporters, easily could make matters worse. Modest improvements are possible, but the voters have grown accustomed to the system and the Democrats will have to make the best of it, enjoying what promises to be a Republican donnybrook in 1988. In any case, the Democrats have more fundamental problems.

The New Deal Coalition and the New Deal Strategy

After the election, the *New York Times,* while urging a new Democratic agenda, observed that Mondale had won substantial majorities among racial minorities, Jews, trade unionists, big-city residents, and the unemployed, and concluded that "the old New Deal coalition remains very much alive."[32]

The *Times'* prescription for the Democrats makes sense, but its political history is in error, and that mistake says a great deal about the failure of the Democrats in presidential politics.

The New Deal *coalition* — the majorities that four times elected FDR — began with the Democratic Party that Roosevelt inherited, a party built around southern whites and northern Catholics, the latter providing the crucial base of the urban Democratic organizations. The New Deal *strategy* took both groups more or less for granted, and it set out to add enough votes to create a national majority. New Deal tacticians, consequently, courted liberals (in those days, more likely to call themselves "Progressives"), Jews, the unions and — half-incidentally — blacks and racial minorities.

Like any such strategy, the New Deal's political design gave special attention to the groups it aimed to win. In the event, the New Deal strategy attuned Democrats to the values and sensibilities of the target groups and made the party increasingly tone deaf, if not hostile, to the sensitivities of Catholics and southern whites. In order to hold the New Deal coalition together, Democratic strategists relied on historic loyalties, on the power of the urban party organizations, and on an appeal to the economic interests of all those who benefited from New Deal programs — the poor and the working class, of course, but also protected groups like subsidized southern farmers.

Loyalties and memories erode with time. Even while Roosevelt was alive, southern conservatives grew restive. In 1944 an anti-Roosevelt ticket, the "Regulars," ran unsuccessfully in Texas, and in 1948 the growing conflict over racial policy erupted in the Dixiecrat revolt that eventually took Strom Thurmond, among others, out of the Democratic Party. Similarly, party organizations grew weaker, partly because of secular changes in American life, but also because of the hostility of liberals, who promoted legislation and party rules designed to weaken or break up the "machines."[33] Today, party organizations are no more than an interest group — and not always a strong one — in local party politics, much too confined to their own supporters to be able to deliver votes to the national party.[34] In 1984, for example, white Democratic leaders in Chicago made relatively little effort to dissuade their constituents from supporting Reagan; instead, they offered to forgive their friends for such defections and hence to preserve social harmony and local community, if they would vote for Paul Simon, the successful Democratic candidate for the Senate. In doing so, they were probably making the best available bargain, but it indicates the diminished role of the "regulars."

By 1972 Democrats were left, in relation to southern whites and northern Catholics, with a kind of pseudo Marxism, the hope that an appeal to economic interests would prove sufficient to hold voter loyalties. "If we don't have an economic issue for those people," Robert Squier declared in 1984, speaking of "born-again" Christians, "we don't seem to have any issues."[35] As Democrats are acutely aware, the success of their own policies has lifted the majority of such voters at least marginally out of poverty; as a result, Democrats often feel reduced to waiting for a recession. In any case, Democrats know that economic interests are not a sufficient guarantee of party loyalty. No party leader imagines that the economic ties between lower-class blacks and the Democrats would long survive racial insensitivity, and economic interest in the narrow sense would probably lead liberals to support the Republicans. Political allegiance involves our deepest feelings and our highest aspirations as much as our prosaic needs; in the last analysis, political loyalties are a matter for the soul.

The New Deal strategy has played out, whatever we may think of the prospects for the New Deal coalition. It is exhausted because it has succeeded; the groups the New Dealers courted and cultivated have been *won*. The periphery of the New Deal coalition has become the heart of the Democratic Party and the historic Democratic Party — northern Catholics and southern whites — has moved to the periphery, if it has not been lost to the Democrats altogether. The Democrats need a new strategy — whether they hope to restore the old coalition or to build a new one.

The heart of the new Democratic Party — the liberals, the racial minorities, and the trade unions — so accustomed to being wooed, will have to learn how to do the courting, attending to the values, affects, and dignities of others. And correspondingly, the core Democratic groups will have to adjust to their new position. The unions, the minorities, and the liberals will have to ask which items on their respective agendas they are willing to give up in order to win. It is not easy to break a pattern of institutional sensitivity, especially one a half century old, associated with great names and triumphs and buttressed by ideology. The Democrats may find it impossible. Nevertheless, the electoral logic is obvious.

Liberals, for example, have no place else to go. Given the nature of American national politics, they can choose between the Democrats and the irrelevance of third-party candidacies. It is not even clear that such third parties hurt the Democrats very much: Henry Wallace's Progressive Party in 1948 helped establish Truman as the candidate of the center and freed the Democrats from association with the "extreme left," and while John Anderson's candidacy in 1980 certainly cost the Democrats some votes, it may also have helped to hold some southern and moderate Democrats behind President Carter. Organized liberal groups, moreover, seemed relatively ineffective in the electoral politics of 1984. Feminists — having applied pressure heavy-handedly, making Mondale's selection of Geraldine Ferraro look weaker and less daring than it was — failed to deliver a vote sufficient to support their pretensions. Eastern women did give Mondale and Ferraro a majority, and the Democratic ticket did well among younger, unmarried women, but the majority of women voted for the Republican ticket.[36] In any case, it is not credible that organized feminists, or other groups on the liberal left, will be able to support a Republican candidate in the foreseeable future. Such voters need the Democratic Party at least as much, and possibly more, than it needs them.

Trade unions, similarly, no longer have the ability to play one party against the other. In 1980 Mr. Reagan advertised his terms as president of the Screen Actors' Guild as proof of his sympathy for unions; that argument did not surface in 1984. In fact, Reagan set his administration, and the Republicans, on a firmly antiunion course.[37] The image of organized labor has become undeservedly negative among voters in general; labor's position of power *within* the Democratic Party is one of its few remaining political assets. Walter Mondale would not have won the nomination without the unions, but the embrace of the AFL-CIO helped tag him as a servant of "special interests." Whether it plays its cards foolishly or well, organized labor will continue to be a major power in the internal politics of the Democratic Party, but given its external vulnerabilities, labor will have to walk more carefully and speak more softly.

Of all the elements of the Democratic core, Jewish voters — at least, those who are not identifiable liberals — may be the most likely to defect to the Republicans. Democrats will certainly need, consequently, to continue to support Israel, and they have every reason to censure anti-Semitism. Yet the increasing role of right-wing Christians within the Republican Party seems likely to tie Jews more closely to the Democrats. "The group that Jews love to hate most," Milton Himmelfarb remarked, "is the Moral Majority."[38] Even Jewish Democrats, in other words, can probably expect somewhat less solicitude than they have learned to take as their due.

Blacks and Hispanics may find it hardest to accept the restraints entailed by their position at the heart of the Democratic Party. Both groups, after all, still have a long agenda of demands and resentments; poverty and social injustice aside, they have overcome political exclusion only recently, if at all. It is not surprising, consequently, that Jesse Jackson campaigned in 1984 on the premise that blacks should approach the Democrats as outsiders, a pressure group that cannot be "taken for granted." But black officeholders, and a surprisingly large majority of black voters, recognize a stronger commitment and obligation to the party.

In inner cities, the Democratic Party is increasingly dominated by blacks; it is becoming as much "theirs" as it was the preserve of the Irish during their glory days, and blacks have every interest in preserving or building the party's ties to whites. Black voters supported Jackson in the primaries on symbolic grounds but appear to have preferred, on pragmatic grounds, that the eventual Democratic nominee be a candidate with a chance to win. Even more striking, only 4 percent of those who supported Jackson indicated that they would be less likely to vote for Mondale — or less likely to vote — if Jackson did not endorse the Democratic ticket.[39] Democrats, of course, would be unwise to underrate Jackson's strength or the mood of assertiveness among new and younger black voters. By and large, however, blacks are straight-ticket regulars; that fact entitles them to greater representation at the highest levels of the Democratic Party and may, conceivably, make them willing to share the party's burdens.

There are compensations for the hard-core Democrats that may encourage them to make the programmatic and affective sacrifices necessary to build a new presidential coalition. They have become the party's establishment, and for practical purposes, the party is their instrument. It is a sign of the times that Walter Mondale, not so long ago regarded as a left-liberal, was identified in 1984 as a "mainstream" Democrat. Yet just as it is hard to change from being cared for to caring for others, it is difficult to accept responsibility for a political institution. Political adulthood, like personal adulthood, is bittersweet. Whatever their regrets, however, the core Democrats have no alternative if they hope to reestablish a national majority.

Old Friends: The Historic Democrats

The most obvious strategy for the Democrats lies in attempting to win back the estranged elements of the old coalition, voters who, for the most part, still think of themselves as Democrats and vote for the party's local candidates. Since Franklin Roosevelt died, this has amounted to the Democrats' only recipe for success. In the elections since World War II, the Democrats have nominated one Catholic, Kennedy, two candidates from the South, Johnson and Carter, and one, Truman, who came from a border state with southern associations. With the exception of Carter's second try in 1980, all were elected. During the same period, the Democrats five times nominated northern Protestants (Stevenson twice, Humphrey, McGovern, and Mondale); all of them have been defeated. Other factors were at work, of course — no candidate, for example, could have beaten Eisenhower — but the pattern is too suggestive to be ignored.[40]

Nevertheless, Democrats should not underestimate the difficulty of reestablishing the old coalition. Even the historic loyalties that still tie so many Catholic and southern voters to the Democrats are a mixed blessing. There is no quarrel more bitter than a family argument. A great many Democrats who grew up thinking of the party as their political home have never recovered from the shock they received in 1972, when they found the national convention filled with strangers and themselves — or people with whom they identified — treated as unwelcome guests. And others have been embittered by what they experience as abandonment and years of neglect.

In 1984 Democrats rested much of their hope on the "fairness issue," the recognition that the burden of Reagan's policies falls disproportionately on poor and low-income Americans. Even more than in 1980, however, the Republicans benefited from their own, half-covert, "fairness issue," the conviction that women, blacks, and Hispanics are receiving more than their "fair share," measured by the standard of equality of opportunity. Affirmative action objectifies the resentment of traditional Democrats who feel they have been shouldered aside by the party and ignored by its policies.[41]

On the whole, Democrats of this persuasion are not defending old-style racism or sexism. The many southern whites who voted for Carter in 1976 and 1980, defecting to Reagan in 1984, have adjusted to a considerable measure of formal equality, as their votes for Carter attest. And while Jerry Falwell may call on women to return to their status as "weaker vessels," Ronald Reagan suggests that a woman soon will, on her "merits," win a place on the Republican ticket. Walter Mondale recognized the strength of this resentment against the felt inequalities of opportunity. He emphasized his own commitment to "opening doors," and he suggested that American success at the Olympics was due to policies promoting racial and sexual equality. It was, however, too little and too late for 1984.

In any case, the Democrats cannot possibly abandon affirmative action. If they hope to conciliate traditional Democrats, they will have to seek new and better remedies. And the Democrats may need new sensitivities even more than a new agenda.

John Kennedy's nomination helped reaffirm the bond between Catholics and Democrats, which dates from the nomination of Al Smith in 1928, and a Catholic at the head of the ticket would certainly help to reconcile defecting Catholic voters to the Democratic Party. Yet it seems unlikely that so simple a solution will be enough. In 1960, making allowance for Protestant fears and hostilities, Catholic leaders did not object when Kennedy declared that, in public life, he would follow his conscience rather than his church. In 1984 Geraldine Ferraro took a position more conservative than Kennedy's only to become embroiled in a long, lacerating argument with Archbishop John O'Connor and other members of the hierarchy over the question of abortion.

In 1960, of course, abortion was not an issue in national politics.[42] It is more important, however, that changes within the church — and in the place of the church in American society — have unsettled many of the old anchors of American Catholicism. Public anti-Catholicism has virtually disappeared.[43] Catholic leaders, on the other hand, have become more anxious and more assertive about the orthodoxy of the flock. At the same time, lay Catholics have developed a new touchiness about their identity as Catholics because commitment to the church has become problematic and personal.[44] Catholics, more likely to disregard the church's teachings in private life, are also protective about the church and inclined to resent any disrespect, in public life, for its leaders and its teachings. Walter Mondale's decision to cancel his appearance at the Al Smith dinner, for example, was probably a political error; a considerable number of Catholics surely recognized that Mondale's decision sprang, at least unconsciously, from anger at Archbishop O'Connor, and many must have suspected that Mondale — even if exhausted, as he surely was — would not have missed a dinner in honor of Golda Meir or Dr. Martin Luther King.

The effect of religiously charged issues on Catholic voting is not easy to assess. Catholic teaching argues that political decisions must be made holistically, not on the basis of discrete, absolute principles. A pro-choice position on abortion, consequently, is not a fatal liability by itself.[45] Ferraro's views, for example, were familiar to her socially conservative, 70-percent Catholic congressional district. In her district, Ferraro was able to balance her position on abortion by support for tuition tax credits and for an antibusing amendment designed to protect neighborhood schools.[46] The national platform allowed no such flexibility. It seems clear that any Democratic effort to win back Catholic voters will have to offer some concessions to Catholic values and social concerns.

The Catholic hierarchy emphasized the possibilities of such a rapprochement immediately after the election. The Bishops' Pastoral Letter on poverty and economic life presented a trenchant critique of the Reagan administration's policies and a call for a national commitment to alleviate economic misery.[47] During the campaign, the hierarchy spoke almost exclusively about issues like abortion; now, Father Paul Steidl-Meier writes, "the other shoe has dropped."[48] Catholic doctrine is sympathetic to economic regulation for the same reason that it often supports social regulation: it sees the law as magisterial, necessarily and rightly involved in teaching morals and shaping character as well as controlling conduct.[49] The hierarchy's campaign role, combined with the Pastoral Letter, amounted, whether by accident or design, to a message to the Democrats: Catholic teaching cannot be opposed without cost, but if accommodated, it can also be a powerful ally. It remains to be seen if the Democrats heard, or if they will respond in the same spirit.

In 1984, after all, the Democrats sent a mixed message to white ethnic communities, their old strongholds. For some time, sparked by the self-assertion of racial minorities, ethnic consciousness has been revivified in communities of east and south European extraction.[50] Governor Mario Cuomo addressed that sensibility when he spoke of the "blood of immigrants," and in the last two weeks of the campaign, Mondale grew eloquent when he spoke of pluralistic political community.

Yet while Democratic Party rules mandate representation of women, racial minorities, Hispanics, and young people in state delegations to the national convention, they do not call for inclusion of Poles, Greeks, Italians, or other, still relatively disadvantaged nationalities. Perhaps, in this respect, the Democrats suffer not from recognizing too many constituencies, but too few.

In fact, the Democratic Party's rules reflect an individualistic liberalism that implicitly disdains community. In the tradition of philosophic liberalism, human beings by nature are separate bodies whose merit is measured by their work. The only natural communities are defined by biological likeness — age, sex, and race — but these communities have no *moral* status. Inequalities based simply on physical differences demand special attention and correction because they breach the wall between *nature* and *political society*. Democratic Party rules, in other words, recognize women, racial minorities, and young people in order to free them from the burden of classifications that are "suspect" because they are based on qualities that were not chosen and that do not reflect achievement.

Cultural communities differ because they are based on convention, custom, and choice. To be part of an ethnic community suggests, in the individualistic view, either that one *chose* not to pursue assimilation into the middle-class mainstream or that one *failed* in the attempt, and hence any discrimination or disadvantage is, to some degree, one's own fault. Ethnic voters do not need to spell out the philosophic principles of this argument to feel and recognize its effects.[51]

It is probably impractical and unnecessary for Democrats to mandate formal representation of white ethnic communities. Any Democratic appeal to such voters, however, must make clear that the party respects ethnic traditions and dignities, and is devoted to the values that, broadly speaking, characterize ethnic voters: "patriotism, a strengthening of families and neighborhoods and the work ethic."[52] Jimmy Carter's campaign in 1976 profited because it seemed to promise such devotion; Carter suffered in 1980 because he had failed to deliver. In 1984 the Democratic candidates said many of the right words, but they failed to develop the Democrats' one great advantage over the Republicans, the willingness to use public power to support their verbal commitments. For ethnic voters, who tend to be economically and socially marginal and whose communities are ordinarily embattled, it is not enough to be decent; one must at least appear to be strong.

The South and Social Values

In the white South, Democratic losses are far more serious and difficult to reverse because they have carried over to the local level, suggesting a thoroughgoing change of party identification.[53] Moreover, southern white defections in 1984 were complicated by the contemporary political problem of race. The South today is hardly an egalitarian society, but memories of Jim Crow are fading; moderate southerners are less likely to feel guilt for the past and more likely to be anxious about the future. Already worried about the increasing black presence in the Democratic Party — and especially, the Democratic Parties of the South — white voters were alarmed by Jesse Jackson's demand for the abolition of runoff primaries, a policy calculated to ensure black domination of state Democratic politics. Voters who would have been ashamed of the simpler forms of racism found it easy to rationalize hostility to Jackson. To white voters, Jackson suggests an inner-city hustler with an aura of financial sleaziness, self-promoting and injudicious, while Jackson's ventures into foreign policy were at least leftist and arguably unpatriotic.

It did not help that the extreme sensitivity with which Democratic leaders approached Jackson was coupled with an almost brutal disregard for the white South. Mondale selected Bert Lance to be national chairman and then abandoned him, under fire, a disloyalty made worse by the fact that the revolt against Lance centered on his connection to Jimmy Carter, not on his alleged financial peculations. To a great many voters, it must have seemed clear that Lance was subjected to public humiliation because of his connection to the South. The 1984 Democratic convention was apparently all too eager to ignore southern whites and to repudiate their leaders.[54]

Across the nation, evangelical religion deepened the revolt against the Democrats, but it was felt in the South with particular force. The members of the theologically conservative churches have traditionally been people of low income, likely to be and vote Democratic. But greater personal involvement in such churches tends to imply a greater commitment to the conservative emphasis on personal virtue and self-reliance and an increased likelihood that this conservatism will be expressed in political behavior.[55] Consequently, the "born-again" movement, with its tendency to heighten zeal and devotion, has been a time bomb for the Democrats, somewhat held in check by Jimmy Carter's very visible Christianity.[56] In 1984 evangelical Christians, North and South, were less likely than any other religious communion to express concern for the fairness of Reagan's policies and the most likely to cite abortion as a reason for their vote.

It is also no accident that the religious right is so deeply associated with television. Television has increased national awareness of moral and social change. It has made any number of traditionally religious people more cognizant of their embattled status, so that the claims of the religious right to speak for a "moral majority" amount to desperate morale building. It is part of Ronald Reagan's appeal, as *Commonweal* observed, that he understands this "sense of grievance" among the religious, the feeling of disadvantage in relation to secular culture. Reagan's apocryphal anecdotes about "court decisions" banning voluntary school prayer speak to the fear that religion is losing its place in American public life, and the president seems to offer religious Americans a chance to reclaim their "fair share" in the nation's civil religion.[57]

Even with all these disadvantages, however, the Democrats' position in the white South is not hopeless. Jimmy Carter's relative success in the South, even in 1980, suggests that recognition of the region — especially when combined with responsiveness to its religiosity — can go a long way toward holding enough white voters to tip the balance. The new Republican strength, moreover, is unstable to say the least; the GOP made similar gains in the election of 1980, only to see them disappear in 1982.[58]

The old Democratic coalition is not quite Humpty Dumpty. Any chance of reassembling it, however, presumes that the Democrats can understand and respond to the "social issue," that touchstone of discontent among erstwhile Democrats. More and more Americans are aware of and disturbed by the growing fragmentation and disorder of American social life, our increasing tendency to privatism and our escalating indifference. They recognize, even if inarticulately, that social institutions — especially the family and the school — are not simply a "private" sphere separate from politics but the foundations of political life, the places where citizens are first and fundamentally educated and shaped. The health of society is necessarily the concern of any democratic regime.

Democrats recognize this, perhaps better than Republicans. They have been willing to help families, especially among the disadvantaged, and they have been deeply concerned about the growth of crimes against children. In 1984 the Democratic candidates invoked and campaigned on the basis of "family values." Yet Democrats have also been unwilling to set a *standard* for policy. They spoke of "family values" without affirming that a social unit including two heterosexual parents is the *norm* for family life on which public policy should be based. To set such a standard does not entail cruelty to single-parent families; quite the contrary, it calls attention to the difficulties under which such parents labor, and it implies the need for special public support — stronger federal laws, for example, enforcing the payment of child support. In the same sense Democrats cannot abandon their concern for the rights of gay Americans, even though that support entails political costs, but they need not maintain that homosexuality is anything but an exception to the social rule.

Liberals have been unwilling to set such a standard, fearing its punitive potential, but the lack of regulating norms makes Democratic policies seem directionless, so much formless sentimentality. Democrats will find it impossible to address the social issue successfully unless they are willing to affirm *some* moral center for social life; the fear that we are coming to lack such a foundation is what all the fuss is about. Certainly, the Democrats must accept the fact that the troubling aspects of the social issue will not, as so many liberals have hoped, simply fade away, at least not in the near future.

Finally, the Democrats would be well advised to reconsider their commitments on the vexing issue of abortion. In a sense, the abortion issue is similar to Prohibition, which split the Democrats into "wets" and "drys," except that the argument over abortion concerns first principles, the very definition of human life, and the argument is correspondingly more serious. The moral rights and wrongs aside, it is arguable that the "great experiment" in national abortion policy has failed, as Prohibition did, because it involves unacceptable political costs. Even the relatively small number of voters who cite abortion as a reason for their vote can hold the balance in a national election, and the figures overlook those voters for whom abortion is not decisive but contributes to their final choice. Americans appear to be divided into three almost equal camps: only 29 percent would ban all abortions, but only 35 percent are in favor of "free choice"; the rest would permit abortion only in specified cases.[59] Roughly 60 percent of Americans, in these terms, regard abortion as at best an exception to the rule; support for unqualified "free choice" not only costs the Democrats strategic support, it aligns them against a conditional majority.

Of course, the Democratic Party cannot endorse any constitutional amendment that would ban abortions. It may be possible, however, to explore alternatives. Abortion could, for example, be returned to state jurisdiction, or the Democrats could accept the principle that abortion should be permitted only in some defined set of cases.[60] In any case, the Democrats will need to do some hard thinking about the principles that should govern social life.

Over the years, social conservatives have imagined, foolishly, that self-seeking and unrestrained liberty in economic life will not carry over into public life and moral conduct. They are wrong. We commit ourselves to communities, to people, or to the future only to the extent that we are confident of our knowledge of what is and will be. Instability and change make our knowledge of one another more superficial and the future more unpredictable. Since the free market implies an economy open to unregulated change, it weakens our commitments and promotes social decay.[61]

The liberal left, on the other hand, has been devoted to the decencies of sympathy and generosity, but liberals have also defended a permissive private morality, confident that it would end repression but leave compassion intact. Confronted by so many new cruelties and the insouciant selfishness reflected in Reaganism, liberalism ought to recognize its own complicity: a doctrine that defends self-expression and self-gratification lays the foundations of selfishness and self-interest and may even point to enormities. George Orwell spoke to the point:

> For two hundred years we have sawed and sawed and sawed at the branch we were sitting on. And in the end our efforts were rewarded and down we came. But unfortunately, there had been a little mistake. The thing at the bottom was not a bed of roses after all, it was a cesspool full of barbed wire.[62]

Even amid Reagan's jerry-built recovery, Americans are rightly worried about the moral foundations of the country. Walter Mondale did the Democrats good service for the future by championing decency. It remains to be seen if the Democrats — and, especially, the party's liberals — can learn that decency is an exacting creed, premised on self-denial. Caring for others presumes that we make their need prevail over our desire, and even a modest civility requires that private feeling yield to public form.

After 1984

The nation's moral and political future certainly lies with its youth. Today's younger voters lack a sense of their ability to change the world. Their relative conservatism, as Bernice Buresh writes, is "personal, not political," rooted in their sense of vulnerability, their desire to be reassured against the threats of a world that seems too much out of control.[63]

It makes matters worse that young Americans feel the weight of their elders so heavily. Social Security, of course, is increasingly costly, but it matters even more that older Americans clog the routes to employment, opportunity, and power. Increasingly healthy, older Americans want to work longer and, on the whole, have been able to make good their claims. Buttressed by seniority clauses and tenure provisions, older Americans are relatively protected against unemployment and economic insecurity; of workers laid off between 1979 and 1984, 40 percent were under thirty-five.[64]

White youth, in fact, has its special reasons for resenting affirmative action: since the Supreme Court has held that seniority clauses do outweigh the claims of women and minorities, the burden of racial and sexual equality falls almost entirely on the young.[65] Senator Hart's hints that he might consider limiting increases in Social Security did not hurt him with younger voters, and Democratic charges that Reagan cannot be trusted to protect Social Security entitlements may, in this respect, have helped the president. Social Security and collective bargaining, those pillars of the New Deal, are no great assets for the Democrats among the young.

At the same time, however, younger voters have no real commitment to the GOP. They seem fond of Reagan, but it is a soft sentiment, not a strong devotion; Hart's neoliberalism attracted young voters, many of whom voted for Reagan in November, at one point giving Hart a lead over the president in the polls. Younger voters are decisively *not* ideological conservatives. They voted for Reagan on pragmatic grounds, giving him credit for strong leadership and for the recovery, but they rarely cited traditional values or conservatism as reasons for their choice. Roger Stone, a Reagan strategist, worries that too close an identification with social conservatism and the religious right may shake the fragile bond between the Republicans and the young.[66]

Shaped by change and uncertainty, younger Americans are inclined to be self-protective and fearful of deep commitments. Loyalty — especially loyalty to institutions — does not rank high on their list of virtues and disciplines. A generation shaped by television, they are more likely to judge on the basis of images and styles; as in Johnny Carson's version of Hart's campaign, "Vote for me, I have Kennedy hair," the young are more likely to be guided by the shifting externalities of appearance than the inward bonds of soul.

Democrats can hope to recover lost ground among the young, and that possibility inspires much of the Democrats' recent concern for toning up the party's image, with its vulgar fixation on Tip O'Neill's weight and rumpled appearance and its neglect of his legislative craft. Within limits, however, there is room and reason for Democrats to think about new images and new ideas. There is a conflict, however, between wooing traditional Democrats, who tend toward social conservatism, and pursuing younger voters who do not. The problem is not insuperable — Democrats have coped with a radically diverse coalition in the past — but it is a challenge to political art. The Democrats will need, in Theodore White's phrase, "to make new friends without losing old ones."[67] That exacting task demands new ideas and more; in 1988 and beyond, the Democrats will need to combine statesmanship and party government.

Some directions offer obvious possibilities. Work is the great theme uniting any prospective Democratic majority, and while there are tensions between old and young, whites and minorities, men and women, a policy of full employment aims to keep those conflicts within civil bounds by guaranteeing decent jobs for all Americans. In our society, as the New Dealers knew, employment is a virtual prerequisite of social dignity. As Robert Kuttner remarks, "American liberals went off the track when they opted for income transfers rather than full employment as the centerpiece of their economic strategy. Means-test income transfers are very destructive. You create a separate welfare class, which is encouraged to become dependent."[68] The Democrats may very well want to phase down welfare in favor of some forms of "workfare," through public service employment — as in proposals for a national Police Corps or a revived Conservation Corps — or through programs — such as wage subsidies, following the Swedish example — that stimulate employment in the private sector.

There are also good reasons for the Democrats to continue Walter Mondale's late campaign theme, developing programs that support community. For some time, social disintegration has sparked somewhat sporadic efforts to preserve or create community.[69] By the 1980s almost half the country, according to Daniel Yankelovich, at least *claimed* to be deeply involved in the quest for community.[70] The Democrats have at least a chance to become the champions of community, and theory as well as practice may encourage them to make the attempt. Small, reasonably autonomous, and stable communities and neighborhoods are still our best schools of citizenship, and we all pay a cost for their decline.[71]

In general, the Democrats will need to reclaim their old position as the party of those who are outsiders in the labyrinths of bureaucracy. Wherever possible, the Democrats should embrace simplification and decentralization, but they can and should argue that to dismantle the federal government would only leave citizens at the mercy of private power. With good reason, voters want to simplify the *process* of government, but that does not necessarily mean that they want *weak* government. Quite the contrary, it may mean that they want a government that has discretion. There is considerable evidence that the suspicions of the 1970s are waning. The Reagan administration demonstrates, rather paradoxically, that Americans want a government that at least appears strong, direct, and decisive; and in 1984, state referenda suggest that the "tax revolt" is ebbing. It may be that the electorate wants a government that is checked, not by denying it power, but by holding it accountable before the law and in political life.

The election of 1984 symbolized the beginning of the politics of the electronic age. The coming political era has its bright possibilities, but it is full of dangers as alarming as those of Orwell's imagining. Citizenship and statecraft will be more necessary than ever, but they will have to rest on new foundations. Ronald Reagan has presided over the demolition of the old politics; in the years after 1984, it will be necessary for Americans to see if they can build anew.

CHAPTER FOUR
Enchantment's Ending
The Election of 1988

By 1988 the bloom was off the Reagan Revolution. Americans still liked Reagan, but the Iran-*contra* scandal — along with other revelations — had undermined confidence in Reagan's administration and, especially, in his personal competence. Cracks were showing in the still-expanding economy, and voters were more inclined to question the country's direction. Neither George Bush nor Michael Dukakis was star material as a candidate, but Dukakis, the challenger, needed — and lacked — an agenda for change, a moral direction sufficiently attractive to overcome the voters' fears and distrust.

＝＞—«⦿»—＜＝

> *Yet some men say in many parts of England that King Arthur is not dead... but rather I will say: here in this world he changed his life.*
> — *Morte d'Arthur*

A quarter of a century ago, John F. Kennedy was assassinated, and the American Camelot began to evanesce into the mists of a political Avalon. Three years earlier, in 1960, Michael Dukakis had been caught up in the enchantment of Kennedy's New Frontier; in 1988 he sought to call it back. He failed. The time for Camelot has passed, even for a candidate with more magic than Michael Dukakis possessed.

In 1988 the Democrats came back to the "Boston-Austin ticket" that had succeeded in 1960 — a Massachusetts liberal with ethnic credentials paired with a moderate Texan. Electoral logic now works against a northeasterner at the head of such a ticket, however; in 1988 Democrats suspected (with reason) that they could have won with Bentsen as their presidential nominee. In 1960 the combination of Lyndon Johnson and traditional party loyalty was strong enough to enable Kennedy to carry most of the South. In 1988 Bentsen's presence on the ticket was insufficient to win even one southern state.

Race and economics have reduced Democrats to a minority of southern whites, an unreliable constituency, sufficient to win in coalition with black voters, but one that requires special cultivation.[1] Locally, biracial coalitions are frequent and often decisive in the South, as they were in 1986; but no Democratic presidential nominee other than Jimmy Carter has assembled such a majority since the federal protection of voting rights transformed southern politics. For Democrats, this trend is probably crucial: southern votes were essential to three out of their four postwar presidential victories, and in the fourth, LBJ's 1964 landslide, Democrats carried all but the Deep South.[2]

These days, moreover, the Democrats have no support to spare; Michael Dukakis did a good job of bringing Democrats home, only to discover that this was not enough. Conservatives outnumber liberals; Dukakis did not approach Kennedy's appeal to Roman Catholics; the political weight of the cities and industrial states, "the last Democratic trench" — is in decline.[3] Even the good news for the Democrats in 1988, their gains in the Midwest and West and their ability to stall or roll back Republican gains among the young, only emphasized the decreased importance of the Northeast and the party's heritage. In 1987 Robert Shrum gave the Democrats good, if unheeded, advice: "The Democratic Party has lived off the legacy of John F. Kennedy for twenty-eight years. The torch will go out unless it finally passes to a new generation. We need to invent a new legacy."[4] The "Kennedy business" did not help Dukakis, A.M. Rosenthal wrote at the end of the campaign, because "the young do not vote for the dead."[5]

And yet, Rosenthal is right only in a very narrow sense. Yesterday's events shape today's allegiances, language frames thought, and dead kings and citizens do live on, shadowy, in the body politic.[6]

A century ago, in *A Connecticut Yankee in King Arthur's Court,* Mark Twain described another effort to update Camelot. Sent back in time, Hank Morgan, the Connecticut Yankee, tries to bring Arthur's Britain into the nineteenth century through a combination of technological mastery and showmanship. In 1988 each of the Yankee candidates — no one was deceived by Bush's pose as a Texan — had his technical credentials — Bush's Washington experience set against Dukakis's managerial miracles — but neither was much for flair. Bush, guided by his media "handlers," did better than his rival (although Hank Morgan would probably have called Bush's posturings the "magic of fol-de-rol"), and inevitably, many Democrats incline toward the argument that Dukakis's defects as a campaigner cost them the election.

It may be so. But in Twain's story, for all his gifts as a performer, Hank Morgan fails to transform Britain. The Connecticut Yankee relies on technology and material progress to produce a republic; but the church, the Yankee's nemesis, keeps control of birth, marriage, and death, the events that punctuate the life of the human spirit. Hank Morgan's politics fail because he neglected the soul. His catastrophe can serve as a cautionary tale.[7] The election of 1988 sent an urgent signal that something is wrong with the political soul of American democracy.

Public Life and Private Media

The campaign was more than "negative." It was a year when civility "took it on the chin," one in which, on talk shows as in politics, nastiness "became a commodity."[8] Even so, it had precedents.

In 1888 President Grover Cleveland, who had survived considerable tarring four years earlier, faced smears and distortions at least the equal of 1988.[9] His former opponent, James G. Blaine, charged that Cleveland had appointed to office 137 convicted criminals, including 2 murderers, 7 forgers, and several brothel keepers. Mrs. Cleveland was forced to deny the rumor that the president beat and abused her. It was said that Cleveland was a dogmatic liberal (of the nineteenth-century variety) and the equivalent of a "secular humanist" because he was reported to have said "I believe in Free Trade as I believe in the Protestant religion."

Most notoriously, Matt Quay, the Republican boss of Pennsylvania, engineered a scheme by which a Republican supporter, posing as a former British subject, wrote to the British ministry, asking which candidate would best advance Britain's interest. The minister, Lionel Sackville-West, injudiciously replied that Cleveland's free trade sympathies made him preferable, and Republicans exultantly portrayed Cleveland as unpatriotic and, especially in Irish wards, as the tool of British imperialism.[10]

Nevertheless, there is something new and alarming about the incivilities of the presidential campaign in 1988. In the first place, the electronic media give greater force and currency to scurrilities, just as television makes innuendo visible: Blaine's attack on Cleveland's appointments had nothing like the impact of a glowering Willie Horton, illustrating Republican claims that Dukakis had been "soft on crime," or of pictures of garbage afloat in Boston harbor. Moreover, contemporary voters are more exposed to and dependent on mass media.

In Cleveland's day, the press could still be described, in the terms Tocqueville used earlier, as a form of political association. There was a mass press, but the great majority of newspapers were local, the voices and guardians of community. Information from national campaigns and leaders reached most voters only through local editors, leaders, and opinion makers who interpreted it and passed on its propriety and authenticity.[11] In 1988 the media spoke to more and more citizens directly, without intermediaries; gatekeepers could not protect us when the fences had been trampled or pulled down.

In 1888 American politics was still dense with associations, and for both parties, the presidential candidate was only the chief figure in a campaign made up of a myriad of local campaigns in states and wards. Cleveland, in fact, did not campaign at all, considering huckstering beneath the dignity of his office, and Benjamin Harrison's more active office-seeking was very limited by our standards.[12]

Law and technology have combined to create a centralized presidential politics dominated by national media and party committees. In campaigns, as in voting, congressional and local elections are sharply distinct from the presidential contest, so much so that it seemed anomalous, on election night, when candidates for governor and U.S. senator in Montana received about the same percentage of the vote as their party's nominee for president.[13]

The "nationalization of the electorate" has been a major political theme of the century, the result of an effort to "open" politics to individual citizens, freeing them from the control of local elites. Progressive reformers, advocates of the primary system, were also inclined to celebrate the mass media, just as their successors urged "a more responsible two-party system."[14] In one respect, the breaking down of racial barriers to political participation, the process has been pure gain. It has become increasingly clear, however, that the grand design of the reform tradition has failed.

Despite prolonged campaigning, despite vast expenditures of money (in which, in 1988, the two parties were virtually equal), despite the advice of experts and the easing of rules for voter registration, turnout fell — as it has, with the exception of the New Deal years, throughout this century. This "demobilization" of the electorate is too profound and too persistent to be explained by the requirement of registration or other barriers to voting.[15] In 1988 the fraction of adult Americans who went to the polls was almost 20 percent lower than it was in 1960, when racial discrimination still kept masses of black Americans off the electoral rolls. In Todd Gitlin's axiom, "As politics grows more professional, voting declines."[16] The affective distance between citizens and public life is great and growing. When they vote for president, voters must evaluate candidates whose characters they know only superficially, for an office in which character is crucial.[17] We lack the "peer review" that, in earlier years, was provided by party leaders and opinion makers who controlled nominations and guided campaigns. In 1884 the discovery that Grover Cleveland apparently had fathered an illegitimate child provoked the response that such private failings, then as now the focus of media attention, are not the most important indices of political character, and Cleveland won the election.[18] In 1988, by contrast, while Gary Hart's derelictions shattered his candidacy, voters did not appear to notice that, after all his years in the Senate, Hart was endorsed by only one incumbent Democratic senator. Judgment by peers is yielding to an "audition" by the media, and private proprieties may now outweigh public virtues.[19]

Be that as it may, citizens are dependent on mass media for news and for the interpretation needed to make sense out of the bewildering ravelments of contemporary life.[20] At the same time, the media are great concentrations of power, remote and distant "private governments" that decide who will speak to us and on what terms.[21] In the media's version of deliberation, citizens have no voices; one cannot "talk back" to a television set, and citizens can assert their dignity only by refusing to listen.[22] Of course, a displeased viewer can also change channels, but this "receiver control" is almost entirely negative, given the media's tendency toward a homogenized message.[23]

Yet media decision makers know that, while the power of the media as a whole is overawing, any single medium is vulnerable, its position still more precarious because media domination invites resentment. Changing channels is as easy as it is because national television has no organic relation to our lives; a local newspaper or radio station is part of, and often indispensable to, the day-to-day life of a community, but there is no reason why I should prefer ABC to NBC or CBS. The older media, especially the local press, had a position that permitted them to offer "cue giving" — guidance as well as protection — and evaluation was an integral part of their reporting. The electronic media are more anxious to "resonate"; more fearful of giving offense, they cultivate nonpartisanship and a professional neutrality.[24]

Better than the Democrats, the Republicans have understood that this desperate neutrality makes it easy to neutralize the media. Fairly consistently, Republican candidates criticize the media, appealing to the public's fear of "hidden persuaders" and joining its resentment of media power. George Bush virtually began his campaign with a contrived faceoff with Dan Rather, and he continued to fault the media's coverage of the election. This "media bashing" takes the form of asking for fair play or "balanced" treatment, but its real aim is to insulate a candidate — or a president — from criticism, Teflon-coating its beneficiaries.

The success of this strategy was evident in the media response to this year's presidential and vice-presidential debates. After the first debate, the media pronounced the exchange a draw, a defensible stance even if a plurality of viewers thought Dukakis had edged Bush. Even John Chancellor's astonishing claim that Dan Quayle had done well, despite Lloyd Bentsen's one-sided victory, might be explained as a too-rigid refusal to take sides. But television newsmen showed no reluctance to declare that Bush had won the second presidential debate. Taken as a whole, these comments suggest that if the media did not approach Republican candidates "on bended knee" — Mark Hertsgaard's description of the Reagan years — they did bend over backward.[25]

Even at its best, however, television reporting (and increasingly, all reporting) shies away from evaluating the substance, or even the accuracy, of what is said in campaigns, preferring to discuss the strategy and process of campaigning.[26] Nominally neutral, this emphasis on stratagems effectively tells citizens that the public side of politics — and, especially, those questions being argued — is of secondary importance. Even pure quantities, like results of polls and elections, need to be interpreted in the light of "momentum" and "expectations." In this implicit teaching, "real politics" is covert, "a business for professionals" that can be approached only through "inside" information supplied by the media.[27]

Parties and candidates, of course, struggle to control the process of interpretation, bypassing the press whenever possible and controlling "photo opportunities" through carefully contrived events. In 1988, for example, the Dukakis campaign, after beginning with relatively frequent press conferences, followed the Republicans' example in shielding the candidate from the press.[28] Similarly, both national conventions were transparently staged to avoid any appearance of conflict and to project optimism, harmony, and concern for "family values." Ironically, the 1988 conference of the Communist Party of the Soviet Union featured heated debate, resembling an old-style American party convention as much as the 1988 American conventions called to mind the traditional, totalitarian gatherings of the Communist Party.[29]

"Packaging," however, only redefines the role of the media; by pushing debate and decision offstage, it makes citizens even more dependent on the media to search what is said in public for clues to the real deliberations behind the scenes. Public life, increasingly, is mirroring the media's art; portrayed as trivial or superficial, political events become lifeless and shallow, arguments for cynicism and indifference.[30]

Inherently, the electronic media emphasize the private, self-protective, and individualistic side of American culture at the expense of citizenship and public life. Traditional politics, like older forms of entertainment, drew citizens into public places; the media bring politics to individuals in private retreats. In those settings, private concerns are naturally uppermost, making it harder than usual — and it is always difficult — to appeal to public goods and goals.[31] Politics is dramaturgical: it asks us to step beyond the day-to-day, to see the present in the light of the possible, judging practice by theory. Great politics, like great theater, requires a special space, a precinct for its particular sort of fantasy, from which we reemerge into everyday life. Such distinctions hone and heighten experience; by blurring fantasy and reality so pervasively, television weakens reality's force and fantasy's charm.[32]

Above all else, television is a visual medium, confined to what can be seen and hence to externalities. Sight is our quickest sense, but it is also superficial, and the media's discontinuity of image and affect encourages emotional detachment, adaptation rather than commitment. A politics of the visible comes naturally to, and teaches us to be, a "world of strangers."[33]

At the most fundamental level, politics is about invisible things. A political society can be symbolized — for example, by the flag, George Bush's talisman in 1988 — but it cannot be seen. Especially in a polity as diverse as the United States, political community is not a matter of outward semblance but of inward likeness, common ideas and ideals. In this sense, television almost necessarily distorts politics, since it is forced to visualize and personalize things that are impalpable or objective.[34] When events suit the medium, as in television's coverage of the southern civil rights movement, it speaks with unique power, but more often it is apt to be misleading, silly (Dukakis's tank ride), or mischievous.

To classical political theory, speech, not sight, is the most political of the faculties because it is in and through speech that we discover the boundaries and terms of political community.[35] But political speech — and, especially, listening to political speech — is a skill and pleasure that must be learned; it demands an extended span of attention, the capacity for critical reflection, and that art of hearing that lets us separate meaning from its disguises. Always difficult, that command of rhetoric is harder to cultivate in a society as supersonic as ours, and the electronic media actually undermine the arts of speech and hearing.[36]

Preoccupied with holding their audience, television programmers shun anything that might bore us (the Republican argument, this year, against more than two presidential debates), a logic that tends toward the lowest common public denominator.[37] The 1988 debates were question-and-answer sessions in which no comment could run longer than two minutes; in 1960 Kennedy and Nixon began their debates with eight-minute opening statements. In the 1970s the average "sound bite" allowed a public figure was 15 to 20 seconds, and the president was given as much as a minute. Pretty thin at best. But in the 1980s the figure has declined to 10 seconds for all public figures.[38] It symbolizes the decline of speech that George Bush, admiring the refrain, made "Don't Worry, Be Happy" into a campaign song, either ignoring the words or trusting that American voters would not notice their very contrary lesson.[39]

"Almost the only pleasure of which an American has any idea," Alexis de Tocqueville wrote, "is to take part in government and to discuss the part he has taken," and even women "listen to political harangues after their household labors."[40] More recently, Frank Skeffington, Edwin O'Connor's fictional mayor, spoke of politics as America's "greatest spectator sport," in which performers could, at least, rely on a critical mass of knowledgeable fans, but Skeffington was already sounding "the last hurrah."[41] In 1988 public speech seemed to be degenerating into shouted incivility, the tough talk of playground squabbles, at best a preface to politics.

The Parties and the Nominations

The primaries worked, in a sense, although the nominating process was too long, too costly, and too much influenced by unrepresentative electorates. The cost in time and dignity helped keep out some of the most attractive Democratic possibilities, but the primaries sorted out a number of flawed candidates, and the eventual nominees were sensible and able. The electorate, however, did not like the choice, with some reason. Democratic Party discontent has a special point, since the primary system puts the party at a strategic disadvantage in presidential politics.

Contested primaries, the rule for Democrats, are associated with defeat in presidential elections. In the last quarter-century, the only Democratic victories occurred in 1964 and 1976, when Republicans had their own bitter internal struggles.[42]

In any election, candidates of the center have a tactical advantage, since they have the best chance of making themselves "acceptable" to a broad coalition. In primary elections, this edge is not always decisive: candidates "win" primaries by coming in first, and they do not need majorities. In 1988 Dukakis received 42 percent of all Democratic votes cast in primaries, but until the Pennsylvania primary he was under a third, and his victory in Texas, crucial to his eventual nomination, was won with just less than 33 percent of the vote. The primary victor, consequently, can be, like Goldwater or McGovern, the candidate of party militants, who are more likely to participate in primaries. In a contest for the nomination, a centrist is usually the best a party can hope for.

Nevertheless, a candidate who stands in the center of his or her party will be considerably to the right or left of center in relation to national opinion. Primaries pull candidates away from the national center, especially since primaries deemphasize economic issues, about which parties agree, and emphasize intraparty disagreements on foreign policy and social issues, the rallying points of party militancy.[43] Michael Dukakis is a centrist Democrat and no hero to liberals in his own state, but, as George Bush happily observed, Dukakis was forced by the logic of the primaries (especially in Iowa and New Hampshire) to stress his liberal credentials, his membership in the ACLU, and his devotion to peace. These sincere convictions, identifying Dukakis as substantially left of center, indicated his vulnerability. Before his contests with Jackson and rise in the polls induced temporary blindness, it was clear that Dukakis, unable to stir voters anywhere, was too liberal to win even moderate conservatives. Dukakis, James Reston wrote, would "lose the South and bore the North," and so it proved.[44]

For Republicans, it was a near thing: a shift of 7,300 votes in New Hampshire would have made Senator Dole the victor in that state, at least lengthening the contest and, given Dole's gift for vituperation, raising the possibility of a donnybrook. As it was, the Republicans avoided a prolonged primary campaign, and they wound up with a candidate at least moderate and possibly better described as part of the party's liberal wing. Beginning with the nominee closer to the center of national opinion, the Republicans enjoyed an advantage that could be countered only by a superior Democratic campaign.

That campaign, of course, did not materialize, for which the primaries also bear some limited responsibility. The effort to capture a nomination establishes habits that persist, in the candidate and his or her staff, in the campaign proper. Part of Dukakis's primary success derived from his refusal to be drawn into intraparty conflict; his reliance on vague, liberal, but relatively unprogrammatic appeals; and his rejection of negative campaigning. Part temperament, part calculation, Dukakis's tactics within the party foreshadowed his failure in the national campaign.[45]

The problem posed by the primaries is bad news for Democrats, since their party is much less cohesive than the GOP. Republicans declare themselves the party of individual liberty and opportunity, which translates broadly into a defense of property and profit; the Democrats' standard is "equal justice," a much harder term to define. Democrats require deliberation and tests of strength to work out the terms and frame of party coalitions.

There is some balm for Democrats in the offing. Blessed with an incumbent president, the Republicans will probably be able to avoid a primary battle in 1992, though even that is no sure thing. "Main Street" Republicans — the ideological right, buttressed by the party's growing evangelical wing — are almost certain to be frustrated and enraged by the "Wall Street" cast of the Bush administration. That partisan fault line, already rumbling, seems likely to shake Republican foundations, in 1996 if not sooner.[46]

Democrats cannot afford to be much comforted. For the immediate future, Democrats must expect primaries shaped by the candidacy of Jesse Jackson, based on Jackson's support among blacks and the white, middle-class left, the "Peugeot proletariat."[47] Jackson's vote is remarkably stable — from Super Tuesday to the end of the primary campaign, Jackson's percentage of the Democratic vote rose only from 26 to 29 — but numbers are not the whole story. Jackson inspires negative coalitions; race injures him with many voters, and by most, he is perceived as too radical, possibly anti-Semitic, and certainly unelectable. Consequently, unless another candidate can dent Jackson's support in either of his two constituencies, the primary campaign is likely to be defined by the effort to establish which candidate is the alternative to Jackson. And that goal, obviously, will exaggerate the already disproportionate influence of the early primaries.[48]

It makes matters worse for the Democrats that money plays so decisive a role in primary campaigns. In general, Democratic money comes from liberal donors, which accentuates the pressure on candidates to establish their ideological bona fides. Since the material interests of liberals often run counter to their political commitments, they have no reason to value an electoral success that is not a victory for principle. Republicans also have their ideologues, of course, but in general, Republican donors see an economic interest in victory that moderates their zeal for pure doctrine. Nevertheless, even Republicans know the problem: the primaries displace those who live "off" politics in favor of those who live "for" politics, which imposes a strain on the political center.[49]

In what has become a quadrennial ritual, the Democrats will tinker with the nominating process. (In fact, they began to do so at the 1988 convention where Dukakis made important concessions to Jesse Jackson.) But the primaries are almost certainly too well established to permit a return to a nomination controlled by professionals, and more modest reforms have so far proved ineffective.[50] For example, "superdelegates," introduced to strengthen the role of professional judgment, have been pretty much irrelevant. Largely elected officials, they are bound to be leery of opposing any candidate who leads after the primaries, even if they think him a loser. In a democracy, it is never safe to resist the "people's choice," and the interest of superdelegates in doing so is lessened by the fact that their own chances of election seem so independent of the national ticket. There is something to be said for Robert Beckel's suggestion that 60 percent of the delegates be chosen by primaries and the rest by state parties, but that proposal almost certainly offends too many interests to be adopted.

Democrats can and may do something to establish a national campaign staff, independent of the retinues of candidates, which can make plans for a campaign against the Republicans while the primary season is still going on. Such a planning staff might lessen an important Republican advantage: it might attract senior Democrats, who are disinclined to commit their time and prestige to the uncertainties of a primary campaign.[51] Even the shrewdest and best designed reforms, however, will only better the ability of Democrats to cope with their inherent disadvantage in the nominating process and the difficulty it implies for the campaign.

Politics and Memory

In one important sense, the Democrats, as the "out party," began the campaign one-up on the Republicans. The party in power must defend the whole of its record; the opposition can choose the aspects of that record on which to base its challenge. The "outs" can promise to continue the popular aspects of the administration's program while correcting its flaws; if the "ins" pledge to do likewise, they will be asked why they have failed to act before. Discontent and the desire for change were the foundations of Dukakis's early lead and shaped his strategy of limiting criticism of Reagan and his policies in favor of the "upbeat" theme, "The best America is yet to come."[52]

But the choice between change and the status quo is never the whole story. The appeal to political memory may allow the party in power to present a different choice: not what they promise as opposed to what we have done, but what they did as contrasted with what we have done. Fear or resentment of the past wars with hope for the future in our judgment of the present.[53]

Until recently, memory was a Democratic fortress, recalling the Great Depression and World War II, the glory years of the Roosevelt era — and in the South, where memories faded more slowly than in the North, nursing the straight-ticket heritage of Reconstruction. Now those old remembrances are quieting into whispers, losing their connection to contemporary partisanship, especially since, wounded by change and the media, our political memory is growing shorter.[54] Even the Kennedy years, so important to Dukakis, were only a flickering of the Democrats' candle of memory, obscured by the dark years that followed.

Increasingly, the focus of American political retrospection is Vietnam and the turbulence of the 1960s, permissive morality, stagflation, and the decline of America's imperium, the "greening of America" turned overripe. Out of that half-remembered experience, conservatives — but preeminently Ronald Reagan — have shaped a new, mythic history epitomized by the "L word," liberalism identified with the Carter years, but also with all the excesses of the late 1960s and the 1970s.[55] Ironically, Republicans also benefit from the New Left's critique, which, by portraying liberals as hypocritical and lukewarm, helped build the image of liberalism as morally soft. It is part of Reagan's art, moreover, that implicitly he ran against Nixon as well as Carter, appealing to the distaste for government reinforced by Watergate, assimilating Nixon's era to the "night" dispelled by Reagan's "morning." Where Democrats once ran against Hoover, Republicans ran against McGovern in 1988, and George Bush argued repeatedly that "neighborhood Democrats" should prefer him to a leadership dominated by "the remnant of the '60s."[56]

Up to a point, Democrats recognized the problem and sought to correct it. Dukakis emphasized work rather than welfare and party leaders insisted on a shortened platform, unburdened by many controversial planks. The Democratic convention featured the author and folk-hero Garrison Keillor, surrounded by children; and Jimmy Carter, praising past Democratic candidates, asked, "Wouldn't Ed Muskie have made a wonderful President?" Symbolically, Carter was reversing the verdict of 1972, attempting to write George McGovern out of Democratic history. In the same spirit, Michael Dukakis, despite his supposed disregard for symbols, was careful, early in the campaign, to invoke Harry Truman and to make a pilgrimage to Lyndon Johnson's birthplace, and it was Truman's liberalism with which he identified himself toward the end of the contest.

Yet to overcome the Republican version of the past, Dukakis needed a vision of the future, a language of the common good. He never articulated one, and the lack was more noticeable because the appeal to "community" in his acceptance speech was the rhetorical high point of the campaign.[57] More was involved than Dukakis's too-apparent shortcomings as an orator. He betrayed an uneasiness with the idea of community in both the infrequency and artificiality of his references to his ethnicity (despite its obvious political potential) and his choice to respond legalistically to slurs on his patriotism.[58]

It cost him. After the convention, Dukakis's severest losses were among Catholics, a decline most visibly linked to his views on crime, but most fundamentally to the emphasis, in Catholic teaching, on the idea of political society as a moral order.[59] The second presidential debate, his last real chance, was a disaster. Asked what his reaction would be were his wife raped and murdered, he responded with an abstract — and rehearsed — statement of his views on crime; portraying himself as one to make "tough choices," he declined to say what taxes he would raise should it become necessary, refusing to deal with the possibility, even as a hypothesis.[60] Dukakis was unwilling or unable to find words that, validating personal experience, would subordinate it to citizenship, bridging the distance between private feeling and the public good. But that is what his campaign required.

Michael Dukakis came of age in the 1950s, the Silent Decade, when politically interested students were preoccupied with totalitarianism and McCarthyite repression, and intellectuals elevated the "separation between facts and values" into a dogma, convinced — wrongly — that it leads logically to tolerance.[61] Ideology was "unmasked" to reveal its roots in the interests of groups and classes, and social scientists discerned its impending end.[62] Politics, in these terms, could be reduced to "brokerage," the arrangement of compromise between groups, perfected by able management and skilled administration.

Political science helped make "interest-group liberalism" into "the new public philosophy."[63] A political generation learned to cultivate "realism," a pragmatic "tough-mindedness" that scorns sentiment in favor of "hard fact." That teaching lies behind Michael Dukakis's extraordinary assertion that the issue between him and George Bush was "competence"; it was also the weakest side of the Kennedy years, the illusion of "the best and the brightest."[64]

For all his faults, however, John Kennedy retained a certain Irishness: he set his pragmatism to a poetry that sent hopes dancing. Yet Kennedy was surely no ideologue; suspect on civil liberty and no enthusiast for civil rights, he often seemed to the right of Nixon on issues of foreign policy. In this sense, George Bush's charge was appropriate: Michael Dukakis is a liberal, at least when compared with his hero, and the campaign in 1988 could not be a replay of 1960.

In one critical respect, however, George Bush is more akin to Michael Dukakis than either is to the great presidents. Bush gave little indication of any idea of public purpose beyond an individualist's devotion to the private sector, the "thousand points of light." His hope for a "kinder and gentler America," consequently, seems to amount to no more than a promise to administer and broker private initiatives so as to moderate conflict. Bush, wrote George Will in disgust, "skitters like a waterbug on the surface of things," and James Skillen observed that both Bush and Dukakis are fundamentally "managerial coordinators," who use language to "buy time" rather than articulate an idea of the common good.[65] The candidates in 1988 reflected the fears and hesitancies of the contemporary public mind, but not the ability to lead or elevate it, and in the end, they confirmed the electorate's disenchantment.

Liberalism, Politics, and Economics

Republican success in attacking the "L word" obscured the fact that political liberalism, more broadly defined, was a world-beater in 1988. Modern liberalism grew up as the advocate of the Positive State, exemplified by the New Deal, urging the use of government, "the common instrument of political democracy," to meet human needs and take on problems that, as individuals, we are too weak to address.[66] In 1988 regulation and intervention were climbing back into favor, and active government commanded broad support.[67]

The Republican platform did not advocate the elimination of a single government program, and George Bush plumped for day care and youth employment. Nevertheless, economic policy was basically a Democratic talking point, and Michael Dukakis scored when he talked about such economic programs as nationwide health insurance. The Republicans gained the whip hand, however, because they were more willing to extend the positive state into foreign policy — Dukakis was hurt by his questions about the Grenada invasion and by a fear that he would endanger "peace through strength" — and into social life.

Bush moved ahead by advocating public support for "values" in civic education, most visibly in his zeal for the Pledge of Allegiance and his defense of school prayer.[68] His stance on abortion also helped, although his waffling entailed some embarrassing moments. Having expressed sympathy for a "Right to Life" amendment, Bush upheld abortion in cases of rape and incest or to protect the life of the mother, and once he had "sorted out" his views, advocated criminal penalties only for the doctors performing illegal abortions, not for the women who obtain them. Yet even this moderate — or muddled — persuasion favored more government intervention than Dukakis's position in favor of a woman's "right to choose." Bush rejected abortion on demand, as Dukakis did not, and Bush's vacillations put him squarely in the center of American opinion.[69]

Most important, Bush succeeded in portraying himself as the champion of stronger law enforcement, chiefly by arguing for the death penalty for "cop killers" and "drug kingpins." This deprived the Democrats of what had looked to be a major asset. The Democrats began with an unwonted claim on the social issue because the administration looked weak on drugs: "Just Say No" failed to make use of state power, and the government seemed compromised and craven in its dealings with Panama's Noriega. Dukakis, however, offered no distinctive antidrug program, and his views on the death penalty, together with Willie Horton's infamous furlough, helped establish the image of Dukakis as a militant civil libertarian and soft on crime. In this, as in so many things, it seemed a bad year to oppose big government and public power.

That conclusion, however, is one-dimensional. Our culture has always been divided between the individualism of philosophic liberalism and the communitarian strain most powerfully expressed by biblical religion.[70] It is not surprising, consequently, that Americans look to government for more services but also regard it suspiciously and support it grudgingly, demanding tough laws but distrusting public authority, recognizing their own vulnerability but clinging to private liberty.

Modern America magnifies the reasons for skepticism. Government and politics are baffling and frustrating, especially at the national level. To enter public life is to be convinced of one's unimportance; political life forces a confrontation with indignity, even when it hints that the "arts of association" may hold the key to another sort of honor. Private life, by contrast, affords an illusion of control, especially in relatively prosperous times.

John Kennedy's grace helped give a charm to politics, but Kennedy's assassination (and the assassinations of Dr. King, Malcolm X, and Robert Kennedy), together with disillusioning experience, emphasized dangers and limitations, weakening the personal attractions and moral claims of public life. Dan Quayle, as Lloyd Bentsen observed, is no Jack Kennedy; today, the rich and the would-be rich, the bright and the handsome, are apt to gravitate toward private pursuits. Shrunk to the measure of the yuppie, Kennedy's image is caricatured by Donald Trump and Alex Keaton.

So much of government's recent record, after all, seems to tell against it. Lyndon Johnson, so forceful and adroit, overreached in Vietnam and overpromised in the War on Poverty. Nixon, despite his reputation as a Machiavelli, stumbled into Watergate; and Carter, who profited from mistrust of government, proved a marplot, additionally cursed with bad luck. For a time, the public thought Ronald Reagan had "taken charge," but the Iran-*contra* affair revealed him to be feckless, ill informed, and indecisive, a virtual figurehead whose best defense was that he did not remember, or had never known, what was going on. Reagan retained his popularity, but the electorate, forced to recognize his shortcomings, received another jolt to its confidence in government and its judgment of political leaders.

Paradoxically, Reagan's pratfall may have helped George Bush. Bush was a safe candidate, a known quantity. Many voters felt that Michael Dukakis might be a great president, but prodded by the Republican campaign and Dukakis's own missteps, they came to fear that he might be terrible. Given the recent record of failed presidencies, most such voters preferred not to take the chance. Dukakis's vagueness only made matters worse, since it left voters without a clear sense of what he would do.

Moreover, Dukakis's appeal to his "competence," like Bush's own managerialism, may have fed the suspicion that democratic politics, including the presidency, no longer controls the nation's destiny. In the first place, we know that American life is more and more affected by events and decisions in foreign countries over which the U.S. government has only a measure of influence. We bluster, but we are becoming accustomed to the limits of American power.

Second, in the sphere that does remain to government, bureaucracy plays an often esoteric but increasingly central role. Authority has everywhere a tendency to pass downward, "into the body of the organization."[71] The Executive Office burgeoned in order to help the president control the executive branch; now the agencies of the Executive Office enjoy a sometimes startling independence from presidential control. For years, political scientists have warned that the president is in danger of being made a captive of his own machinery, and while the best modern presidents have fought that tendency, the drift is there.[72]

Harry Truman insisted that "the buck stops here" precisely because he understood, following *The Federalist,* that the price of presidential authority — and, especially, of the "inherent power" of the prerogative — is a willingness to be held accountable for mischances and the misdeeds of others.[73] The diffusion of power, however, makes it seem more and more inappropriate to think of the president in terms of rule and unfair to hold him strictly responsible for execution. By contrast, it is now common to refer to the president as a manager, a coordinator of policies initiated and carried out elsewhere.

When John Kennedy accepted responsibility for the Bay of Pigs, he meant that it was his decision and that he held himself accountable for the plan, its execution, and its failure. When Ronald Reagan declared himself "responsible" for the Iran-*contra* imbroglio (and before that, for the bombing of the Marine barracks in Beirut), he meant that he was *legally* accountable, but he went to some lengths to disclaim *personal* responsibility, and his language — "Mistakes were made" — directed the blame to a subjectless organizational process. Reagan's preposterous innocence made it easier for him to make such arguments; Lyndon Johnson could never have persuaded us that he did not know the details of the Iran-*contra* policy. Nevertheless, Reagan indicates the direction of things: accountability is shrinking into a thin political fiction.

Kurt Vonnegut saw it more than thirty-five years ago, imagining a future America in which government had become separate from politics and hence from civic deliberation and direction. In Vonnegut's fantasy, the president was a former actor — "he had gone directly from a three-hour television program to the White House" — and his job amounted to a kind of media show:

> All the gorgeous dummy had to do was read whatever was handed to him on state occasions: to be suitably awed and reverent, as he said, for all the ordinary, stupid people who'd elected him to office, to run wisdom from somewhere else through that resonant voicebox and between those even, pearly choppers.... Just as religion and government had been split into

disparate entities centuries before, now, thanks to the machines, politics and government lived side by side, but touched almost nowhere.[74]

The doubt that politics makes, or can make, more than a trivial difference to our lives calls into question the possibility of self-governance and hence the basis of the American republic. This evidently concerns all parties and all citizens, but it should be particularly disquieting to Democrats, since theirs is preeminently the party of the state, the champion of "citizenship values against market values."[75]

Democrats need to remind themselves, moreover, that this "civic ethic" holds, in principle, that economic interests are subordinate and do not deserve to rule, in the country, in the self, or in the party. For Democrats, this is not an entirely comfortable teaching. Divided between the culturally most modern and most traditional groups in America, Democrats would prefer to avoid "social issues" and broader questions of value; scarred by Bush, the Dukakis campaign hoped to "drive such questions off the political, agenda and replace them with economic concerns."[76] In general, most voters did see the Democrats as the defenders of their interests, and Dukakis's late campaign — "I'm on your side" — drew most Democrats home. It was not enough. Economic concerns will blot out everything else only when economic problems are overwhelming, as they were in the Great Depression. They could not do so amid the relative prosperity of 1988.

In any case, economic interests are clearly inseparable from questions of foreign policy, just as social concerns are linked to economic phenomena like the two-wage-earner family. In fact, the need to shore up our economic culture — pride in work, commercial rectitude, and willingness to save — is probably the most important economic issue confronting the republic.[77]

The "American Century" is ending in a mood of dread; Americans worry about the country's future even when they are more or less confident about their personal fortunes. Conservative cheerfulness seemed forced — "Be Happy," the Bush theme song, is eerily parallel to the depression favorite, "Ain't We Got Fun" — and a great many Americans voted for Bush not so much because they believed he could avert the day of reckoning but because they expected him to postpone it.[78]

Debt towers. In eight years, America has changed from the largest creditor to the largest debtor nation, and public and private borrowing has become an economic way of life. To alarm Americans with memories of the Carter years, George Bush did not refer to the magnitude of inflation; he recalled the sky-high interest rates of Carter's last year, imposed in the (successful?) attempt to drive inflation down. Implicitly, Bush realized that Americans do not mind paying dearly if they can borrow cheaply, but the public is never quite able to forget that we are discounting the future to pay for the present.

Americans are also uneasily aware of the trade deficit and the apparent decline of American products in the international economy. They see foreigners buying U.S. assets and suspect it is "on the cheap."[79] Long accustomed to something like economic autarky, Americans are still uncomfortable with our increasing dependence on foreign economic decisions, even though our new vulnerability is subtler and easier to ignore than the oil shortages of the 1970s.[80] And as Paul Kennedy argues, political power tends to follow the path of economic decline.[81] Pridefully, Americans used to quote Berkeley's vision of America's future, "Westward, the course of empire takes its way." No more: American preeminence seems to be passing, like that of the ancient empires, moving farther west across the Pacific.[82]

About their personal economic prospects, Americans are mostly optimistic, but there are reasons for disquiet. Poverty, although increasing, is still distant from most, but they are disturbed by homelessness, its most visible form.[83]

More and more Americans sense — and many know by experience — that upward mobility, the opportunity celebrated by Republicans, is becoming difficult, and even a middle-class standard of living is harder to attain. Jobs are less secure, and the preponderant evidence indicates that the new jobs being created are not "good jobs at good wages." From 1980 to 1986, average personal wages fell 2 percent (discounting inflation), and household incomes rose 10 percent only because of women entering the workforce, a resource now substantially spent.

Americans have long been accustomed to achieving a middle-class standard through borrowing, a strategy made even more necessary by the fact that college costs are rising faster than families' ability to pay. Young Americans, however, are likely to find this burden heavier, and perhaps unsupportable, because future gains in prosperity are likely to fall short of expectations. Over the succeeding decade, the wages of a thirty-year-old worker in 1950 increased 58 percent, and in 1960, 44 percent; by 1977, the figure had fallen to 21 percent.[84] "It is a true rule," John Winthrop argued, "that particular estates cannot subsist in the ruin of the public."[85] He was right: Our personal economic destinies cannot be separated from the country's shadowed future. The private centers of power in American post-industrialization are a source of problems rather than solutions. Americans are unsettled by mergers, "junk bonds," and "leveraged buyouts," and they are troubled by corporate power generally. In a *Washington Post* poll, 66 percent of Republican voters (as opposed to 14 percent of GOP convention delegates) agreed that corporations have "too much power."[86]

In 1932 Berle and Means described the separation of ownership from control, the growing ascendancy of managers over stockholders in the modern corporation.[87] Today, however, managers seem unable to protect themselves against takeovers, even with such innovations as the "poison pill" defense. Finance, always powerful, has become imperial, and it sometimes seems that managerial bureaucracy, displacing politics in public life, is *being* displaced in economic life.[88] On Wall Street, observers note a radically short-term orientation in which wealth and control have become separated from production. At the center of our economic life, a contemporary version of "conspicuous consumption" is undermining the discipline of productivity.[89]

Liberalism, Values, and Community

Yet, discontent with this "conservative permissiveness" in the economy is only part of the broader feeling that society is out of control, falling toward Gehenna. Every day's news — if not everyday experience — testifies to the frequency of disordered families, child abuse, child neglect, and teenage suicide. And for millions of voters in 1988, the drug problem ranked first among political issues.[90]

The difficulty is more fundamental than such tumults; it can be heard even in the silences of contemporary life. American households are radically mobile — somewhere around 20 percent of Americans move every year — and we learn to be fearful of attaching ourselves to people or places in order to avoid the pain that comes with uprooting. Divorce, now commonplace, underlines that lesson, and even stable families are more and more apt to be limited to two generations (only about 25 percent of American children have a significant relationship with a grandparent), a setting that teaches Americans that important relationships are short term.

Illustratively, in a 1988 television ad, a young girl, separated from her friends by her family's move, complains that she does not make friends easily. A motherly employee of the moving company reassures her, "You've already made one. Me." Yet, obviously, this slight acquaintance with an adult who, because of her job, will also soon be moving on, is no substitute for the intimate ties the girl has lost. The ad offers only the cool counsel that such transient relationships may be the best we can hope for, and, as at least one news story reminds us, closer bonds may not be safe. In Wisconsin, two teenage friends, unable to bear the separation when one family moved away, ended a weekend reunion in suicide.[91] Experience cautions Americans to keep their relationships shallow, their liabilities limited, and their obligations minimal.

Shouting that individuals are insignificant, contemporary America also whispers the more seductive lesson that, in consequence, they are free from responsibility and that it is not even legitimate to hold them accountable. Lewis Lapham describes that temptation:

> A man can feel shame before an audience of his peers, within the narrow precincts of a neighborhood, profession, army unit, social set, city room, congregation, or football team. The scale and dynamism of American democracy grants the ceaselessly renewable option of moving one's conscience into a more congenial street.[92]

And it is predictable, if unedifying, that the dominant moral doctrine of the media is a version of relativism and the ethic of success.[93]

Despite all that, Jimmy Carter was right to discern a "moral hunger" in the electorate, a yearning attested by the remarkable success of Allan Bloom's *The Closing of the American Mind,* with its appeal to natural right and to the enduring classics of Greek antiquity.[94] Yet America is too diverse and Americans are too accustomed to the benefits of modern commercial society to admit of a return of traditional morality and community, especially since Americans have enough memory of Jim Crow to know that community can be repressive. The past that holds the broadest appeal in popular culture is recent, though stabler: *Who Framed Roger Rabbit?* is likely to be contemporary America's closest approach to the trial of Socrates.[95]

At the same time, civil order — and, especially, a democratic one — does require and rest on shared beliefs and principles.[96] In regimes that are not democratic, the culture of the ruling elite can be the foundation for political life; democracy presumes a much broader sharing of civic ethics and culture. Democratic debate is possible only about matters we are willing to submit to the judgment of majorities, and so presumes that we are minimally confident in the public's decency and idea of justice. It is the things not in debate that make democratic argument possible, as Tocqueville observed in an earlier America:

> Thus, in the moral world, everything is classed, adapted, decided and foreseen; in the political world, everything is agitated, uncertain and disputed: in the one is a passive, though voluntary, obedience; in the other an independence, scornful of experience and jealous of authority. These two tendencies, apparently so discrepant, are far from conflicting; they advance together, and mutually support each other.[97]

Tocqueville worried, however, that individualism, embedded in the laws, would eventually eat up those public and private virtues he called "the habits of the heart," and there is evidence that just such an imbalance is developing in American culture. Robert Bellah and his associates found that Americans are losing the languages of biblical religion and civic republicanism, the historic rivals of individualism in our national dialogue. Even when Americans act in terms of these older values, they tend to explain and justify their lives in the language of utilitarianism, calculated self-interest, or "expressive individualism," the appeal to private feeling.[98] Too many "modern people" have "sadly concluded" that "greed is the universal motive, sincerity is a pose, honesty is for chumps, altruism is selfishness with a neurotic twist and morality is for kids and saints and fools."[99] At the same time, like Glaucon in Plato's *Republic,* they long to be persuaded that it isn't so.[100]

A great deal of Ronald Reagan's abiding popularity reflects his effective appeal to patriotism and "traditional values," but this rhetoric, while important, must be set against a record of symbols and policies that forward individualism.[101] Neither Ronald Reagan nor George Bush has been willing to ask Americans for sacrifice, and where their policies have imposed burdens, they have almost universally fallen on the less fortunate.

In foreign affairs, the Reagan administration celebrated cheap victories, but it shied away from policies that involve significant costs. Verbally firm on terrorism, the Reagan administration hesitated to risk the lives of hostages, pursuing its secret negotiations with Iran. Despite the importance of Nicaragua in Reagan's worldview, he preferred covert action to either an open use of prerogative or an all-out, popularity-risking effort to persuade the public.[102] And conservatism's social issues, with their challenge to contemporary middle-class lifestyles, were never high on Reagan's political agenda and probably rank even lower for George Bush.[103]

In part, this reticence derives from the accurate calculation that Americans are unwilling to make more than modest sacrifices. At bottom, however, Republicans are individualists in principle, devoted to the private sector and to private gain. In the second debate, George Bush assailed Michael Dukakis's plans to make tax evaders pay, saying that they would lead to "IRS agents in your kitchen." (Characteristically, Dukakis let slip the chance to call his opponent soft on law enforcement.) On the other hand, Democrats have failed to make clear that they understand that political community is more than "inclusiveness," that it imposes duties as well as rights.

This was the deeper dimension of the argument over the death penalty and law enforcement that hurt Dukakis in 1988. At the Democratic convention, Dukakis's invocation of community spoke, as his citation of John Winthrop indicated, to the biblical elements of the American tradition and to all the resonances in our culture that are older than the individualism of liberal philosophy. Political community, however, presumes, as a ruling principle, some idea of the common — and, ultimately, of the human — good. Communitarianism sees political society as a moral order, and the laws of such a regime, designed to strengthen what is admirable and right, entail penalties for the wicked as well as rewards for the virtuous.[104]

By contrast, philosophic liberalism begins with autonomous individuals, and it rejects the idea of a single human good. Political society, in this view, has no moral mission, no goal to shape the soul. It exists to advance private rights more effectively, and public policy is properly a calculation of utilities.[105] Liberalism is always hesitant to punish because it doubts that, strictly speaking, there is any wrong: there are only rights carried to excess, as in the saying "We have a right to do as we please, so long as it does not infringe the rights of others." Obviously, liberals can and do punish, but they are more comfortable with the effort to cure the "underlying conditions" of crime by providing positive incentives to civil behavior.[106]

To ask whether the death penalty "deters," as Dukakis did, is to range oneself on the liberal side of the debate, seeing punishment in terms of utilities and from the criminal's point of view. It also misses the vital communitarian point that decent citizens are not "deterred" primarily by the likelihood of punishment — if that were the case, America would be in even worse straits — but by the idea that crime is wrong.[107]

In a troubled society, citizens look to government to vindicate their decencies and to protect public life from simply private-spirited calculation. Periodically, any political society must call on its citizens to risk their lives, to suffer economic loss, and to disrupt their relationships on behalf of the public good. Citizenship, like civility, begins with a form of self-denial, a willingness to see oneself as a part of a whole. Punishment balances the scale, imposing on vice a homage to civic virtue, and a political society that is too gentle with crime or avarice will find, in the not so very long run, that it has lost its citizens.[108]

Toward Public Renewal

Abler and less hollow than his predecessor, George Bush may be willing to grapple with the nation's deeper problems.[109] Republicans have no immediate interest in tampering with their formula for success in presidential elections (although as memories fade, it will grow harder to run against the late 1960s and the Carter era.)[110] By contrast, Democrats have every reason, at least as a presidential party, to attempt to articulate a view of the common good.[111]

In the first place, Democrats need a more positive, less apologetic foreign policy.[112] This is a matter for delicacy, since Democrats are far more divided than Republicans in their attitudes toward international affairs; in a 1987 poll, Democrats divided almost equally when asked whether the United States should "support anticommunist forces around the world."[113] Even that polarization, however, argues against dovishness and for moderation, and there is a special urgency to the need for a new Democratic perspective on foreign policy.

There are unmistakable signs that the "Vietnam syndrome" is ending. Even more dramatically than the Vietnam memorial, Jane Fonda's apology to veterans signals the war's new place in national remembrance, and the rise of courses on Vietnam in nonelite colleges is a political omen Democrats cannot afford to ignore. This change is an opportunity for Democratic reconciliation, since lines are softening on both sides of the Vietnam divide. The controversy over Dan Quayle's military record established or revealed a new, lower conservative standard, by which patriotism is satisfied by law-abidingness: one did one's duty, George Bush implied, by refraining from burning draft cards or flags.

This is as clear a portent as Ronald Reagan's divorce was in social policy: conservatism is adapting, and opinion in contemporary America, while not dovish, is also not on the side of the hawks.[114] If Ronald Reagan can become an apostle of arms control, it should be possible for Democrats to lose their reflex against the use of military force, avoiding their recent tendency to overgeneralize the "lessons" of Vietnam. (Senator Bill Bradley has already set an excellent example.) Perhaps some Democrat may even observe that both those who fought in Vietnam and those who resisted the war filled a fuller measure of patriotism than those who merely obeyed the law.

In any case, Democrats surely need to offer some examples of "toughness," some instances of willingness to punish and to enforce standards of civil conduct, if they are to be credible advocates of political community. Locally, even very liberal Democrats, like Assemblyman Jack O'Connell in California, are apt to support stricter sentences, including the death penalty, and Congress was wise in voting to enforce child-support payments.[115] Beyond particular policies, Democrats have a special reason to demonstrate that their party has a vertebral moral identity. The Democratic Party cannot weaken in its advocacy of racial and gender equality; it is probably committed to a pro-choice position; and the list goes on. Committed to change in so many areas of life, Democrats must demonstrate to the electorate that, more than weathervanes, they have some principles that do not change.[116]

This is nowhere more evident than in relation to race, the "dirty little secret" of the election of 1988.[117] Actually, it was not much of a secret. There is more and more willingness to speak about the drift of whites away from the Democratic Party, and not only in the South. Among Democratic candidates since Franklin D. Roosevelt, only Lyndon Johnson received the support of a majority of whites, and Johnson's revolution helped persuade a large number of working-class white voters that, in the last analysis, Democrats will prefer the interests of blacks to their own.[118]

At the same time, it is harder to overcome such feelings by an appeal to guilty consciences.[119] Legal segregation is a hazy memory, and for the most part, overt racism has yielded to subtler forms. For example, in the media — and hence in the view of most Americans — race is visible largely in relation to crime and the sleazier forms of interest-group politics.

Philosophic liberalism offers little help. The primacy of individual rights in the liberal tradition implies that equality, "before the law" and in politics, exists to protect earned inequalities in economic and social life. Enforced integration of low-income housing runs against property rights; busing menaces plans to give one's children the benefit of superior public schools; affirmative action seems to endanger the basic principle of equal opportunity, that jobs should be awarded on the basis of demonstrated ability. Liberal doctrine does recognize the claim of minorities to compensation for past injuries, but its individualism, rejecting the idea of collective guilt, argues that I am responsible only for my own deeds, not those of the past. Policies to promote racial equality are increasingly likely to be seen, in these terms, as "reverse discrimination," violations of the unequal prerogatives of private achievement.

Democrats cannot counter that persuasion, let alone overcome it, without a language of collective obligation. In the biblical view, for example, membership makes citizens participants of the whole of a political society's life, including its heritage. When citizens say that in 1776, "we" declared our independence from Great Britain, they identify with the American past, but this appropriate pride also entails guilt: our Constitution included slavery, and our society perpetuated racism. "In Adam's fall," the Puritans taught their children, "we sinned ALL."

In that understanding, all Americans have an obligation to make those sacrifices that are necessary to atone. The burdens this involves should be shared as equally as possible: working-class whites in cities like Yonkers should not be expected to welcome low-income housing when rich neighboring cities like Scarsdale are left alone. When individual Americans suffer some loss in the interest of racial equality, however, it is no different in principle from conscription, which may call some to serve in time of war while leaving others at home. Every citizen has a civic calling to repay his or her debt to the common life.

Implicitly, by pledging "equal justice," the 1988 Democratic platform went beyond pluralistic inclusiveness. Equality makes its own discriminations. We are not equal in the way we look or in what we have achieved; since equality rejects the testimony of such appearances, it points politics toward the soul. Moreover, a politics founded on the belief in equality excludes racism and relativism, for it holds that what is human is more important than biology or culture.[120] There is also a contemporary truth in the promise of just equality, with its suggestion that equality can be unjust.

America cannot be an ancient Greek *polis* or a homogenous community; political life must find room for our diversities and our privacies, just as prudence must acknowledge the impact of technology and economic change. American democracy needs, and can stand, only so many stanzas of epic poetry; contemporary politics calls for the more prosaic effort to protect and rebuild locality, association, and party, the links between private individuals and public goods. Even such limited goals, however, presume policy guided by a ruling principle, that middle term between repression and relativism whose better name is citizenship.[121] For both Republicans and Democrats, the election of 1988 indicates the need for a new civility, and for the kinds of word and deed necessary to affirm, for the coming century, the dignity of self-government.

CHAPTER FIVE

Thinking about Tomorrow Worriedly

The Election of 1992

In 1991 George Bush, victorious in the Gulf War, had seemed unbeatable, and the Democrats' stars had decided to pass up the race. But by election time, a prolonged recession — the natural result of Reagan-era economics — had made Bush supremely vulnerable. Bill Clinton, dogged by stories about various improprieties, was the class of an uninspiring Democratic field. Millions of voters were unhappy with the choice, flirting with or voting for Ross Perot. In the end, however, Clinton's ability to reassure and tantalize proved most appealing to America's discontents.

⸻ ⦿ ⸻

> *And all the unsettled humours of the land . . .*
> *Have sold their fortunes at their native homes,*
> *Bearing their birthrights proudly on their backs,*
> *To make a hazard of new fortunes here.*
> *— The Life and Death of King John* (II, i)

Half a millennium ago Columbus, unwitting, landed in a new world, and Americans in 1992 suspected that, like him, they had arrived at some unexpected place, full of unfamiliar shadows.[1] In the election, most Americans allowed themselves to be drawn by hope, but they went wistfully, driven by worries and without much confidence, convinced that they had more to fear than fear itself.

Change was in the air: for the first time in more than half a century, a presidential election was not framed by war, present or rumored; voters were restless; new concerns and constituencies made themselves felt; and the victorious Democrats proclaimed themselves a "new" party. Yet no election has so often or so pervasively been compared to the American past; Americans wanted assurance of comparability if not continuity, looking for old landmarks and fixed stars in the strange new world they confronted.

The election was likened to the contest in 1932 and to earlier third-party elections, especially the races in 1912, 1968, and 1980.[2] Observers drew parallels between Bush and other defeated incumbents — Taft, Carter, and most insistently, Herbert Hoover.[3] On the other side, analysts sought

Clinton's prototype in Carter, in Kennedy, even in Franklin Roosevelt.[4] For obvious reasons, Clinton was not often compared to Truman, that tower of straight talk and private rectitude, but he did claim Truman's legacy. It was a heritage much in demand: Perot had designs on it and so, even more implausibly, did George Bush. Both comparisons were bizarre, and not only because Bush, a dutiful son of a Republican family, had voted for Dewey in 1948. Unlike Perot, Truman was a partisan and an insider, whose life was spent in the environs of politics and who never shook — or really sought to shake — his association with the Pendergast machine. And Truman, the come-from-behind campaigner Bush hoped to emulate, himself ran an almost completely partisan campaign, with few references to his opponent and no attacks on his character.[5] Lyndon Johnson, however, was not used as a model for the three candidates, although through Vietnam and racial politics he was a presence in the campaign; in 1992 Americans showed signs of making their peace with Johnson's lacerating failure and his equally troubling success.

In any event, a great many Americans, viewing the present, found themselves attracted to earlier times, especially to their moments of strength and exuberance. After the "numbness" of the presidential debates, Russell Baker wrote, "the mind finds itself shamefully yearning for a benighted time when vigor, sassiness, confidence, even arrogance, expressed itself in the national spirit."[6] In 1992 confidence did not point Americans to the future, it drew them to the past; and the election, a vote for change, was also a hope for renewal.

Economic Disorder and the American Civil Order

In one sense, the election is easily explained: Bush, R.W. Apple Jr., noted, was "the economy's casualty."[7] The bad portents began to be apparent early on; by August 1991 Warren Brookes was arguing that the economy's woes might make Bush a "sitting duck" for the Democrats, and so it proved.[8] Democrats refused to be distracted and, in the end, achieved something close to their old fantasy, an election fought out simply on economic terms.[9]

The numbers were depressing. Unemployment was relatively high, job creation had virtually stopped, and the gross national product (GNP) was going nowhere.[10] Yet as Bush complained rather plaintively, the data were not *that* bad, especially when compared to other countries, and there were bright spots, such as low inflation and low interest rates.[11]

The greatest problem for the president lay behind the figures. Short-term calculations and immediate economic experiences, and even self-interest, narrowly defined, are less potent politically than judgments about the future and about the country as a whole.[12] In 1988 Bush parroted Ronald Reagan's 1980 question, "Are you better off than you were four years ago?" and the promise of improvement haunted him in 1992. But Reagan himself withstood worse economic conditions in the congressional elections of 1982, when the Republicans suffered relatively light losses because voters were convinced he had a star to steer by. In 1992, by contrast, the country felt no such assurance about times to come. Even during the Great Depression, Americans could take comfort in being the world's largest creditor, an industrial powerhouse with a favorable balance of trade and little public debt. All those consolations are now turned upside down, and the recession in 1992 differed from any since World War II "in the near certainty that it is not a prelude to any substantial recovery."[13]

Voters had been inclined to say that the country was on the "wrong track" even when Bush's ratings were high, and time only added to their pessimism.[14] Material well-being was only a part of the story: for many of the electorate in 1992, the economic issue was dignity for themselves and their country.

In the beginning of the Republic, Jefferson observed that virtually all free men could enjoy the degree of economic independence necessary to self-governing citizenship. He relied, in his familiar thesis, on the existence of abundant land, available to yeoman proprietors, but it was also important, he wrote later on, that even those who worked for wages could expect to find "comfortable subsistence" and the ability to provide for old age.[15] In the latter argument, the critical factor is not income, although Jefferson presumes a socially adequate wage; his case relies on the worker's confidence that he will be able to find work at "satisfactory" pay so that no worker feels unduly dependent on a particular employer. And through much of our history, with only a little distortion, Americans have been able to take that condition as the ordinary rule.

Contemporary Americans are less likely to enjoy that good fortune. Blue-collar labor, once a kind of aristocracy, has been watching its position deteriorate for years: the 1991 *Economic Report to the President* indicated that the average weekly wage of blue-collar workers had fallen 20 percent since 1972.[16] Middle-class families generally have been able to keep incomes stable or rising, but only by relying on second wage earners, working longer hours, and borrowing, caught in the cycle of "work and spend."[17] More and more households, too, have found their health insurance threatened as employers seek to control costs.[18]

By a good many reckonings, the income of Americans in the middle sectors of society has been stagnant for a decade, and the U.S. Census Bureau recently noted a long-term decline in the percentage of Americans ranked in the middle class.[19] Inequality is growing, reaching "Great Gatsby levels," Paul Krugman says; even on the right, Charles Murray is troubled by the disparity between a considerable elite (10 to 20 percent) that can "bypass institutions it doesn't like" and the rest of the public, foreshadowing a society divided into the exempt and the trapped.[20]

During the Reagan years, this increase in inequality could be treated, in middle-class America, as only the other side of opportunity.[21] The recession of 1992, however, struck at the jobs of white-collar labor, its threat magnified by the fact that the middle class carries a burden of debt and expectations that makes its way of life exceptionally vulnerable.[22] Whole layers of management are disappearing, apparently for good, as companies strive to become "lean." Moreover, such jobs as are being created — blue and white collar — include a growing number of temporary positions, evidently less secure, with lower wages and benefits.[23]

Economic troubles, bad enough by themselves, were interwoven with concern for civil order and the decencies of private life. Despite devotion to "family values," the deterioration of families escalated during the Reagan-Bush years: the number of single-parent households increased by almost 50 percent, and too many of those families are desperately poor, while even in economically better-off homes with two parents, the demands of work drain time and quality from family life.[24] At best, families are losing autonomy; the media begin to inculcate their "hidden curriculum" in infancy, before literacy and to some extent even before speech.[25] Visible in the media, if not in day-to-day life, divorce, feminism, and the demand for gay rights, to say nothing of new ethnic diversities, are undermining old certainties. Change and mobility continue to make us hesitant about commitments to persons and places, and in a more overtly sinister way, crime keeps citizens away from public spaces, barring doors when it does not prompt a retreat to some place of relative safety.[26] The affluent are inclined to seek private solutions and immunities, while the less fortunate have their own forms of privatization, most destructively in the autoanesthesia of drugs.[27] Too many Americans are alone, frightened, or uncivil, and all of us are at least a bit bewildered. Living in a state of anxious vulnerability, if not privation, multitudes of Americans in 1992 were disgusted with an administration that they saw as out of touch, indifferent, and ineffective.

Foreign policy, George Bush's strong suit, gave him little help. With some pride, the president argued that because of Republican successes, Americans could sleep without fear of nuclear war, but that claim moved few voters.[28] The collapse of Soviet communism softened the glue that had held the conservative coalition together, and for most Americans, foreign threats seemed distant, hypothetical, or unpersuasive.[29] In August, Bush tried a little showy "toughness" with Iraq, but no other "October surprise" materialized, apart from the self-wounding search through the Clintons' passport files. Possibly the administration realized that, as Leslie Gelb observed, presidents "have so often abused the national interest for their own political ends" that Americans have come to take partisan purposes for granted.[30] Disillusionment hovered even around Bush's triumph in the Gulf War, which appeared more and more suspect and inconclusive, a mood typified by the bumper stickers that read *Saddam Has a Job. Do You?*[31]

In fact, foreign policy added to the American sense of economic and civic vulnerability. American borders are now permeated by foreign products, capital, and labor.[32] Foreign governments, too, play increasingly evident roles in American politics, as Ross Perot, with some exaggeration, so often observed. In 1988, Kevin Phillips claims, the Bank of Japan helped Bush so much "it should have registered as a Republican political action committee," and this year, the Miyazawa government, similarly inclined, ordered Japanese companies to ship fewer cars to the United States than they were allowed under Japan's self-imposed quota.[33] Americans became accustomed to hearing that their economy is no longer "world class," and already wounded by slighting comments from Japanese leaders, they were not reassured by Bush's feckless assertiveness in Tokyo, which came across as "bashing on bended knee."[34]

Clinton, an internationalist and, in these days, a moderate hawk, demonstrated a respectable aptitude for foreign policy, and many observers ended by sharing Gelb's verdict that Bush, an able leader in dealing with the "old security and power issues," was not up to the economic concerns that now occupy center stage in international politics.[35]

The Skeptical Search for an Active Government

The clearest message of 1992 was the majority's demand for active government, engaged to relieve America's discontents and reclaim the future. Even in 1988, opinion had tended to side with the candidate who, on any given issue, supported the use of public power.[36] This time, the tide was unmistakable: 62 percent voted for the differing, but undeniably activist persuasions of Clinton and Perot.

It was a hard year for laissez-faire. Rhetorically, the high point of the Democratic campaign was Mario Cuomo's attack on Bush for relying on "the invisible hand of some cyclical economic god" to save the ship of state, and less elegantly, the Democratic campaign featured denunciations of "trickle-down economics."[37] Even conservatives, of course, now accept a considerable degree of economic intervention: Ronald Reagan promised a "safety net," the Reagan and Bush administrations committed billions to protect depositors in failing banks and savings and loans, and the administration took it for granted that the Federal Reserve should manage interest rates to promote growth.[38] In 1992 the current of activism ran even stronger. Among economists, there was something of a generational shift, reminiscent of the advent of Keynes, with practice brought to the critique of economic theory.[39] Clinton found no shortage of economists willing to agree, for example, that government is needed to promote saving and investment, especially since Reagan's reliance on the classical "equivalence theorem" — that government spending will lead to private saving — had proved misplaced.[40] By itself, moreover, investment may not be enough: counter to much conventional wisdom, there is good evidence that American productivity is not low.

The problem may be that relative efficiency is being purchased at the price of employment, so that government is needed to link investment, productivity, and work.[41]

Americans were only a little less likely to look to government to shore up the social and moral foundations of society or to build new ones. Most were inclined to think that government should support the family in some way or other.[42] Conservative noise about family should not obscure the fact that liberals, though they differ in their definitions of the family and the policies they recommend, are eager to extend help.[43] The willingness to involve government in civil life extends beyond the family: the communitarian movement has attracted support from a broad spectrum of intellectuals, while in practice, 1992 saw several states attempt to link welfare rights with obligations.[44] Even the vogue of environmental protection, limits to growth, and historic preservation, while often tied to fairly narrow self-interest, also reflects an effort to enlist policy on the side of community.[45]

This is part of an old story, for conservatism's concern for "values," often bigoted and bumbling, touches a truth. Government by itself cannot make us good, but it can encourage decency by reducing its costs and by raising the price of indecent behavior.[46] In America, that role of government has been vital: our customs and culture are not immemorial, but the result of a more or less conscious design, a people engaged in making itself.[47] American culture has been a perennially political issue, so it is no surprise that the contemporary "culture war" finds its way into democratic politics.[48] In fact, we ought to hope that the conflict can be expressed in, and confined to, democratic forms.

Unfortunately, our confidence on the point cannot be very great. Although Americans turned to government in 1992, they distrusted it and were apt to despise politics; a year earlier, Peter Hart and Douglas Bailey found that although voters "desperately want to believe in government," they were deeply disillusioned, so there was a "dangerously broad gulf between the governors and the governed."[49]

All our public pillars were more or less damaged.[50] Congress, which never stood too well with the public, was injured by legislative delay, the "scandal" at the House bank, and most of all, by the hearings on Justice Clarence Thomas's confirmation. Watching Thomas and Anita Hill before the Judiciary Committee, voters divided on the basis of gender and class, but virtually all felt contempt for politicians, and David Rohde saw the hearings as one event in the long-term "undermining of respect for institutions."[51]

Historically, the presidency has been less exposed to scorn than Congress, but a long series of abuses — Watergate, Iran-*contra*, and what the media began to call "Iraqgate" — has worked its hurt. Carter's perceived failure left its weight of doubt, as did Reagan's increasingly evident ineptitude, and George Bush never had Reagan's Teflon charm.[52]

The decline of political parties, of course, has long been apparent, and this year the low level of partisan allegiance was reflected in the oscillation of the polls.[53] Voters, seeing money as dominant in elections and increasingly convinced that corruption is the political rule, feel a lack of voice and representation; in a 1990 *Times-Mirror* poll, 57 percent of respondents agreed that "people like me don't have any say about what government does."[54] This mood of disaffiliation and deauthorization in turn encourages citizens to look outside the institutions or to the negations of protest politics, a disposition especially clear among those attracted to Ross Perot — a candidate by "immaculate conception," Garry Wills said, untainted by politics.[55] Perot voters, Richard Morin and E.J. Dionne Jr. found, had no good words for political parties, and while a large number expressed a desire for a third party, they did so not because of any positive convictions or any confidence in democratic politics, but simply because they were applying a free-market *model to* politics, relying on the logic of competition.[56]

It was to be expected, then, that along with some hope, the electorate harbored an abiding doubt that government can succeed.[57] And although it has been almost twenty-five years since an active president dealt with a legislature of the same party — in many ways, Carter was suspect on both counts — the voters' lack of confidence is not simply instrumental. It reflects an accentuated mistrust of government's moral title and the suspicion that politicians have no goal except self-perpetuation.[58] Divided government, after all, has been the creation of distrust, the mirror of deauthorization.[59] It also set in motion its own vicious cycle: the voters' disaffiliation has made leaders shy away from any policies with immediate costs, resulting in a "no pain" politics, full of posturings, such as the Balanced Budget Amendment, frustrating for leaders and citizens alike.[60] Political leaders have become more contemptuous of the electorate, not always so secretly, while the voters — on a generous reading — were left with a "grumpy cynicism."[61]

The prevailing discontents made it all the more striking that voter turnout in 1992 reversed the long decline in participation.[62] That the race was apparently closing undoubtedly helped, as did the fact that so many voters felt themselves immediately threatened by the recession. These factors, more or less specific to 1992, suggest that voters may easily lapse into their old indifference; over the long haul, individuals calculating self-interested utilities will find only inadequate reasons for going to the polls. Consistent participation presumes a fuller involvement in community life.[63] The signal in 1992 was faint, but Americans did hint that they are willing to be drawn back into the political system by any relatively entertaining show.[64]

Public Life and Private Politics

Clinton's great challenge, and the Republic's, lies in the need to strengthen the dignity of citizenship and the quality of democratic consent. Knowing this, Clinton plans something approximating a permanent campaign, but the media, a part of his intended solution, are an even bigger part of the political problem.

Earlier in our history, Alexis de Tocqueville had no doubt that the press was an essentially representative institution, deriving much of its authority from the power of communities to hold it accountable. Like the media we know, the press of Tocqueville's day was inclined to slight principles in favor of personalities and to pursue public figures into their private lives. Tocqueville saw a press, however, that was local and intimate with its readers, enjoying less power than a mass press, but more authority, so that it was less likely to "give way to the current of the multitude."[65] Bound up with its communities, Tocqueville thought, the press was better able to instruct them and might even suggest from time to time that private and local interests should yield to the public good.[66] The "old news," Bill Moyers writes in the same spirit, "drew people to the public square" and helped teach the "vital habits of democracy."[67]

In contemporary America, in contrast, the dominant forms of the press are media by which information is communicated *to* us, but without any serious element of reciprocity or accountability.[68] We depend on the media and recognize their power, but our dependence is a mark of voicelessness and indignity.[69]

Recognizing our resentment and their lack of authority, the media are desperately anxious to please us, as Tocqueville would have expected, especially since few things are easier than changing channels. But in the first place, that disposition makes the media contemptible and incapable of self-regulation without limiting their power. In 1992, for example, the media's early resolution to forego sensational inquiries into the private lives of candidates crumbled under the impact of the supermarket tabloids, and the whole of the press was soon engaged in what one British paper called "sexual McCarthyism."[70] Similarly, concerned with criticism of the ever-shortening "sound bite" — down to 7.3 seconds, by one calculation, in 1988 — CBS decided that all sound bites would, henceforth, be 30 seconds or more. But news editors, reaching the conclusion that such "bites" were unavailable or "unwieldy," eliminated them almost altogether, showing reporters more and candidates less.[71] And second, even the determination of *how* to please us is made by the media, on the basis of criteria and evidence they choose. This unauthorized decision making fuels the fear of some secret political design. In 1992 conservatives were particularly apt to detect a hostile conspiracy, or at least a tilt to the left, but plenty of liberals heard a tune called by Republican elites.[72] In fact, the media are probably shaped less by political intent than by "mass circulation images, themselves squeezed by commercial pressures," a principle just as troubling.[73]

The opinions that guide the media are not genuinely public, though they come from the people. The media reach us in private settings and address largely private concerns and feelings, relying on images more than words.[74] Where radio, as Russell Baker remembers, "intoxicated us with voices," the contemporary media discount speech, continuing the grand modern impulse, initiated by Machiavelli, to exalt the visible and nonverbal, the deed as opposed to the word.[75] To the extent that they are treated by the media at all, political speech and deliberation are presented as a kind of theater of deception, in which content matters only as clue to covert forces and schemes. In response to the president's State of the Union message, John Tierney noted that "the chief question raised by analysts on television was not whether his proposals made any sense, but how the Democrats would respond to his staff's strategy."[76]

This year American resentment of the media turned so explosive that suddenly the campaign was dominated by "new" news — "weird media," Bush said — the talk shows and tabloids, Don Imus and Arsenio Hall, Larry King and the "infomercial."[77] Ross Perot was the first to see the advantages of the new vehicles; Clinton, damaged by the more orthodox media, soon followed. The new media have undeniable benefits: they are apt to be free, and they allow candidates to develop positions in depth, or at length, at any rate. Clinton turned to them in some relief. After a frustrating, much-trivialized primary in New York, Clinton sought to use his victory speech to direct public attention to the substance of his campaign, but after four minutes, all the networks except CNN and C-Span stopped their coverage, and CNN dropped out after nine minutes. Network news reduced the speech to sound bites, and the next morning, on the *Today Show,* Clinton's remarks had been shrunk to "I love Wisconsin, Minnesota and Kansas, and I really love New York."[78] The talk shows, by contrast, allowed Clinton to display his virtuosity and command of the issues.[79] The new media, moreover, worked to diminish the advantage the party in power draws from its ability to dominate television news, and Republicans can be expected to cultivate them in force in 1996.[80]

For viewers, what mattered in the "new news" was face-to-face interaction with hosts and with audiences, or hearing candidates field called-in questions, an approximation, even if weak, of town-meeting democracy. But the "community," produced for the media, is only another image that can be managed. It comes into being around and because of leaders — the hosts or their guests — so that the talk shows only emphasize, as Ellen Hume put it, "that the media are our new political bosses — the direct filter that parties used to be."[81] The media audience cannot hold its studio "representatives" accountable, nor can the individuals who make up the "community" of questioners speak to one another without the assistance of the media themselves. The "electronic town hall," Gerald Marzorati wrote, is what passes for civic community when people live among strangers and the "friendliest colleagues are the computer, database and fax."[82] The new media, in sum, did not renew American citizenship, although they may have made citizenship seem interesting; as David Broder noted early on, they offered only the "catharsis" of "highly contrived dramas."[83]

Nothing in 1992 changed the fact that masses of Americans, inundated with information, know they lack the means of separating the false from the true.[84] As Michael Rogin argues, all too many citizens find themselves facing a baffling, overwhelming, and often arcane government in the "paranoid position" of "disordering powerlessness" and are tempted to equally paranoid analysis.[85] They are nudged further in that direction by the media's blurring of the line between politics and fiction, exemplified by the rise of the docudrama and movies like Oliver Stone's *JFK*.[86] This aspect of the media weakens the check of reality and encourages "splitting," the psychological process by which heroes or times past are idealized — as with John Kennedy or the "inheritance" denied to young Americans — while their negative qualities are disowned and identified with demonized and conspiratorial enemies.[87]

There were plenty of examples in 1992. Ross Perot, pushing aside evidence of his own use of investigators and personal threats, as well as his dealings with foreign governments, talked a good deal about the plots of Republican dirty tricksters and foreign agents in major-party campaigns.[88] Most pervasively, however, homosexuals — as Rogin pointed out — were identified with erotic and social disorder; this was true of the leftist fantasy of Oliver Stone, of the falangist rhetoric of Patrick Buchanan on the right, and of Perot's fear that appointing a gay cabinet member would cause "controversy" or that his daughter might be portrayed as a lesbian.

There was no shortage of Americans who, sharing such persuasions, were eager for a leader able to cut through the thicket of democratic politics. And others, less troubled, shared the same impatience.

The candidacy of Ross Perot epitomized many of the themes of 1992, but it would have been impossible without the media. On their battlefield, Perot proved a master strategist. He opened and promoted his candidacy through talk shows, trailing a stream of one-liners; he demonstrated the viability of the "infomercial"; and week by week, he spent more money purchasing time for his interrupted campaign than any previous candidate.[89] Perot showed that with grand salesmanship and enough money it is possible to become a major force without passing through the primaries or the parties, and dodging the press where he could not dominate it, he avoided almost all the scrutiny that goes with a traditional campaign.[90]

Of course, even Perot could not entirely sidestep the old modes, and Perot the candidate repeatedly undermined Perot the strategist, revealing too much of his testy, autocratic, and paranoid streak.[91] Yet at the beginning of the campaign, Perot was able to present himself as a candidate of force who could solve all problems magically, virtually without cost — "without breaking a sweat," as he liked to say — and otherwise, as a tabula rasa on which voters could write their own scripts and fantasies.[92]

Recognition that ending the deficit would call for taxes and for sacrifice of a high order helped persuade Perot to quit the race.[93] When he returned, he retained the image of "can do" forcefulness, now combined with a "message" that — vague in so many details — was presented as complete and tied to Perot's persona.[94]

The common thread of Perot's two campaigns was his demand for quick solutions and his unwillingness to do the prolonged work of persuasion and compromise within institutions. Hostility to institutions, in fact, was a major part of his appeal. In May the great majority of Bush and Clinton supporters, while critical of Congress generally, approved the job being done by their own House members, but 55 percent of those supporting Perot disapproved.[95] That unhappiness fit neatly with Perot's discounting of representative government and his disdain for conflicts of interest and party, the messy charms of democratic politics.[96] The instinct of the entrepreneur, Michael Schrage observed, is the desire to create new forms, and hence to reject established institutions; Perot had the special attraction of an "outsider" who was knowledgeable about the system, one who did not offer to dismantle government but promised to make it stronger and more effective.[97] In addition, the nationalism of his antiforeign themes amounted to a pledge to restore the American imperium as a part of America's inheritance.

Repeatedly, Perot's campaign was linked to the "tradition of prairie populism," but the stark differences between his movement and the old Populism illustrate the difficulties of contemporary democratic life.[98] The Populists of 1892 grew out of and were composed of a dense forest of membership groups and face-to-face communities, so the People's Party was a federation of localities and associations, held close to the grass roots.[99] The party abounded in policies, many spelled out in detailed plans: the Sub-Treasury system; free silver; the graduated income tax; the government ownership of railroads, telegraph, and telephone were only the most prominent.[100]

But the Populists of 1892 had trouble finding a candidate. Their best bet, Polk of North Carolina, died before the convention, and Judge Walter Gresham turned them down. In the end, they nominated a veteran but rather uninspiring radical, General James B. Weaver, more or less because "there was little else left to do."[101]

By contrast, Perot's movement was constructed from the top down, its organization at least inspired and certainly sustained by Perot's money. It offered few policies; only the deficit-reduction program, the centerpiece of the second campaign, had much solidity. Above all, Perot's movement was centered on and defined by its candidate. Even Perot's version of the "electronic town hall," George Will pointed out, involved citizens giving information to the leader, not discussing or making decisions among themselves — an image, Will thought, shaped by the mystique of leadership with which Woodrow Wilson had invested the presidency.[102]

"I'm doing this for the American people," Perot often declared, "because they can't do it for themselves." Just so. Whatever the legacy of Perot's candidacy, it pointed to our distance from Populism's promise and to the endangered status of democratic citizenship.

The State of the Political Parties

Perot's candidacy, of course, also testified to discontent with the nominating process. In droves, voters rejected the primary system, grumbling about the choices offered and staying away from the polls. Many, a plurality at one point, found themselves supporting Perot despite the fact that he had avoided primaries altogether. The system, Russell Baker wrote, "is dead, dead, dead and ought to be buried before it kills the two major parties."[103]

Baker's obituary was premature. The primary system was wounded, but it will survive, especially because the Democrats won the election. Bush's nomination made many voters unhappy, but they saw that it was more or less inevitable; Clinton's candidacy was the source of more murmuring, and his success will quiet many critics.

Yet Clinton did emerge from the primary season as a flawed candidate, so damaged by doubts about his character that crowds of Democrats would have preferred someone else, just as they would have done when campaigning began.[104] The primary system, however, forced candidates to choose early, when Bush looked like a sure winner. The leading Democrats opted to wait for more likely times, leaving the field to long-shot players. Mario Cuomo might have entered relatively late in the game, but he took himself out, and the Democrats were left with the candidates in the field. The primary system has enough residual democratic legitimacy to prevent the party conventions from setting aside the verdict of its long string of elections.[105]

The primaries gave the Democrats two consolations in 1992. In the first place, President Bush was also scarred by Pat Buchanan's challenge. Moved to confess that he had made a "mistake" in agreeing to higher taxes, Bush added evident weakness to the sin of broken promises. And the president and his advisers responded curiously to the returns. In New Hampshire and after, Buchanan's supporters were mostly independents intent on "sending a message," voters who crossed the ideological spectrum. Bush, however, seemed to hear only the clamor on the right, setting a pattern for the campaign.[106]

Second, although the primaries ended with Perot ascendant and the Democrats near desperation, Clinton proved a supremely resilient candidate who played his hand well. Happy with the result, Democrats need to remember that Clinton's nomination was itself a chancy business, since it turned on Jesse Jackson's decision to stay out of the race and on the fact that Governor Douglas Wilder did not prove to be a viable candidate. Everywhere, Clinton had a decisive advantage among black voters, and that edge was critical to his victories. Had he lost those votes to Jackson or another

African American candidate, he might have done no better on Super Tuesday than Senator Al Gore did in 1988, when Jackson won some southern primaries and Michael Dukakis squeaked by in Texas and Florida.[107] In this sense, Jackson, absent, was still a master spirit. His decision to forego the primaries allowed Clinton to build a class coalition across racial lines, the foundation for his success in November.

The Democrats have always been the more fractious party, a coalition of localities, ethnicities, and interests full of inner conflict and including ancient enemies united only by a sense of exclusion and opposition to the status quo. The GOP ordinarily has more positive bonds, with the defense of the established order — especially the private economy — as the party's bottom line.[108]

Social Issues: The Democrats and Race

For contemporary Democrats, race has been the bittersweet apple of discord. This is not an entirely new story, since Democrats began to lose support in the South in the 1940s; but since 1964, Democratic championship of blacks and other minorities has led to defections that have been nationwide, chronic, and ordinarily decisive in presidential elections. Liberal Democrats did not acknowledge quickly enough that middle- and working-class whites were bearing a disproportionate part of the social and economic burden of the quest for equality, and their failure to redistribute those costs made it seem, to many traditional Democrats, that the party had deserted them in favor of minorities on one hand and liberal elites on the other.[109] And Republicans have been forward and effective in cultivating that view.

In 1992, however, race was a dog that did not bark, noteworthy for its relative absence as an issue in the campaign. In the second presidential debate, Carole Simpson had to prod her audience to ask about the politics of race, and even her insistence brought only a vapid inquiry about how soon minorities or women might be elected president or vice-president. The silence was more evident because the occasions of racial conflict were so thunderous: the rioting in Los Angeles that followed the verdict in the trial of the police officers who had arrested and beaten Rodney King, only an extreme case of urban ethnic conflict, forced more insulated Americans to look, briefly, at the ravaged ground and human desperation of the inner city. The sight was so dreadful that most Americans were happy to turn to something else, while for Americans of all races, economic conditions helped to discount other concerns.[110]

More specifically political factors were also at work. Ron Brown's visibility as national chairman symbolized the fact, recognized by an increasing number of African Americans, that blacks are no longer outsiders pressuring Democrats, but the new regulars, the heart of the party.[111] That perception strengthened the impulse, at least among leaders and activists, to find common ground, and with it, a willingness to speak the language of class rather than race.[112] Some of the most compelling African American voices showed themselves uneasy with the old shibboleths.[113] For Democrats of all races, moreover, the Los Angeles riots emphasized the need to win, making ideology less compelling than the need to end the decade of neglect, to do something to ease the agony of the inner city and the sense of superfluity that is the most terrible affliction of the underclass. It was part of the temper of 1992 that a surprisingly wide spectrum of African American leaders supported the principle that, just as all citizens have contributions to make, public assistance is rightly tied to responsibilities.[114] Clinton, William Julius Wilson wrote, spoke to "those who have grown weary of destructive racial rhetoric," and this year, that disposition counted.[115]

It allowed Clinton to distance himself from Sister Souljah and from Jesse Jackson, a decisive gesture to "Reagan Democrats," without any significant loss of support from African Americans.[116] Although not enough blacks went to the polls, Clinton gathered the percentage of support among African Americans that Democrats have come to expect, in part because, whatever his other maneuvers, he addressed and appealed to their dignity as citizens.[117] Intermittently, in Clinton's rhetoric, there were intimations of a Republic of equals.

Social Issues: The Republicans and Religion

Where the Democrats achieved a reasonable degree of unity, the Republicans called attention to their most troublesome divisions. The Reagan years made the GOP more discordant; its new accessions of strength, especially among social conservatives and the religious right, are also occasions for quarrel. The old rift between Main Street and Wall Street was, in large measure, a difference of interest; the new dissensions are matters of faith and culture.[118]

This year's Republican convention, the party's opening to the nation at large, was more or less given over to the cultural right. Its stridency, mirrored in the early part of the Bush campaign, presented Republicans in a role that, since 1964, had been claimed most often by Democrats, a party captured by ideologues and zealots.[119] The prominence of the right helped fracture the Republican coalition: in 1988, 90 percent of Republican voters supported Bush, but in 1992 his share fell to 73 percent, most of the defectors going to Perot.[120]

Still, while the Republicans ran a maladroit campaign, marked by arrogance and misjudgment, their strategists had reason to think that a turn to the right and an emphasis on "family values" was their best alternative.[121] Bush, always a poor candidate, was saddled with the stumbling economy, and it made matters worse that, by pledging to make voters "better off," he had invited them to desert him in hard times.[122] Unlike Reagan, Bush has no gift for political poetry. He is guided by certain working rules —

good manners, confidence in the market economy, and devotion to the national interest — but, notoriously, he regards the "vision thing" as a word-spinning disturbance to the logic of practice, propriety, and power.[123] In 1988 Dukakis's emphasis on "competence" allowed Bush to present himself as the candidate of principles, but that opportunity was not offered in 1992, and in fact, Bush frequently seemed to be a weather vane, pointing in whatever direction he was blown by opinion or perceived political advantage.[124]

Needing an appeal that would be proof against economic distress, at a time when foreign policy no longer galvanized voters, Bush and his advisers fell back on the social issues. Bush's dependence on the right was greater, and the risks of that dependence smaller, in a three-way race, since Perot had already shaken Republican loyalties.[125] Despite all of Bush's liabilities, it was the right that kept him in the race: in 1992 the core support of the Republicans came from social conservatives, and the party will need their loyalty in the years to come.[126]

To assemble a winning coalition, the Republicans will need to moderate their stance on social issues, but doing so will call for art and delicacy. Social conservatives cannot be taken for granted: evangelical Protestants — and even more, socially conservative Catholics — can lean to the left on economic questions, and many might change sides if they feel abandoned, especially since Clinton keeps an open door.[127] Even in 1992, while white, born-again Christians heavily supported Bush, Clinton did better than Dukakis, winning about one vote in four, where Dukakis received only one in five.[128]

Paradoxically, the need for moderation points the Republicans right and not left. Bush had to curry favor with the right, stepping up his rhetoric where Reagan could be temperate because, unlike Reagan, the right did not see Bush as one of its own.[129] After all, in 1984 Bush had confessed his discomfort with the "elevation of the religion thing," and in practice, his support for the right-wing agenda had been modest at best.[130] Feeling its oats in 1992, the right made Bush pay the price. If Republicans want to lower that cost in 1996, they will need a candidate who is pragmatic but is perceived by the right as one of its champions, and that may be a tall order to fill.

On the other side, Democrats have reason to pause amid their ecstasies. Clinton's skillful race still fell far short of a national majority, and his victory can be explained by third-candidate defections more than any increase in Democratic strength.

Republican hopes of realignment were blunted. A higher percentage of college students began calling themselves liberal, and there was much comment about Clinton's appeal to the young.[131] But in the end, about the same percentage of younger voters went for Clinton as had gone Democratic four years earlier, while among younger married voters with children, Clinton did very badly indeed.[132] On the other hand, he apparently won an overwhelming majority among homosexuals.[133] Still, comparing Democratic support in 1988 and 1992, change was the exception and continuity the rule.

The Emerging American Politics

Clinton's victory, however, hinted at broader possibilities for redefining the Democratic coalition. On election night, Al Gore asserted that the election demonstrated the "end of sectionalism," and in a sense, it did confirm sectionalism's long decline.[134] But Clinton's southernness still made him seem alien to many northern audiences, and even Gore's argument pointed to the special sectional character of the Democratic ticket.[135] As the nomination of two border staters, it was not unprecedented; rather, it turned away from Dukakis's effort to re-create the Boston-Austin axis to that earlier success, the Truman-Barkley ticket of 1948. But unlike those predecessors, Clinton and Gore came from states that were members of the Confederacy: the 1992 nominations were a strong symbolic gesture to the South, part of a successful effort to dent that now-Republican bastion.[136]

The geography of the election was suggestive in another way. Sweeping the Northeast and the West Coast, Clinton and Gore also were almost universally successful in the broad, middle American region that Meredith Nicholson once called the "Valley of Democracy."[137] Except for Mississippi, Clinton carried every state bordering on the Mississippi River and every state on the Ohio except Indiana, equaling Lyndon Johnson (who took Indiana but lost Louisiana).[138] Only on the upper Missouri did Clinton's pluralities disappear.

Our stereotypes associate the two areas with the Democratic Party's fundamental agon. We think of the coasts — somewhat unjustly, of course — as the homeland of liberals and neoliberals, a diverse grouping uniting partisans of high-tech industry and the cultural elite, mostly internationalists disposed toward free trade, almost all secular and inclined to relativism, people who defend policies in the idiom of rights.[139] Middle America, by contrast, symbolizes those in the middle sectors who "do the work, raise the kids, and pay the bills," the people to whom Clinton offered himself as champion and who probably gave him his margin of victory. For all their variety, these middle Americans are often tied to place and apt to be religious, not often moralists (at least, not those who voted for Clinton), but concerned with decency and justice — with families and safe communities and fair taxes — at least as much as they care about rights. And less confident about international politics, they include many unashamed patriots who sympathize with protection.[140]

The "character issue" chafed the line of friction between the two persuasions. The most bothersome side of Clinton's account of his doings during the Vietnam era was not that he tried to avoid military service — as the warm reception to his American Legion speech showed, that could have been dealt with rather easily — but that his stories varied, suggesting, as Dan Quayle argued during the vice-presidential debate, that "Bill Clinton has a problem telling the truth." It stirred fears among middle Americans that Clinton was too close to what they see as liberalism's moral flabbiness, too unwilling to offend, too prone to seek compromise, lacking any standard of justice except civil peace.[141]

The problem of guiding principles was exemplified in the debate over "family values." When they responded to Quayle, Russell Baker observed, liberals too often sounded "as though they're against love, marriage and family."[142] Unnecessarily so; recognizing that single-parent families face special difficulties does not entail rejection or ostracism but calls for appropriate assistance. Paradoxically, the liberal inclination to denounce as repressive any idea that the two-parent family is a standard leaves liberals only a limited, economic justification for aiding single-parent households, while conservatives, who accept the standard, are too niggardly to offer help.

Clinton avoided that ideological trap. He defused a good deal of the Republican appeal to "family values" by observing that, apart from restrictions on abortion and on gays, it was largely talk. And in his soft way, he was just as clear about the defects of liberalism: "Family values alone won't feed a hungry child, and material security can't provide a moral compass. We must have both."[143] Yet Clinton's shrewd claiming of the sensible middle ground left his family policy vague, like much of the agenda of the Clinton administration, still waiting to be defined.[144]

At the beginning of the campaign, the need for a moral compass led E.J. Dionne Jr. to recommend the earlier, tougher liberalism symbolized by Humphrey Bogart in *Casablanca*.[145] To his detriment, a great many voters could not shake the fear that Clinton might be something closer to Claude Rains's portrayal of a smooth, unprincipled opportunist. But in the end, Rains's policeman went off with Bogart's Rick to join the Free French, and there is reason to hope that Clinton will do at least as well.

As a campaigner, Clinton kept his coalition pretty much together, but the presidency will be a harder test. More or less united against Bush and the Reagan legacy, Democrats will be more apt to squabble when the question is what they are for.[146] Even during the campaign, many of Clinton's middle-American supporters were bothered by the exclusion of Robert Casey, Pennsylvania's antiabortion governor, from a convention platform that had been opened to pro-choice Republican women.[147] It was an example of the abiding fear of middle-American Democrats that liberals will be more at ease in the corridors of power and that, in a Clinton administration, the "new" Democratic Party will be swallowed by the "old." It will not help that some items high on the liberal agenda, including many aspects of abortion and gay rights, can be achieved fairly easily by executive order, while the hopes of middle Americans call for structural solutions, a long process of legislation and considerable pain.[148]

Judged by the campaign, Clinton can be expected to attend to such feelings and to the demand that burdens be shared fairly. But sacrifice, likely to be asked of all of us, will call for more than a gift for conciliation and the brokering of interests. It will demand a scale of justice and the conviction that our dignities and destinies are bound up with the common good.

Clinton shows every sign of concern to strengthen the government's title to rule and its claims on our allegiance. If he is wise, he will promote the use of public policy to rebuild the links between citizens and their government, not simply media gimmicks, but local governments, parties, and associations with the "power of meeting," where citizens can learn the habits of democracy and the arts of politics.[149]

Yet ultimately, both in relation to his party and the country as a whole, Clinton's success will depend on his ability to articulate measures of public purpose and policy. For a Democrat, equality is the enduring grail, and in his best moments, Clinton's rhetoric of citizenship pointed to equality's vital contemporary meanings. Civic equality is no prescription for uniformity, not even in the form of enforced diversity. As Barbara Jordan told the Democratic convention, equality and equal rights are the conditions of civil variety. For Americans, their differing faiths and cultures are sources of strength, but no one needs to be told, these days, that cultures are not always easily compatible with each other or with democratic politics, that cultures often include racism and sexism, or that some nurture a hunger for dominion or are otherwise at odds with democratic life. America's version of multiculturalism accepts diversity, but only on the understanding that all cultures yield any claim to rule that runs counter to equality and equal rights. From an egalitarian point of view, cultures are not "separate realities" but more or less adequate answers to the human problem, to which equality and the rights that go with it are qualitatively superior because, unlike stories and legends, they rest on the stark truth of human nature.[150]

An excellent campaign slogan, "Putting People First," also hints at broader meanings, just as the reconciliation with nature to which Al Gore calls America implies more than our relation to the nonhuman environment. From its Columbian beginnings, America has been caught up in the modern quest for the mastery of nature, the rejection of whatever humans have not chosen or made. It becomes ever clearer, however, that technological mastery subordinates us to the things we have made and, left to itself, tends to dispense with human craft and devotion.[151] Yet the United States also began by asserting the proposition that both our equality and our rights are things that we did not make and about which we have no choice, an unalienable heritage from nature. If people are to come first in public policy, human nature must be given its due. Human beings are more than consumers, and their dignity — their need to be needed — deserves to be afforded at least equal status with the pursuit of abundance and mastery. Equality implies more than rights; it suggests that, within the limits of our circumstances, we can and should be held accountable to equal standards, offered and expected to live up to the opportunity to contribute to the common life. Even in speech, Bill Clinton's promise of a "new covenant" sounded chords of memory; it remains to be seen how far he can take Americans toward a rediscovery of the Republic.

CHAPTER SIX

Uncertainties at Midcrossing
The Election of 1996

By 1996 not even the White House was talking about a new Camelot. Bill Clinton, though pursued by scandals and burdened by failures, was still probably unbeatable, riding the wave of comparative good times. It helped, of course, that the Republicans — once General Colin Powell decided not to enter the race — had no really attractive candidate. But probably even the majority of Clinton supporters felt more resignation than enthusiasm about their choice, and with reason.

————)((◍)) ————

I stood in Venice on the Bridge of Sighs,
A palace and a prison on each hand....
— Lord Byron,
Childe Harold's Pilgrimage

In the election of 1996, the tumult and shouting were mostly contrived. There were no great captains and certainly no kings, and the parties' overfunded armies fought out the campaign on the dreary edges of political life.

The result amounted to a decision not to decide, dividing government between bitterly partisan rivals but issuing what Garry Wills called a "mandate to get along."[1] Uneasy about the direction of things, most Americans were unready for big changes, balanced, like a vampire's lover, between fascination and dread.[2]

Not much inclined to cheer, the voters found even fewer reasons for doing so. They didn't like the Congress or trust the president, but they re-elected both, and the percentage of Americans who even made it to the polls was the lowest since 1924, the second lowest in the history of mass democratic politics.[3] It didn't help that the race was one-sided — Clinton's victory was predictable from the end of the primary season, if not earlier — or that both candidates, whatever their defects, were safe and sane, so that staying home was unlikely to do damage.[4] But more ominously, millions of Americans believe or suspect that democratic politics, even at its best, has become largely irrelevant; in America's developing postindustrialism, economics and technology seem to call the tune even where government plays the fiddle.

Conservatives have profited from and encouraged this mood, linking it to their own critique of government, and neoliberals have embraced it, albeit with less enthusiasm. But the conviction that politics is impotent rests on a relativism that, while it deprecates government and law in the first instance, goes on to devalue all institutions, all promises and choices, and even the idea of human freedom and responsibility.[5] Ultimately, that logic is bound to provoke contradiction. Human beings are creatures, but they are also made to be creative; the products of a society, they are also its shapers.[6] And it bears remembering that many, if not most of us would rather be governed by someone than be subjected, voicelessly, to the ordeal of change. Jean Bethke Elshtain is right: democracy is "on trial," challenged to demonstrate that its politics is equal to the time.[7]

Americans have been there before. Back in 1896, during our transition to industrialism, intellectual orthodoxy held that government should not meddle with socioeconomic evolution; William Graham Sumner had proclaimed, more than a decade earlier, that the "inadequacy of the State to regulative tasks is agreed upon, as a matter of fact, by all."[8] The incumbent president was Grover Cleveland, the first Democrat to be reelected since Andrew Jackson [though for non-consecutive terms], as Bill Clinton was the first since F.D.R., and also like Clinton, Cleveland practiced "third-way" politics, cracking the GOP majority by adopting large parts of respectable Republicanism — sound money, internationalism, and a frugal government suspicious of welfare.[9]

Discontent divided both parties. The old distinctions, defined largely by the tariff and memories of the antislavery struggle, were coming to seem outmoded, and the third-party Populists had won significant support in 1892 and 1894. In 1896 the minority Democrats took the gamble: their convention was dominated by a large majority — a little fast footwork provided the two-thirds then needed to nominate a candidate — dedicated to the repudiation of Cleveland's policies. In the process, they redefined and revived American party politics and signaled the advent of the age of reform.

In the short term, however, the nomination of William Jennings Bryan on a "free silver" platform was a political flop. The accents of the campaign were agrarian and Protestant, and while Bryan added a number of Plains and western states to the then-Solid South, he lost the East and the Midwest.[10] But Bryan's oratory formulated what, ever since, has been the Democrats' ruling image: a rejection of "trickle-down" economics in favor of the proposition that "if you legislate to make the masses prosperous," their well-being "will find its way up through every class which rests upon them."[11] Bryan's rhetoric pointed beyond free silver and the gold standard, ranging the Democrats as partisans of a government active in the pursuit of civic equality.[12]

There were no Bryans, however, in 1996.[13] In fact, it is tempting to regard the election as the revenge of the Cleveland Democrats: Bill Clinton, like Cleveland, played down the claims of government, urging a moderate social liberalism informed by internationalism, and his areas of electoral strength paralleled those of McKinley and the Republicans a century ago.[14] But where Cleveland's party was fractious, Clinton's was surly but willing to check its discontent in the interest of checking or reversing 1994's swing to the right.[15] Democrats are less likely to be compliant, four years down the road. For that matter, Republicans cannot expect much serenity in their own future. In the shallows and silences of 1996, it is possible to make out signs of a political redefinition waiting for its season. Half postponement and half prelude, the election of 1996 let Americans off the hook for a while longer, and they were happy to be spared.

Clinton's Victory: The Uncertain Economy

To most observers, Clinton's victory was easily explained. In the first place, the economy was prosperous, the country was at peace, and most Americans were enjoying a decent level of well-being: R.W. Apple's postelection column was subtitled, "Good Times Lead to Second Term."[16] Second, Clinton had the good fortune to be opposed by Bob Dole, a candidate who was famously inarticulate and startlingly out of touch.[17] In both respects, however, this account is only the beginning of the story, and each of its parts — the economy and the opponents — deserves exploration.

By all accounts, the economy was doing reasonably well in 1996, but prosperity hadn't saved the Democrats in 1994, when economic conditions were so good that Fred Greenstein could only describe the voters' discontents as "iatrogenic," produced by the diagnoses of gloomy economic experts and would-be healers.[18] Politically, immediate economic circumstances are apt to matter less than judgments about the economy as a whole, and especially, about its future.[19] In politics, economic questions are not narrowly material; our reactions are affected by loyalties and memories and by culture generally, and the crucial issue is less dollars than dignity, the hope of winning and preserving a socially honorable station.[20] And Americans, so long confidently expectant, are showing long-term uncertainties and even fears of decline.[21]

It seemed logical that when the voters' estimates of the direction of the economy turned down in June 1995 — 47 percent said things were "getting worse," as against 34 percent the year before — Richard Morin counted it as "disturbing news for Clinton's reelection team," and by May 1996 the figures, if anything, were a little worse.[22] The public's feeling was more than subjective: economic growth was slow, as Bob Dole repeatedly pointed out, often in rather shrill hyperbole, but the fact did Dole very little good.[23] Economic expectations proved to have an unexpected effect: by July the economy was getting fairly good marks, but those who thought its direction "good" divided the credit almost evenly between Clinton and Congress; those who said conditions were "bad" were more than twice as likely to blame Congress.[24] Those who experienced things as not going well, in other words, tended to regard the president [and probably, his party] as on their side. Clinton benefited from a combination of economic well-being and worry.

Battered by technological change and globalization, most Americans are living with a sense of vulnerability, most immediately in relation to their jobs. In 1996 "downsizing" — and "outsourcing," a parallel term in economic newspeak — became something like the economic rule; in March the *New York Times* ran a seven-part series on "the downsizing of America."[25] It is cold consolation that the problem is international and that conditions elsewhere are generally worse than they are in the U.S.; misery, in this respect, does not love company.[26] Even where there are jobs, the quality of work is, to put it generously, unreliable: wages edged up a little in the late summer of 1996, but the long-term tendency of real wages has been down, and more and more Americans are working as temporary workers in the "contingent economy," with volatile wages and few benefits.[27]

The problem, of course, is most severe among the urban poor, but it gnaws at the people E.J. Dionne calls the "anxious middle" — older workers threatened by technology (which includes virtually anyone over thirty-five), white-collar families whose precarious prosperity rests on debt, retail small businesses facing competition from category-busting superstores, and younger people, comfortable in the "information age" but facing a future shaped by the "hollowing out" of labor.[28]

Americans do tend to exaggerate the country's economic woes, but they are on the mark in seeing an increase in inequality, now more extreme than in any other industrial nation.[29] Russell Baker called it "disgusting": the affluent are virtually rushing away from middle- and working-class Americans.[30] Upward mobility is slower, and elite incomes are exploding, so that the average corporate CEO, who earned 35 times the salary of the average production worker in 1974, now earns 120 times as much.[31]

Too many Americans feel stalked by indignity, and the very idea of civic community is more open to question. Traditionally, it was assumed that growth that benefits elites will also reward the great majority, albeit to a lesser extent; now, Benjamin Schwartz argues, changes that are making upper-income Americans prosperous may actually be hurting something like 45 percent of their fellow citizens.[32] In fact, Robert Frank and Philip Cook make a persuasive case that the United States is becoming a "winner-take-all society," in which highly visible people toward the top of the heap win disproportionate rewards for marginal advantages: the best lawyers or anchor people or corporate executives or sports stars may be better than their rivals in the second tier, but they are not as much better as their salaries would suggest. At the top, the market is oligopolistic, with few sellers and many buyers, and competitive advantage turns on positions as much as abilities. The lure of the brass ring, moreover, is so great that Americans overestimate their chances of grabbing it, while more modest success and local celebrity seem not much better than defeat.[33]

At the same time, while technological change is unsettling old elites, it is also creating new ones. Power gravitates to those who can control or master new techniques, and the great majority, scrambling to catch up, acquire a level of skill only to find that it has already become obsolete.[34]

Clinton's Victory: The Uncertain Community

The problem goes beyond the workplace. Economic and technological transformations demand adaptability and mobility, necessarily weakening commitments to place, to relationships, and to beliefs and values.[35] They encourage relativism and disengagement, undermining trust and loyalty across the board and generally eating up the "civic capital" of our institutions.[36] Growing numbers of Americans live in "common interest developments" specialized on the basis of age or class or — if only implicitly — ethnicity and culture, often walled and gated, essentially seceding from the public into a "culture of nonparticipation."[37] Families, destabilized and pressured, scramble for time, and more and more, children count as economic costs.[38] Meanwhile, the media intrude on and disrupt families and communities, shaping a "collective second identity" based on mass marketing's lowest common denominator.[39]

All of this results from the dynamics of the private sector; despite conservative complaints, government is a very minor player. The criticism of welfare has been critical for conservative politics, in fact, because it is one of the few cases in which it is possible to make a tolerable case that public policy bears a major responsibility for social demoralization.[40] The best conservative voices acknowledge the private sector's depredations: denouncing violence and sexuality in the media in the name of our "better nature," Bob Dole carefully exempted Republican contributors such as Arnold Schwarzenegger and Bruce Willis, but even Dole felt compelled to call attention to the damage done by irresponsible devotion to the bottom line.[41]

Especially where they are touched directly, the great majority of Americans expect government to patch or reweave such tears in the social fabric. They want government to regulate HMOs, for example, by banning "gag rules" or allowing longer hospital stays after childbirth, just as they insist that public authorities oversee the safety of air travel.[42] A significant number probably agree with Edwin Luttwak that the United States needs economic growth less than stability and work. And in less demanding and ambitious ways, very few of us don't look to government for some form of assistance or hope that it can guide change in a way that makes private life compatible with public principles.[43]

In recent years, however, we've become much less certain about what the standards are. Issues that were once handled locally, leaving room for cultural plurality, seem to demand national solutions, so that for some time, Americans have been pulled toward a "culture war" over the nature of morality and the place of religion in public life.[44] There are plenty of people who doubt whether our institutions and our enfeebled civilities will be able to keep debate within the boundaries of democratic politics.[45] And as I have already indicated, a strong current opinion doubts that government has the power to make all that much difference, given the tide of globalization.[46]

In one sense, international politics was invisible in the campaign. In 1992, our first campaign after the end of the Cold War, George Bush still urged his foreign policy credentials, and Clinton's lack of them, as a major issue in the election, provoking Clinton to take hawkish positions, especially in relation to Bosnia, than he came to regret.[47] In 1996 there were criticisms, here and there, of Clinton's vacillations, but the dominant view seemed to agree with Lawrence Eagleburger's judgment, four years earlier, that the United States might be entering "a period of the absence of clear purpose" in foreign policy.[48] Clinton, in fact, had become increasingly sure-handed in foreign affairs.[49] Even his response to Iraq's intrusion into Kurdistan in September 1996 showed a nice calibration of the demands of domestic and international politics.[50] When Dole and Kemp criticized the president's ventures, in fact, they provoked William Kristol and Robert Kagan to charge that they were surrendering Reagan's legacy in favor of isolationism.[51] In fact, both Clinton and Dole are internationalists, free traders and above all, pragmatists who are more inclined to adapt to events than to try to shape them according to some grand design.[52]

Globalization, foreign policy's strong presence in the campaign, was consequently a delicate problem for both candidates, since for millions of Americans, it has come to symbolize the loss of self-government to "uncontrollable forces... with their daily mockery of domestic political agendas."[53] Of course, even more voters value the goods and opportunities that the world economy makes available, and attacks on globalization are somewhat unfair, since domestic technological change probably does more of the damage we complain of than foreign economic competition. Still, the intrusions of international economics are sensitive because they raise, so directly, questions about the value of citizenship, the meaning of nationality, and the reality of the common good.

In the world most of us grew up in, foreign policy, though sometimes a matter for bitter controversy, moderated the tension between the free market and political democracy. It wasn't always that way: early in American history, foreign policy was a major line of partisan and sectional division, partly because, in a society that was still fairly egalitarian, class issues bothered us less and democracy and capitalism seemed more easily compatible.[54] But industrialism, creating a new hierarchy, threatened civic equality, and a major argument for reform — for moderating capitalism in the interest of political community — relied on the need for strength and solidarity in foreign policy, as well as against the specter of socialism. With the Soviet Union as a foe, the two dangers merged, strengthening the hand of politics in its contest with economics.[55] It contributed to the rise of what Alexei Bayer calls "capitalist" as opposed to "market" ideology, an essentially corporatist doctrine centered on an implicit "contract" between management and labor.[56] Modern corporations, it was said, had restored the political relation between classes that had been — or so Marx and Engels argued — dissolved by the market.[57] As American economic dominance weakened, however, management began to find the contract onerous, particularly when victory in the Cold War reduced both the risk of overseas investment and the claim of American business to government protection.[58] In the contemporary global economy, businesses can plead their inability to protect the jobs and benefits of workers — a persuasive argument, apparently, and one that obviously softens any conflict between classes — at the same time that capital is freed from its always problematic relation to country.[59] That the highly-publicized success stories of the international economy are so often authoritarian polities with market economies does not increase confidence about the political future.

American worries along this line help explain the impact of the Indonesian fund-raising scandal that hurt the Democrats in the last days of the campaign.[60] Plenty of observers professed not to see what the fuss was about: realistically, foreign money and influence aren't any worse than their domestic counterparts, particularly if, as in a number of prominent cases, the domestic money comes from companies controlled by foreign nationals.[61] But the voters who were troubled displayed, if only inarticulately, a more refined appreciation for the formal and legal boundaries of political community.

Nationalist sentiment regarding issues like trade and immigration was never far below the surface, full-throated and more than a little pathological in fringe groups fearful of a "New World Order," and only a little more respectable in Pat Buchanan's oratory, but in a quieter way, touching many hearts.[62] Illegal aliens and immigrants generally were a convenient target for worries, and many Republicans were tempted by the success of Proposition 187 in California.[63] Electorally, these flirtations backfired: Hispanic-Americans appear to have been offended, and they were not alone, especially since a group of bemused Republicans in the House proposed repealing birthright citizenship for the children of illegal aliens, running against generations of civics classes which have inculcated the lesson that in America — unlike less enlightened nations — citizenship comes from the soil, not by blood.[64]

Still, even the over-punitive critics of immigration have a point. In our increasingly two-tiered politics, the bond of citizenship is growing thin.[65] Elites, more than ever apt to be cosmopolitan, are tied to place only lightly; most people are less ambiguously national and more dependent on the country. Millions among those less advantaged were attracted by the argument that our obligations to our fellow citizens come first and would have responded to Burke's famous argument that a political community is no "partnership...in a trade of pepper and coffee, calico or tobacco, or some other such low concern, to be taken up for a little temporary interest and to be dissolved at the fancy of the parties."[66] In a blundering way, the critics of immigration, and of the Democrats' Asian fund raising, were pointing to the principle that politics is entitled to primacy over economics. The majority of Americans would probably settle for a wider margin of security.

Virtually all of us are feeling at least somewhat baffled and considerably overwhelmed: our experience is an ever-closer match to the "paranoid position," and in 1996 the sense of being surrounded by shadowy, disordering powers took a giant step toward the mainstream.[67] Forty-eight percent of Americans, *Newsweek* reported, believe in UFOs and similar numbers are convinced that the government is covering up the evidence; 29 percent believe that the government is in contact with aliens.[68]

In many ways, the mood of the electorate is captured by the hit TV series *The X-Files*, in which part of the government is engaged in a conspiracy to conceal the presence of paranormal and extraterrestrial beings among us, but the hero and heroine are *also* government agents. Government, in this story line, is flawed and not always benign, but it is to some degree responsive and certainly our only means of combating the dark forces around us. And the movie *Independence Day*, a smash at the box office, spoke to its mass audience's desire for government to take control, even at great, apocalyptic cost.[69]

For similar reasons, the Oklahoma City bombing played a central role in the drama of 1996. In one sense, it was just another, more terrible evidence of our vulnerability and our exposure to terrorist violence, like the attack on the World Trade Center, but there was a politically crucial difference. Americans had become accustomed to associating political disorders with foreigners [especially Arabs] and with the left. But the turbulence of the 1960s — frequently present as a bad example in Newt Gingrich's speeches — is decades away, and although there were undergrounds, the left we remember was desperately public.[70] Even the Unabomber, that lonely, antitechnological reminder of 1960s violence, was caught because of the manifesto he insisted on publishing. In 1996, however, Americans were forced to confront disorder from the right, in the burning of African-American churches across the South as well as in Oklahoma City.[71] Moreover, rightist terror—secret, apparently respectable, and technologically adroit—epitomized our more paranoid fears.[72]

Most important, the militias and the extremist right were linked to savage attacks on the government by the political right. Freshman Representative Steve Stockman accused Janet Reno of "premeditated murder" in the 1993 attack on the Branch Davidian complex at Waco and spoke of a "gestapo mentality" in government; his colleague, Helen Chenoweth, was comparably extreme; the NRA referred to government agents as "jack-booted thugs" wearing Nazi uniforms — prompting President Bush to resign from the organization; even Newt Gingrich opposed the administration's antiterrorism bill, referring to a "genuine fear of the federal government." And on talk radio, of course, there was much worse.[73]

Conservatives recognized their exposure. When Clinton denounced antigovernment rhetoric, suggesting, sensibly enough, that "words have consequences," the shrewdest among them, like Bill Kristol, more or less agreed.[74] Most Republicans, however, turned civil libertarian, denouncing the president's remarks as repressive, and their response indicated, as Dan Morgan wrote, a sense that the conservative movement had been "sub-liminally tainted."[75] The Oklahoma City disaster greatly raised Clinton's standing and, as Morgan observed, "put a human face on bureaucrats, and revealed a kinder, gentler federal government, with a day-care center on the ground floor."[76] Suspicion of government didn't go away; some 11 million Americans, if the polls are right, regard government as an "enemy," and 40 percent express milder distrust.[77] But right-wing terror reminded most Americans how much they depend on government and need to trust it: as Tom Esker, a youngish Californian, told Richard Morin, "I'm not afraid the feds will blow up our cities."[78] And that sentiment, pretty much, framed the election of 1996.

Republican Alternatives, Democratic Responses

Republicans didn't get it, at least until very late in the day. Bob Dole was the calculated choice of party leaders who knew and discounted his weaknesses. They assumed, back when the campaign began to take shape, that Clinton was a dead duck; in 1993 it was common to say that the president had contracted "Quayle syndrome," and in early 1995 Richard Morin reported, while calling into question, the Washington belief that Clinton's defeat was a sure thing.[79] The Republicans, on this view, didn't need a candidate to win an election, but to avoid losing one, and just as predicted, Bob Dole proved to be a candidate minimally acceptable to all elements of the Republican coalition, and one who could, helped by a front-loaded primary schedule, avoid a prolonged, embittering contest for the nomination.

The problem, of course, was that Republicans misread the mood of the country and the verdict of 1994.[80] The midterm election did show a marked distrust of government and a conservative tilt that shifted the terms of political debate decisively to the right.[81] And it is easy to understand how the exhilaration of victory encouraged Republicans to overreach, especially since so many political scientists saw a political transformation in the 1994 returns.[82] Yet even at the time, it was easy to see ambiguities; the 1994 election did not mark a "chapter" in our politics, Ross Baker observed; it was "somewhere between a page and a paragraph."[83]

Newt Gingrich and his allies, however, seemingly caught up in a sense of destiny, carried the idea of a constitutional revolution beyond the relative moderation of 1994's Contract with America.[84] In their version of ideological politics, social conservatism got little more than lip-service: Gingrich, a "values-based libertarian," put his emphasis on dismantling the government, hoping to undo the legacy of the 1960s, if not the New Deal.[85] The new Republicans, Russell Baker wrote, are "full of ideas, and so young they can't remember they are ideas that have already failed."[86]

The goal of starving the government led Republicans to question programs, such as the Earned Income Tax Credit, aimed at helping the working poor, exactly the sort of policy that conservatives might be expected to support. Similarly, the Republican majority proved unwilling to spend money on "second chance homes," an effort to deal with illegitimacy and family instability, and Cardinal O'Connor was not alone in worrying that niggardliness about welfare might press the poor to have abortions.[87] In all of this, Republicans seemed to miss the point that a large part of popular disenchantment with welfare was concerned, not with the cost, but with the cultural and moral impact of public assistance, and plenty of voters who had marched to the Republican drum in 1994 had no desire to turn cutting costs into an excuse for hurting the poor.[88]

The Republican militants in Congress, convinced they were riding the wave of the future, were led to the belief that "shutting down the government," in their budgetary conflict with the president, would be regarded as an acceptable demonstration of moral conviction and strength of purpose, and that the president would eventually "blink."[89] They were wrong, of course: Republican intransigence was seen as just this side of nutty, and the shutdown was another reminder, for Americans, of the ways in which government is a convenience or a necessity.[90] In all probability, Republicans kept their majorities only by a "switch in time" to modest cooperation in the interest of "productive government."[91]

In fact, the voters who tipped the balance in 1994 did not vote *for* the Republicans so much as *against* Clinton and the Democratic "old gang" in Congress.[92] Having inspired high expectations, Bill Clinton began his presidency with a series of miscalculations, waverings, and botched appointments; his legislative victories, like the deficit reduction plan, were not the stuff to make hearts sing; the anticrime bill barely survived; welfare reform, which could have been both a humane new direction and a political triumph, never really got started; and the Clinton health plan, announced with ruffles and flourishes, died with barely a whisper.[93]

It wasn't entirely Clinton's fault. He was bound to fall short of his supporters hopes, given the polyglot nature of his coalition and the increasing limits on the contemporary presidency.[94] But Clinton so insistently took center stage that he made himself a lightning rod, a fact that helps account for the disproportionate criticism he received from the press.[95] In any event,

Clinton came to seem weak and inept, and what direction he had appeared to follow elite liberalism, though often in a bungling way — NAFTA, gays in the military, the insistence on a woman for attorney general, the hasty and later withdrawn nomination of Lani Guinier. Meanwhile, in Congress, the baronial Democrats moved with ponderous indifference.[96] In November 1994 the voters punished Clinton and his party for offering ineffective government, not because they opposed government per se.[97]

Clinton, of course, bent with the wind. The 1994 results confirmed his disposition toward a "third-way" presidency, an "unabashedly mongrel politics" that leans toward "poaching on the territory" of the other party.[98] In general, the president conceded the relatively abstract and widely popular themes that Gingrich had helped make the Republicans' stock-in-trade — a balanced budget, smaller government, devolution to the states, and "ending welfare as we know it" — while taking visible, relatively conservative positions on social issues, abortion excepted, from support for school uniforms to opposition to gay marriage.[99] Increasingly seen as a moderate, Clinton shifted the debate from ideology to practice, into areas — Medicare, Medicaid, Social Security, education, and the environment — where the public's "operational liberalism" is demonstrated and long-standing, and where the Democrats' reputation as the party of government helps, since it makes their promise to protect such programs more credible.[100]

With Clinton staking out a claim to the center, what interest the campaign might have held disappeared with General Powell's decision not to seek the Republican nomination. As Juan Williams had guessed he would, Clinton ran as a mildly liberal Reagan, reasserting the optimistic themes of the Republicans' 1984 proclamation of "morning in America."[101] The last suspense ended when the president signed the welfare reform bill, outraging people on the left but taking away Bob Dole's best hope for a talking point.[102] In fact, having signed the bill, Clinton could tell critics that its very harshness made his reelection more necessary, to "fix" the law or to keep it from getting worse, turning his apostasy into a commendation.[103]

Bob Dole, haunted by gaffes and a rhetoric so graceless that even the sober-sided *New York Times* was moved to mockery, suffered from what Russell Baker called a "charisma chasm."[104] His campaign was a series of improvisations masking as themes. It began inside the Senate, where Dole hoped to pass legislation that would establish him as a man of action, but Dole found himself outgeneraled and caught up in the Senate's routine.[105] His resignation from the Senate won a few headlines, but it cost him influence with his colleagues, and it didn't change Dole's image, three and a half decades in the making, as a Washington insider.[106] Finally, in desperation, Dole surrendered to the supply side, proposing a tax cut he once scorned, winning brief cheers from libertarians like William Safire, but damaging his own credibility, "whittling himself down to Clinton's size" in his evident opportunism.[107] Nothing worked. The "bump" from the contrived

Republican convention was slight and brief; the presidential debates were unmemorable, except for Dole's conspicuous avoidance of the conservative social agenda; even his best rhetoric — "a bridge to the past" — wound up allowing Clinton to present himself as a man of vision, capable of building a "bridge to the future."[108]

For too many voters, the campaign must have been another argument against democratic politics. Clinton and Dole — and Ross Perot, for that matter — contributed, agreeing that the difficulties of Medicare would be better handled by a bipartisan commission, off the political stage. Neither party, moreover, had much to say about the public's concern for secure and socially adequate work. In 1993 Hobart Rowen noted that Clinton had "no apparent answer to the jobs problem," and things weren't much different in 1996.[109] The administration mostly contented itself with accentuating the positives, complemented with appeals to Clinton's "growth agenda" and references to the obligation of business to avoid unnecessary downsizing.[110]

Republicans had even less to say. On the campaign trail, Dole tended to sidle around the issue of jobs — which had surprised him, after all, back in New Hampshire — and even Pat Buchanan, fulminating, had no program beyond protectionism.[111] For familiar ideological reasons, Republicans weren't willing to offer government has an ally. Gingrich, a technophile, is inclined to treat economic dislocations as a phase, and the Republican-dominated Joint Economic Committee of Congress declared that there is "no positive basis for criticizing any degree of market-driven inequality."[112]

In fact, Republican opposition to an increase in the minimum wage made it easier for Clinton to present himself as a friend of labor.[113] Enough Republicans eventually broke ranks to let the bill pass, but it did Dole no good, although it probably saved some Republican seats.

The Republicans' boldest initiative was Dole's tax plan, but even conservative experts, chastened by experience, had become skeptical, and respondents were apt to tell pollsters that the tax cut, even if passed, would bust the budget or have to be paid for in other ways. And they also frequently remarked that, apart from the promise of "growth," Dole's scheme said nothing about work at all.[114]

The Democrats' advantage, in other words, was largely negative, no long-term answer for the party, especially since Republicans will be able to take advantage of America's abiding individualism and distrust of public authority.[115] Both parties, however, have reason to be at least attentive to the widespread desire to *direct* change, rather than merely enduring it. Failure to address the mounting level of anxiety, continuing to drain support for democratic institutions, encourages citizens to look elsewhere, and that searching will not always be directed to private faiths and lives.[116] The electorate, Kevin Phillips wrote, is "almost out of patience," and rebuilding trust in public life deserves to rank first on any political agenda.[117]

It is not a challenge for which Bill Clinton is ideally suited. In 1996 the president was lucky. Even his early failures provided a basis for the belief that Clinton was "growing" into his job, just as the criticism of his wife allowed him to seem chivalrous in her defense, reversing the pattern of 1992, when Mrs. Clinton was called on to support her husband.[118]

Clinton's virtues of shrewdness and adaptability also mark his limits: no lion, he is at best a somewhat pious fox, not disposed to practice or ask for heroism and inclined to let fundamental issues slide.[119] His very imperfections combine with his deference to the decencies of faith, family, and country in a way that suggests Reagan grown clever — "a flawed man," Richard Ford calls him, "for a flawed time."[120]

It is not altogether surprising that the continuing doubts about Clinton's character made so little difference in 1996. Most voters discounted Whitewater as politically motivated and incomprehensible, and Rob Reiner's film, *The American President,* was virtually a pro-Clinton tract on the question of private conduct.[121] "I trust the hard way," Bob Dole said when resigning from the Senate, but most Americans don't: they belong to a world of suburbs, malls, and credit cards, not the "old railroad towns" to which Dole referred, and they suspect that the old virtues, too exacting for comfort even in their private lives, may be unsuited to contemporary politics. In recent elections, more or less able rogues have bested rivals with sterling character: Nixon beat Humphrey and McGovern, just as Clinton bested Dole.[122]

Our need for effective government is decisive. In a world full of perils and possibilities, Americans have adopted an essentially Machiavellian idea of political virtue: what matters in a leader is the ability to get results.[123] On that test, most Americans this year gave Clinton passing grades. "I think he can run the country," an Arizona Republican told Dan Balz and David Broder, "but he's going to lie to us doing it."[124]

Americans will have to hope that Clinton has high statecraft in his repertoire. The bridge America really needs, in the nearest possible future, is one linking its citizens with their government.

Politics and the American Future

A big part of the problem is inherent in the nature of the regime. In the framing of our institutions, distance between government and people was designed; the unique quality of American constitutionalism, Madison wrote, lies in the "total exclusion of the people in their collective capacity" from any share in rule.[125] And at the time, Antifederalists warned that the Constitution's politics — "intricate and perplexed," Cato said, "and too mysterious for you to understand" — were weighted to the advantage of elites. Effective national action called, even then, for large-scale organization, and Melancton Smith observed that "the great easily form associations; the poor and middling class form them with difficulty."[126]

For much of our history, this aspect of American government was checked by a politics — and a press — rooted in locality, the kind of "retail," face-to-face encounter that personalizes public life, conveys dignity and encourages participation.[127] That sort of politics has been waning for some time now; our lives are shaped by forces that, constitutionally and in practice, can be dealt with only by federal power, if at all. In Washington in 1996, devolution was in fashion, but states and localities remained financially dependent, whatever discretion they gained in dealing with policy; willing to hand over responsibility, Congress was less eager, and probably not able, to transfer power. The local press has long been eclipsed by the electronic media, and the political parties, increasingly, are centralized, fundraising bureaucracies, not federations of precincts and wards.[128]

In 1996 money was politically omnipresent, and very few voters did not at least sense that mass politics, while democratic in form, is more and more oligarchic in content. Money virtually defined our political choices. The Republican primary schedule put a premium on early fund raising, and Bob Dole, staggered in the first contests, needed only to survive until the first big round of primaries overtaxed his rivals' financial ability to compete effectively.[129] Bill Clinton was even better off, so well-funded that, despite his liabilities, he discouraged challengers altogether, becoming the first Democrat nominated without substantial opposition since FDR in 1944. Moreover, the escalating cost of effective political participation discourages people from becoming active in civic life, and tends to make even successful elected officials, weary of incessant fund raising, think better of the attractions of private life.[130] And obviously, greater dependence on money makes it more difficult to champion the interests of working- and middle-class Americans.[131]

There was enough unhappiness about the role of money in 1996 that some kind of campaign reform is likely to pass Congress, though how effective such legislation will be is open to question, and not only because congressional incumbents stand to benefit from the current system. A serious approach to the problem requires taking on the Supreme Court's decision, in *Buckley* v. *Valeo* [1976], that contributions of money are speech entitled to the protection of the First Amendment.[132] That ruling, Elizabeth Drew comments, is "wrong-headed, not to say bone-headed": among other things, donating money is a form of expression, but it isn't speech, since it doesn't give reasons or submit to questions.[133] The purpose of the First Amendment is to protect democratic deliberation, not to turn the public forum into private property.[134] Bill Bradley is right: we should be doing whatever it takes to get *Buckley* v. *Valeo* off the books, even if it proves necessary to amend the Constitution.[135]

Of course, the question of money and democratic speech inevitably involves the media, since the visual media add a special political problem. Robert Putnam's recent findings suggest that television, more than any other factor, works to erode our social capital.[136] Nor is this surprising: speech tends to unite the hearer and the heard, where sight isolates, separating the viewer from the seen.[137]

The technicians who shape the media, in politics no less than other programming, see audiences as consumers, desirous but essentially passive, and the logic of their craft aims to give the people what they want and no more — "stirring up emotions," Walter Goodman writes, "and shutting down minds" — following the tendency of the marketplace toward the lowest, and private, common denominator.[138]

In their professional capacity, political media technicians fear democratic deliberation, and with reason. Controversy, debate, dividing the yeas and nays is always risky, and in primaries and conventions has been associated with defeat at the polls; technicians have a natural preference for controlled, quasi-totalitarian spectacles.[139] In 1992 Republicans let right-wingers, most notably Pat Buchanan, dominate the camera. This year, eager to avoid that mistake, they so tightly scripted their convention that Buchanan's delegates were not even allowed to vote for him.[140] And the Democratic convention was at least as thoroughly managed.

The difficulty, of course, is that this for-media version of politics is not very entertaining. As consumers, the audience knows and can find better shows; as citizens, most people realize that the real show is off-stage.[141] If they miss the point, the news media will tell them: sensing the mass public's resentment and distrust, the news media have made attacks on authority into a way of life.[142] And by covering elections as races, to the near-exclusion of any treatment of issues, the news media imply that what is said in public only matters as an indication of strategy.[143] Challenged about this or that enormity, the media justify themselves by reference to the duty to inform citizens, but — as the president might say — that dog won't hunt. The mass public displays a startling degree of civic illiteracy, seemingly unaffected by higher levels of education: in one *Washington Post* survey, two-thirds of the respondents couldn't identify their representative in the House; 54 percent knew neither senator; and a considerable majority believed that foreign aid costs more than Medicare.[144]

Disenchanted and muddled, citizens resent their estrangement from politics, but in expressing that sentiment, they are too apt to "shout opinions into the wind, then hang up," and they could benefit from greater exposure to the art of democratic controversy.[145] Steve Forbes was right when he urged his party not to shy away from open debate: "It's like making sausage. It's not nice to behold . . . but it's absolutely necessary in a democracy."[146] As Forbes went on to say, discontent will find a voice, through demagogues if not in civil argument. "I don't know where they are going," Howard Baker said of the voters in 1994, "and I don't think they know either. But what frightens me is that, if we do not address their feelings, they may develop a tendency to savage our institutions."[147]

The political parties haven't found the answer. Ross Perot has worn out his welcome and people hate to waste their votes, but an awful lot of Americans are thinking kind thoughts about third parties. At a time of increasing partisanship among elected officials, voters are finding it harder to identify with the parties' broad coalitions, and their loyalties have become more ambiguous, where they still exist at all.[148]

The Republicans suffer a widely-advertised internal division between basically pro-business, often libertarian champions of private liberty, and social conservatives, especially the religious right, who expect government to uphold traditional values.[149] At the level of principle, the contradiction is basic, and since the ending of the Cold War removed that commonality, increasingly visible.[150] Ronald Reagan was able to give the Republicans the atmosphere of a joyous crusade, but Reagan — who still had the anticommunist drum to beat — had a special magic.[151]

Bob Dole didn't come close. He made every effort to conciliate social conservatives early in the campaign, but his pragmatism was never a secret, and in building conservative support, he relied heavily on Ralph Reed's willingness to compromise in the interest of victory.[152] It was no surprise, consequently, that by convention time, Dole had virtually abandoned social conservatism.[153] He even largely ignored the carefully crafted challenge to partial-birth abortions, although the president's veto of the ban on that procedure put Democrats at odds with a strategically important body of opinion.[154] Dole preferred to rely on his tax plan, borrowing one of Reagan's parlor tricks, but even if he persuaded himself to believe it, Dole lacked the sleight-of-hand to pull it off.

In the end, having swallowed their pride and followed Reed and Dole in order to win, social conservatives were forced to endure a humiliating combination of neglect and defeat. Moderate Republicans, of course, have been arguing that the party needs to move to the center, cultivating women voters and practicing "inclusion." Social conservatives read a different lesson. They conclude that, all things being equal, Republicans cannot defeat Democrats in an election that turns on economics and government programs. They believe it is possible to score points on such issues, but they argue for the need to *define* campaigns in terms of social and moral issues, speaking to the public's concern for civil order.

Despite some defeats, the right will be stronger in Congress and at local levels. The growing Republican strength in the South and among religious conservatives, in a year when other groups hesitated or fell away, indicates a "subnational" realignment that is likely to strengthen the voice of social conservatives in Republican councils. It is a sign of the times that the Republican state platform in Iowa accused the 4-H movement of leaning toward socialism.[155]

Looking toward the election of 2000, "mainstream" Republicans will hope, almost desperately, for a Powell candidacy, since the general may have enough personal magnetism to overcome opposition to his moderation. A

"New Deal kid" with traditional values, Powell is no opponent of government, and as a candidate, he might — as Theodore Roosevelt did a century ago — pull dialogue in the direction of civic engagement. All that is high speculation; what's certain is that social conservatives, and the concern for civil order, are not about to go away.

Not that the Democrats are in better shape. The electorate didn't like Newt Gingrich, but as the congressional results suggested, it didn't trust the Democrats to run the country.[156] Clinton did well among younger voters and Hispanics, and he scored gains among Catholics, but Democratic candidates for the House showed little or no improvement with these voters, and with Catholics, may even have lost ground.[157] As a party, the Democrats were still associated with liberalism, and that doctrine doesn't sell.[158] Republican attack ads that waved the "L-word" like a bloody shirt were not successful, but Democrats, including the president, generally tried to put distance between themselves and liberal ideology.[159]

For thirty years or so, liberalism has promoted a greatly expanded government *responsibility* for economic and social life; at the same time, it has defended a panoply of liberties, rights, and entitlements, especially for favored constituencies, that create immunities from politics, reducing government's *authority*.[160] Obviously, those cross-purposes amount to a long-term prescription for frustration and failure. Contemporary Democratic politics is effectively postliberal, but so far, the party has not developed an alternative. In 1996 Democrats managed a relatively harmonic front, but post-Clinton, it is hard not to expect a battle for the party's soul.[161]

So-called New Democrats or neoliberals are inclined to emphasize the limits on government. Broadly "postmaterialist," they defend the individual rights associated with social liberalism and they concern themselves with "quality of life" issues such as education and the environment, but — although they emphasize the importance of economic prosperity — they tend to regard unions as relics and show little interest in economic equality.[162] Their position, Harvey Mansfield remarks, is "less caring than liberalism and less judgmental than conservatism," a stance that, to critics, looks like well-mannered indifference.[163] "Old Democrats," by contrast, are more typically working class and more likely to be partisans of equality. They preserve the New Deal's attempt to make government the ally of families, and they are apt to care about decency and civic order more than the niceties of individual rights.[164]

Bill Clinton, characteristically, has gone both ways, although the Republican majorities on Capitol Hill may push him in a New Democratic direction. For the Democratic Party, however, 1996 may indicate a different path. The party of most Americans at the lower end of the income scale, it will necessarily practice a kind of class politics, especially given the mood of the voters and its debt to labor's contributions in the election.[165] As the unions understood, however, American political culture makes it necessary to speak to class concerns without employing class rhetoric, speaking to Americans as a people in terms of the common good.[166]

That subtler politics of class helps explain why race was so invisible in the campaign. Just as it's hard not to see class frictions — particularly those associated with the rise of the black middle class — in the mounting hostility to affirmative action, evident in the California initiative in 1996, it is also true that addressing our common vulnerabilities in terms of widely shared civic values has at least the possibility of muting the politics of race.[167] In any case, when President Clinton took his usual step to the center, agreeing that affirmative action should be "mended," but denying that it should be scrapped, his concession to the prevailing wind was largely understood and accepted by African American voters. And it is at least a straw in that wind that the five African American incumbents in the South, redistricted out of safe, majority-minority districts by court order, all won reelection. Incumbency helped, of course, but those results at least weaken the case for reverse gerrymandering and suggest that, for enough voters to make the difference, policy preferences can override race.[168]

In the same way, the welfare reform bill can open a new chapter. Passing the bill changed the terms of debate: there will be less talk about "welfare chiselers" and, grim though it is, more evidence of desperate families and suffering children. In the short term, there will be no "fixing" the bill, but Democrats can and should be arguing for compulsory national service and a role for the government as an employer of last resort. The old welfare system always slighted the fact that citizens have a duty and a right to contribute to national life, and defending that moral imperative could realize some of the very unfulfilled promise of Clinton's New Covenant.[169]

But the Democrats' most fundamental problem is one that also transcends party. In the anxieties of the contemporary middle class, E.J. Dionne sees an analogy to the old Progressive movement and the promise of a new one.[170] There is, as Dionne contends, still much to admire in the Progressive support for a government actively using scientific administration and political power in the service of civic duty and community.[171] But the Progressives never solved the problem of accountability, and their innovations — the direct primary and the initiative — did at least as much harm as good. Any new Progressive movement must begin there, aiming to revitalize politics as a condition of policy, limiting the role of money, opening the media to serious democratic deliberation, and encouraging the development of party organizations that are local, closer to citizens, and better able to provide them with a public voice.

As if that were not challenge enough, the administrative state can be held accountable only on the basis of some standard or measure. Liberals and libertarians sometimes speak as if politics could be morally neutral, indifferent to first things, and Democrats, inclined to generosity, have often been disposed to agree. But ultimately, all policy — even a generous and tolerant one — rests on a judgment; for all parties and all citizens, politics comes down to a question of right.[172] American democracy is not formless: it presumes the superiority of citizenship, government by the people and the principle of equality that is the foundation of both. For democracy — and historically, for Democrats — cultures and individuals are not separate islands. Our diverse republic rests on equality's enduring challenge to things seen, in which human differences are only occasions for inquiry and wonder. Cultural "stories," treated with genuine respect, are arguments, efforts to understand what is true and best.[173] Our different perspectives are the starting points of a politics that, as Michael Sandel argues, is "more clamorous than consensual," at least in the first instance, but reduced to civility by a sense of our own limits and the respect due to equals.[174] The election of 1996 offers ample evidence of America's need for leaders and parties who can invigorate the contentious decencies of democratic self-government.

CHAPTER SEVEN

Beyond Disappointment?

Exhaustion and Hope in the Elections of 1998

> *And some say there are signs*
> *The second such has come,*
> *The true Millennium,*
> *The final golden glow*
> *To end it. And if so*
> *(And science ought to know)*
> *We may well raise our heads*
> *From weeding garden beds*
> *And annotating books*
> *To watch this end de luxe.*
> — Robert Frost,
> "It Is Almost the Year
> Two Thousand"

The final year of the millennium began with the president impeached and on trial before the Senate, and the national elections of 1998, the century's last, seemed little more than a scene in that larger drama. Not that it was much of a show: it was sad and shabby, too ignoble for tragedy and too depressing for comedy, full of knaves and villains but lacking heroes. Long before its predictable conclusion, the voters were calling for the curtain, eager only for the farce to end. In the mood of the electorate, discontent with the shortcomings of politics appeared to give way to resigned distaste, and outrage — as conservatives discovered — was as unfashionable as civility in high places.[1] But a considerable majority of Americans kept their heads, consistently showing good enough sense to shame their leaders, and there were whispers of a yearning for self-government — or at least, for government — that may point beyond the politics of disappointment.

•

It looked to be a good year for incumbents, and so it proved in the end. There were problems, of course: American well-being was terribly uneven; India and Pakistan tested nuclear weapons; the Middle East seethed; financial crisis kept reappearing in Russia, Latin America, and Asia. The political parties, moreover, weren't playing on a level field: Democrats, facing the traditional disadvantage of an off-year election, were running far behind the Republicans in raising money and finding it difficult to attract quality candidates or even to persuade wavering incumbents to run again.[2] But economically, the numbers indicated continued growth and comparative good times, and whatever our international troubles, no Americans were in combat; there was even hope for accommodation in Northern Ireland. A year of peace and prosperity, 1998 had the ingredients in the classic recipe for contented voters and easy reelection.

Almost immediately, however, scandal centering on the president's relationship with Monica Lewinsky created year-long counterpoint. That imbroglio, of course, was only an incident in the conservative pursuit of Bill Clinton that had prompted the investigation of Whitewater and the appointment of Kenneth Starr as independent counsel. In its convoluted way, that inquiry was extended to Paula Jones's allegations of sexual harassment; to "misleading" testimony by the president and Lewinsky in the Jones case; to Linda Tripp's tapes and the president's denials; to Lewinsky's eventual appearance, after months of hounding, before Starr's grand jury; to the president's videotaped testimony and public confession; and eventually, to the Starr report, the House Judiciary Committee, and the process of impeachment. The story had a tacky sort of fascination — Maureen Dowd called Starr's report a "Harold Robbins novel" — and featured the president lying to the public, quivering with counterfeit sincerity, only to be found out in the end.[3] Republicans, like most observers, saw all the signs of a major victory.[4]

The electoral result was startlingly unexpected. Incumbents *did* do well, by and large, but Democrats actually gained seats in the House — the first time a party controlling the presidency had done so in an off-year election since 1934, in the heyday of the New Deal — and they held even in the Senate, where almost everyone had expected them to lose three or four seats. In gubernatorial races, Republicans did relatively well, but Democrats won in California, a political jackpot, especially given the chance to redraw that state's congressional districts after the next census. The GOP held its majorities in Congress, narrowly in the House, but recriminations after the election led to the resignation of Newt Gingrich from the Speakership and from his House seat. His designated successor, Robert Livingston of Louisiana, also resigned after the revelation of his earlier lapses from marital fidelity, and Republicans ended by conferring the Speakership on Dennis Hastert of Illinois, whose greatest asset was colorless reputability. When the Senate eventually acquitted Clinton, the irony was complete: having set out to topple a throne, the Republicans succeeded in overthrowing their own.

Democrats, celebrating the outcome, knew that they had not really won, although their opponents surely *lost*. The president's troubles, combined with the party's other strategic advantages, gave Republicans a winning hand in 1998, but they played those cards miserably. GOP leaders knew the game called for finesse: one of Senator Trent Lott's aides called the impeachment inquiry "kryptonite," referring to the risk that Republicans would seem partisan, extreme, and sex-obsessed, but that was exactly the tone set by the majority on the House Judiciary Committee and by congressional Republicans in general.[5]

The Republican insistence on broadcasting the president's videotaped grand jury testimony may have been a decisive miscalculation. It was clearly a political maneuver, one that at least hinted at unfairness and was certainly inconsistent with any pretense of bipartisanship. More important, it made the mistake of giving the president, always a plausible talker, a national audience for his explanations. And Republicans, who expected viewers to focus on the president's evasions, misread the dramaturgy of the tapes: the president was the only human face, standing alone against intrusive, relentless questioning by an impersonal voice — a scene out of Kafka, Everyman assailed by a power both invisible and malign, the constant nightmare of mass society. The president did not emerge as a hero, but he did evoke sympathy and no small measure of identification. In any case, the crusade against Clinton never attracted most Americans: there were ups and downs, but the polls consistently showed substantial majorities rating the president as doing a "good job" and opposing his removal from office.

Despite that support, Republican strategists made criticism of the president's misconduct the centerpiece of the party's 1998 campaign, to the virtual exclusion of other issues. The plan had a kind of crack-brained cunning: it deflected attention from the undistinguished record of the Republican-controlled Congress; more important, a focus on Clinton pleased the GOP's right wing, while allowing candidates to avoid giving much attention to the conservative agenda on social issues, with its tendency to offend moderate Republicans and independents.

To put it mildly, the design had flaws. For one thing, it undid or lessened a major Republican advantage, the fact that, in off-year elections, the Democrats' core voters — lower-income, socially disadvantaged, and always disproportionately hard to turn out on election day — are even less likely to make it to the polls, especially when compared with committed conservatives. In 1998, however, the Republican assault on the president helped energize black voters, who tended to see Clinton as the strongest advocate of racial equality since Lyndon Johnson. This was especially notable in the South: in Georgia, for example, where Democrats retained the governorship, blacks comprise 24 percent of the electorate, but 29 percent of voters in 1998. At the same time, it was a bad year to cold-shoulder the right: Democrats — again, particularly in the South — had been at some pains to recruit candidates with at least some conservative credentials on social issues, and while the great majority of religious conservatives continued to vote Republican, the Democratic percentage edged up, possibly enough to make the difference in a number of tight races.[6]

Moderate Republicans, of course, saw a clear message in the 1998 results, that the party had become too identified with extremists and with the religious right. Evidence to support this view is easy to find: Matt Fong's promising race for the Senate in California was seriously hurt, for example, by the revelation that his campaign had made a substantial donation to a notoriously homophobic organization. And there is little doubt that Republicans have underrated the strength of social liberalism among Americans: even the majority of Americans who hold traditional moral beliefs, Alan Wolfe finds, are unwilling to "judge" others or "impose" their views, caught up in a culture of tolerance that is necessarily uneasy with right-wing militancy.[7]

There are some signs of disarray and demoralization on the religious right; Paul Weyrich, for example, speaks of the appeal to the "political process" as a failure, urging social conservatives to build "parallel institutions" and emphasize moral education.[8] Most Republican conservatives, however, have a different reading of events. At the polls, conservative candidates have been at least as likely to win as moderates — more likely, according to some data — and in 1998 the right won victories against affirmative action, gay rights, and gay marriage even in relatively liberal states.[9] Republicans did poorly in 1998, from this perspective, not because they were conservative but because they were *empty*, without any principles or programs beyond opposition to Clinton.

By the end of the impeachment process, in fact, Republican leaders were trying to build a more positive image for the party as the advocate of broad tax cuts — a return to the magic of the Reagan years, acceptable to moderates and conservatives alike. But Clinton's emphasis on the importance of paying down the deficit and saving Social Security — combined with a few, well-targeted tax cuts of his own — enlists powerful interests and claims the banner of fiscal rectitude. What enchanted Americans in the 1980s, moreover, has lost some of its spell, and Republicans will need a new recipe for a new time.[10]

Not that Democrats have found Excalibur. The party had plenty of worrisome moments in 1998 — "I thought the money was going to kill us," Dick Gephardt said, referring to the Republicans' advantage in campaign finance.[11] The GOP's stance in the election and the impeachment crisis, however, allowed Democrats to subordinate their differences and do what they do best: run as the party of things-as-they-are, the defenders of Social Security, Medicare, and programmatic liberalism generally. It helped that most voters, with admirable good sense, did not hold Democrats responsible for Clinton's misdeeds, but *did* consider Republicans accountable for the inactivity of Congress. And the Democrats' allies in the unions, newly energized, turned away from campaigns in the media — vulnerable to attacks on the influence of "big labor" — to a "retail politics" successfully aimed at drawing union members to the polls. (Union members made up 22 percent of the electorate in 1998, as against 14 percent in the Democratic disaster of 1994.[12])

In the impeachment battle, moreover, congressional Democrats wisely said little or nothing in defense of the president; many of them, in any case, despise him — as a man, as a leader, or both.[13] They limited themselves to the higher — and politically safer — constitutional case that the charges against Clinton were not proved or not impeachable, and especially, were no basis for overturning the result of a democratic election. Those convictions, united with their even stronger distaste for the president's opponents, allowed Democrats to maintain an unheard-of degree of party unity through the whole process.

That solidarity, in turn, may have enabled the party to avoid what looked to be a lacerating battle in 2000 between Old Democrats and New: it insulated the administration — and particularly Vice-President Gore — from intra-party criticism, inhibiting the development of rival candidacies at a critical time, so that Gore's most prominent potential rivals for the nomination, former Senator Bill Bradley aside, have decided to forego the race.

So much for the Democrats' good news. The party's internecine quarrels, though temporarily suppressed, are certain to recur. The positive bases of Democratic unity, these days, do not go much beyond vague compassion and the determination to keep a social-service state at least minimally intact. Despite Mr. Clinton's talk of vision, Democrats, like their Republican rivals, are still groping for a program adequate for the nation's political future.

It doesn't help that America's political institutions have sustained serious damage. The Supreme Court's contribution to the Lewinsky follies — its decision that allowing the Paula Jones case to go forward would not distract the president from his duties — suits a comic opera better than *U.S. Reports*. Congress, already low in public esteem, fell into a political sub-basement, and the impeachment process shattered individual reputations: at the beginning, for example, most observers were fitting Henry Hyde, the chairman of the House Judiciary Committee, with the laurels of statecraft; by the end, he was reduced to the role of Polonius, a partisan moralist, somewhat baffled and pathetic. And of course, Bill Clinton, the central player in the Grand Guignol, has taken most of the remaining shine off the presidency, at least for the moment.

As a person, the president inspires little trust or respect. Nevertheless, a majority of Americans have continued to give him good marks for his performance in office, indicating a shrewd understanding of one side of executive leadership.[14] In the theorizing of the Framers, as Hamilton implied in *Federalist* No. 70, constitutionalism and the rule of law are artifacts, the creations of human agreement and effective only within its limits. Outside those boundaries — and beneath the surface of society — nature and other regimes, unbound, threaten those conventions and decencies. And change always tends to make old laws obsolete. Even Locke, that paladin of limited government, argued that every government needs "prerogative," the power of acting without and sometimes even *against* the rules in the interest of the common good or the country's survival.[15]

Most Americans know that, while it is not necessary for the president to be a knave or a thug, presidents have to deal with people who *are,* especially given the terrors and transformations of contemporary life. (For that matter, it isn't enough for voters to be law-abiding: inside the voting booth, exercising sovereignty, they have to *evaluate* laws and policies, placing themselves, for that moment, above the law.) The president, consequently, can't afford to be too conventional or too tied to the decencies: the most conspicuously moral of recent presidents, Carter and Ford, are generally rated as failures, and voters in recent elections have showed a fairly consistent preference for supple rascality over hobbled rectitude. In these terms, the greatest damage to Clinton's standing during the Lewinsky affair may have come not because he lied, but because he did so ineptly, in ways that were almost certain to be found out. From the beginning of the scandal, Alan Wolfe observed, the voters, more than their leaders, were informed by a Machiavellian "realpolitik."[16]

A great deal of this popular opinion, however, reflects the view of people whose attachment to democratic institutions and politics has been unsettled by the transformations of global markets and new technologies. Civic life seems less able to govern the forces of the time, and also less necessary. Given the diminished stature of political community, Americans are tempted to offer it less of themselves. The feeling of being "unencumbered" (the term is Michael Sandel's) encourages an ethic of personal liberation easily offended by intrusions on the president's "private life."[17] Yet that spirit also promotes a *public* life that is increasingly *privatized,* not only through deregulation and government downsizing, but through a politics in which money and lawsuits — most sensationally, Paula Jones's — administrative hearings and "rights talk" replace the effort to persuade and organize majorities.[18] Even civic participation is likely to take the form of volunteering, an individualized politics tailored to burdened schedules and guarded loyalties — fluid and informal, often intense but largely episodic, a reaction to events more than a committed effort to shape them.[19] It is no surprise, consequently, that we are more apt to think of political leaders as lawyers or CEOs, people we hire for essentially private purposes. In these terms, Bill Clinton's character is largely irrelevant unless it shows up in the economic bottom line. If you were O.J. Simpson, would you care about the state of Johnny Cochrane's soul? And it follows, as in the recent thriller *Air Force One,* that presidents also put private motives first, which is fine, the movie teaches, so long as the terrorists get killed in the end.

Other problems aside, that privatized image of politics ignores the fact that political leaders — especially in times of rapid and perilous change — may have to ask us to do things that cost or hurt, that trouble the existing order, or that challenge the way we see ourselves and our country. The authority to do great things requires a strong relation between people and president, one in which we give our allegiance and our willingness to sacrifice, but in which we receive assurance of moral direction and personal responsibility from those who lead us into new ways and times. Presidents, in their highest role, mediate between convention and nature, the laws and the divine. Able to dispense mercy, presidents can bring down the apocalypse; at bottom, the presidency is hierophantic and tinted with regality, a truth partly captured by FDR's hyperbolic likening of his administration to Christ's driving the moneychangers from the temple. But the price of that dangerous authority is the president's willingness to sacrifice his or her private self while in office, to assume a wholly public *persona*: in great monarchies, like the papacy, rulers often surrender their private names, just as high kings must be willing to die or offer up those they love.

In liberal democracies, the price of office, like its authority, is ordinarily not so steep. Still, if our rulers want to be taken seriously, they have to give up most of the liberty they would enjoy as private citizens. Above all, they have to show personal respect for the forms, for the very conventions and laws that a president's extra-legal public power may have to reframe or reform.

Bill Clinton has never approximated that standard. In August 1998 *Newsweek* asked "Can He Still Lead?" but Clinton was never much of a leader: his style is conciliatory, championing consensus rather than party, accommodation over confrontation. After 1994 his ambitions, never very grand, were scaled back to the terms of privatized politics, offering little in the way of vision and making less in the way of demands. Seen in retrospect, Clinton's conduct in office, especially in his second term, looks like an episode from *Seinfeld,* or an anecdote without a punch-line, content to keep the ship of state afloat and the president himself unimpeached, but making almost no effort to shape events to democracy's measure.[20] Bill Clinton is genuinely engaging, and even his misdeeds suggest a Tom Sawyer-like kind of mischief, the sometimes very hurtful frivolities of a basically good kid. But his term of office has left the presidency damaged and in urgent need of repair.

The presidency also suffers from old wounds. Vietnam, Watergate, and their sequelae popularized fears of an "Imperial Presidency" growing out of the recognition of real dangers in the president's prerogatives, especially in national security policy.[21] Yet such perils have to be weighed against the risk that the president will be unable to control the executive branch, allowing its horde of agencies and unelected officials to pursue their own interests and policies. Weakening the *president* does not reduce the power of *government:* it only lessens the extent to which we can hold government accountable or shake bureaucracies out of established routines. That our worries about the misuse of authority should weaken public institutions is paradoxical, because what we fear most is the shadowy power of administrative agencies, so often covert and faceless, speaking in whispers and monotones, adroit at the use of insinuation and terror. Kenneth Starr's prolonged inquisition demonstrated that the Independent Counsel Statute opens the door to abuses of power that at least rival those it was designed to curb. (Since Congress now seems likely to let the statute expire, Starr's excesses may have the unintended good result of dooming the law that made them possible.) At least part of the public's support for Clinton during the impeachment process derived from a perceived need for a president able to exert the full constitutional authority of his office. That attitude, in turn, offers some hope for political reconstruction.

On the other hand, the battle over impeachment was remarkable for the Republican persistence in disregarding that majority voice even after the 1998 returns, pushing ahead with charges that, lacking Democratic support, were bound to fail in the Senate as they had already failed in the court of public opinion. Even former Senator Dole, that celebrated broker, was unable to persuade his party's congressional leaders to accept censure as an alternative. In the Senate, a handful of Republican moderates — predominantly from the Northeast — did eventually tip the balance so that neither charge against the president commanded a majority, let alone two-thirds. But the GOP's moderate minority — in the House as well as the Senate — could have stopped the process much earlier: instead, almost unanimously, they sided with their conservative colleagues on every key vote, soldiering on right up to the last trench. Congressional Republicans seemed to have turned self-destructive, rejecting the pragmatism traditionally thought to be a hallmark of American politics.

Republicans had their reasons, however, even if their calculations prove to be in error. The great majority of members of Congress can afford to ignore national polls: they are elected in districts that are safely partisan and, in the case of Republicans, predominantly conservative. Even those Republicans who are sure bets in a general election, however, find it wise to worry about primaries, and hence about the party's right wing: conservatives are disproportionately strong among primary electorates, since the less zealous are apt to forget or stay home. A primary challenge hurts even when it fails: a contest for the nomination drains campaign funds and leaves scars. In competitive states or districts, moreover, primary contests pull candidates to the right, away from the center that tends to be decisive in November. Moderate Republicans, consequently, walk on eggs wherever the right might take mortal offense. (Obviously, Democratic moderates have a parallel problem, most visibly in New Mexico, where the Green Party is delighted to mount a third-party challenge to any candidates who depart from its version of the fundamentals.)

Moreover, in the internal life of the House and Senate, careers — and projects that benefit a member's district or state — are highly dependent on party leaders. And the dominant presences on the Republican side of the House, after the departure of Newt Gingrich, have been right-wingers like Tom DeLay and Dick Armey, militant ideologues who are not at all hesitant to punish deviants, as Peter King (R-N.Y.) has discovered since voting against impeachment. In the Senate, Trent Lott spoke a little more softly but carried the same big ideological stick. Any Republican with a legislative agenda had plenty of grounds for going along.

Wavering Republicans also knew that the president wasn't going to be removed from office when the final vote was taken, making it easy to dodge responsibility, relying on the fact that, for most voters, the whole affair would eventually drop out of sight and out of mind. Conservatives would be apt to *remember* how you voted; moderates, who probably care less or are distracted by other issues, are more likely to forget, particularly if they ultimately get the result they want.

Former Senator Alan Simpson, a shrewd head, recommended that strategy, encouraging Republicans to discount the polls, trusting in the electorate's fabulously short memory and its capacity for inattention. Up to a point, Simpson is right: most voters do forget political specifics, and in no very long term. Also, when they are discontented, they tend to blame Congress as an institution and to adopt a more favorable view of their own representatives. But political events, half-remembered, do form voters' images of a *party*. A few years after 1972, relatively few Americans could have said much about George McGovern's actual proposals and platform, but they were left with an abiding impression of Democrats as dovish and permissive liberals, a notion that still haunts American politics. The Lewinsky affair, similarly, has worked to solidify the view that Republicans are partisan ideologues in the grip of the religious right, willing to shut down the government or wreck the country. A good deal of Republican ingenuity will be devoted to the attempt to soften the colors of that picture, but it will surely cost them, in 2000 and after.[22]

The Republicans' willingness to pay that price comes back to the peculiar intensity of the right's hatred for Clinton (a man transparently too weak to be grandly evil), a loathing evident since the earliest days of his presidency and strong enough to override any countervailing prudence.

In the first place, for social conservatives Clinton symbolizes the culture of the 1960s, and with it, the forces of moral decay — a draft-dodging McGovern supporter, sexually promiscuous, tolerant of homosexuality, and above all, a challenge to traditional gender roles. Mr. Clinton is soft, pliant and conciliatory. Mrs. Clinton (until recently, much less popular than the president) is a person with convictions and commitments who does not shrink from the fray; worst of all, before his presidency, Mrs. Clinton made more money than her husband. For the evangelical right, it accentuates Clinton's faults that he is, at least nominally, a born-again Christian, so that the anti-Clinton crusade takes on the tone of a trial for heresy.

Moreover, American social conservatives need to demonize the president in order to preserve what's left of their characteristic illusion. After the Democratic debacle in the elections of 1994, Clinton's commitment to a liberal economic agenda, always modest, became even more marginal. The president signed the welfare reform bill, embraced and took credit for the balanced budget, and — his political fortunes visibly dependent on America's very uneven prosperity — has become ever more enthusiastic about free trade and market economics, with only an occasional gesture toward trade unions or human rights. Mr. Clinton's economic turn rightward forces conservatives toward the terrifying truth that the market, left to itself, panders to desire and undermines social institutions, teaching relativism more effectively than legions of intellectuals. In its devotion to individualism and unregulated change, the right has been savaging the values and virtues it professes to love, so it was appropriate for congressional Republicans to fall on their swords.[23] Diminishing government does not lead to a flourishing of civil society: families, communities, and associations are being battered by economic and technological change, and to stand a chance in that unequal contest, they will need government's support.[24] ·

Internationally, opinion has been edging in that direction. The 1980s were dominated by the right, with Mrs. Thatcher its commanding spirit, willing and even zealous to let the market reshape society in the pursuit of growth. Hesitantly but clearly, the 1990s have tilted toward invoking government to protect social order against the unsettlings of change. Mostly, this mood has meant a moderate turn to the left — wrong about socialism, Marx looks more and more prescient as a critic of capitalism — but it also finds expression in support for cultural nationalism, as in India.[25]

In the United States, the signs have been more ambiguous. Clinton's election in 1992 was a straw in the wind, reflecting the hope for a government able to take charge of events — "we force the Spring," the president said in his first inaugural — but his first two years in office were full of missteps, while the baronial Democratic Congress, believing itself invulnerable, showed no eagerness for change. The landslide in 1994 — badly misread by Republicans — was a vote against ineffective government as much as a cheer for Newt Gingrich's Contract with America. And in 1998 great numbers of voters were offended by a Republican Congress that, its obsession with the president's misdeeds aside, was chiefly notable for inactivity.

For most Americans, these are relatively good times, but also uneasy ones.[26] They worry about education and Social Security, dislike HMOs, and fret about the environment and newly-prominent issues such as "suburban sprawl."[27] And above all, they recognize that economic and technological mega-forces — "globalization" and the "information revolution" — are shaking and shattering relationships and communities. "Downsizing," layoffs, and the rise of temporary and part-time employment are creating unstable and anxious workplaces where loyalty and trust are scarce commodities — possibly "leaner," Kristin Downey Grimsley concedes, but "definitely meaner."[28]

Middle America is anxious, feeling the squeeze: economic inequality in America is the greatest in the industrial world. In fact, for a quarter century, the trend of real hourly wages has been downward, and it has been possible to keep up only by working longer hours, taking second jobs, and sending more family members out to work.[29] "Domestic insecurity," as Theodore Lowi writes, has become virtually the first principle of economic and social life.[30] The comparative prosperity of most Americans only emphasizes their sense that things could easily get worse, and they yearn for a greater measure of predictability and civil order.

At the most basic level, Americans want to have some say about the direction and form of change, at least some taste of self-government in the great stew of events. They know that government can be bumbling or even malign — in February 1999, the Center on Public Attitudes found that only 19 percent of Americans thought that the government acts rightly most of the time — and they also doubt that its power, so overwhelming in relation to individuals, can do more than qualify or adapt to the global forces shaping the time.[31] They fear, Lance Bennett writes, that government is "at worst responsible for the economic conditions that dominate their private lives, and at best, of little use for remedying them."[32] Across the industrial world, there is evidence of a decline of allegiance to parties, governments, and nations.[33]

Yet whatever their discontents, voters do not have, and surely are not getting, any persuasive vision of change for the better, so that, cherishing their comforts, they tend to get the shivers from any talk of rocking the boat. They are, however, anything but serene: in popular culture, there are all too many indications of a broad suspicion that our civilization is stalked by nemesis, and of a hankering, not always confined to fantasy, for an heroic leader capable of cutting through the hedge of constitutional forms and asserting some sort of human mastery over the times. Any whiff of hard times, any serious slackening of prosperity, could have nasty political consequences. But through the impeachment crisis and the election of 1998, the majority of Americans demonstrated at least passably good sense, civility, and political shrewdness.[34] If Americans' confidence in public life shows signs of exhaustion, so do many of the illusions, left and right, that have befogged politics since 1980. They may realize, too, that in politics as well as in computers, Y2K points to both the threat of a crash and the possibility of reconstruction.

In their better moments, most Americans still appreciate the higher calling of democratic self-government, a discipline that protects and cherishes private differences and inequalities, but only insofar as they are compatible with a republic of equal citizens.[35] After a generation and more of disappointment, restoring or rebuilding the foundations of democratic politics will require us to translate that ideal into a language and practice adequate for the new century.[36] Risks, obstacles, and all, that venture, like the Yellow Brick Road, is our only way home.

Appendixes

Appendix A: The 1980 Presidential Vote

State	Electoral Vote		Popular Vote		Percentage of Three-Candidate Vote			Percentage of Two-Party Vote	
	Carter	Reagan	Carter	Reagan	Carter	Reagan	Anderson	Carter	Reagan
Alabama	—	9	636,730	654,192	48.7	50.0	1.3	49.3	50.7
Alaska[a]	—	3	41,842	86,112	26.5	54.7	18.8	32.7	67.3
Arizona	—	6	246,843	529,688	28.9	62.1	9.0	31.8	68.2
Arkansas	—	6	398,041	403,164	48.3	49.0	2.7	49.7	50.3
California	—	45	3,083,652	4,524,835	36.9	54.2	8.9	40.5	59.5
Colorado	—	7	368,009	652,264	32.0	56.7	11.3	36.1	63.9
Connecticut	—	8	541,732	655,210	38.9	48.7	12.4	44.4	55.6
Delaware	—	3	105,754	111,252	45.3	47.7	7.0	48.7	51.3
District of Columbia	3	—	130,231	23,313	76.8	13.7	9.5	84.8	15.2
Florida	—	17	1,419,475	2,046,951	38.9	55.9	5.2	41.0	59.0
Georgia	12	—	890,955	654,168	56.4	41.4	2.2	57.6	42.4
Hawaii	4	—	135,879	130,112	45.6	43.6	10.8	51.1	48.9
Idaho	—	4	110,192	290,699	25.8	67.9	6.3	27.5	72.5
Illinois	—	26	1,981,413	2,358,094	42.2	50.4	7.4	45.6	54.4
Indiana	—	13	844,197	1,255,656	38.1	56.8	5.1	40.2	59.8
Iowa	—	8	508,672	676,026	39.1	52.0	8.9	42.9	57.1
Kansas	—	7	326,150	566,812	34.0	48.9	7.1	36.6	63.4
Kentucky	—	9	617,417	635,274	48.1	49.5	2.4	49.3	50.7
Louisiana	—	10	708,453	492,853	46.4	51.9	1.7	47.2	52.8
Maine	—	4	220,974	238,522	43.1	46.5	10.4	48.1	51.9
Maryland	10	—	726,161	680,606	47.5	44.6	7.9	51.6	48.4
Massachusetts	—	14	1,053,800	1,056,223	42.2	42.4	15.4	49.9	50.1
Michigan	—	21	1,661,532	1,915,225	43.2	49.7	7.1	46.4	53.6
Minnesota	10	—	945,173	873,268	47.6	43.7	8.7	52.2	47.8
Mississippi	—	7	429,281	441,089	48.6	50.0	1.4	49.3	50.7
Missouri	—	12	931,182	1,074,181	44.7	51.6	3.7	46.4	53.6

State									
Montana	—	4	118,032	206,814	33.3	58.4	8.3	36.3	63.7
Nebraska	—	5	166,424	419,214	26.2	66.5	7.1	28.4	71.6
Nevada	—	3	66,666	155,017	27.9	64.8	7.3	30.1	69.9
New Hampshire	—	4	108,864	221,705	28.7	58.3	13.0	33.0	67.0
New Jersey	—	17	1,147,364	1,546,557	39.2	52.8	8.0	42.6	57.4
New Mexico	—	4	167,826	250,779	37.4	56.0	6.6	40.1	59.9
New York	—	41	2,728,372	2,893,831	44.8	47.6	7.6	48.5	51.5
North Carolina	—	13	875,635	915,018	47.5	49.6	2.9	48.9	51.1
North Dakota	—	3	79,189	193,695	26.8	65.3	7.9	29.1	70.9
Ohio	—	25	1,752,414	2,206,545	41.6	52.4	6.0	44.3	55.7
Oklahoma	—	8	402,026	695,570	35.4	61.2	3.4	36.6	63.4
Oregon	—	6	456,890	571,044	40.1	50.1	9.8	44.5	55.5
Pennsylvania	—	27	1,936,540	2,261,872	43.1	50.4	6.5	46.1	53.9
Rhode Island	4	—	198,342	154,793	48.0	37.5	14.5	56.2	43.8
South Carolina	—	8	430,385	441,841	48.6	49.8	1.6	49.4	50.6
South Dakota	—	4	103,855	198,343	32.1	61.3	6.6	34.4	65.6
Tennessee	—	10	783,051	787,761	48.8	49.0	2.2	49.8	50.2
Texas	—	26	1,881,147	2,510,705	41.7	55.8	2.5	42.8	57.2
Utah	—	4	124,266	439,687	20.9	74.0	5.1	22.0	78.0
Vermont	—	3	81,952	94,628	39.3	45.4	15.3	46.4	53.6
Virginia	—	12	752,174	989,609	40.9	53.9	5.2	43.2	56.8
Washington	—	9	650,193	865,244	38.2	50.9	10.9	42.9	57.1
West Virginia	6	—	367,462	334,206	50.1	45.6	4.3	52.4	47.6
Wisconsin	—	11	981,584	1,088,845	44.0	48.8	7.2	47.4	52.6
Wyoming	—	3	49,427	110,700	28.7	64.3	7.0	30.9	69.1
National Total	49	489	35,483,820	43,901,812	41.7	51.6	6.7	44.7	55.3

a. Alaska third-party vote includes 18,479 votes for Ed Clark, Libertarian Party, as well as 11,156 votes for Anderson.

Appendix B: The 1984 Presidential Vote

State	Electoral Vote Reagan	Electoral Vote Mondale	Popular Vote Reagan	Popular Vote Mondale	Percentage of 1984 Two-Party Vote Reagan	Percentage of 1984 Two-Party Vote Mondale	Percentage of 1980 Two-Party Vote Reagan	Percentage of 1980 Two-Party Vote Carter
Alabama	9	—	872,849	551,899	61.3	38.7	50.7	49.3
Alaska	3	—	138,392	62,018	69.1	30.9	67.3	32.7
Arizona	7	—	681,416	333,584	67.1	32.9	68.2	31.8
Arkansas	6	—	534,774	338,646	61.2	38.8	50.3	49.7
California	47	—	5,467,009	3,922,519	58.2	41.8	59.5	40.5
Colorado	8	—	821,817	454,974	64.4	35.6	63.9	36.1
Connecticut	8	—	890,877	569,597	61.0	39.0	55.6	44.4
Delaware	3	—	152,190	101,656	60.0	40.0	51.3	48.7
District of Columbia	—	3	29,009	180,408	13.8	86.2	15.2	84.8
Florida	21	—	2,730,350	1,448,816	65.3	34.7	59.0	41.0
Georgia	12	—	1,068,7222	706,628	60.2	39.8	42.2	57.6
Hawaii	4	—	185,050	147,154	55.7	44.3	48.9	51.1
Idaho	4	—	297,523	108,510	73.3	26.7	72.5	27.5
Illinois	24	—	2,707,103	2,086,499	56.5	43.5	54.4	45.6
Indiana	12	—	1,377,230	841,481	62.1	37.9	59.8	40.2
Iowa	8	—	703,088	605,620	53.7	46.3	57.1	42.9
Kansas	7	—	677,296	333,539	67.0	33.0	63.4	36.6
Kentucky	9	—	821,702	539,539	60.4	39.6	50.7	49.3
Louisiana	10	—	1,037,299	651,586	61.4	38.6	52.8	47.2
Maine	4	—	336,500	214,515	61.1	38.9	51.9	48.1
Maryland	10	—	879,918	787,935	52.8	47.2	48.4	51.6
Massachusetts	13	—	1,310,936	1,239,606	51.4	48.6	50.1	49.9
Michigan	20	—	2,251,571	1,529,638	59.5	40.5	53.6	46.4
Minnesota	—	10	1,032,603	1,036,364	49.9	50.1	47.8	52.2
Mississippi	7	—	582,377	352,192	62.3	37.7	50.7	49.3
Missouri	11	—	1,274,188	848,583	60.0	40.0	53.6	46.4

Montana	4	—	232,450	61.3	38.7	146,742	63.7	36.3
Nebraska	5	—	459,135	71.0	29.0	187,475	71.6	28.4
Nevada	4	—	188,770	67.3	32.7	91,655	69.9	30.1
New Hampshire	4	—	267,050	68.9	31.1	120,347	67.0	33.0
New Jersey	16	—	1,933,630	60.5	39.5	1,261,323	57.4	4.26
New Mexico	5	—	307,101	60.3	39.7	201,769	59.9	40.1
New York	36	—	3,664,763	54.0	46.0	3,119,605	51.5	48.5
North Carolina	13	—	1,346,481	62.0	38.0	824,287	51.1	48.9
North Dakota	3	—	200,336	65.7	34.3	104,429	70.9	29.1
Ohio	23	—	2,678,560	59.5	40.5	1,825,440	55.7	44.3
Oklahoma	8	—	861,530	69.1	30.9	385,080	63.4	36.6
Oregon	7	—	685,700	56.1	43.9	536,479	55.5	44.5
Pennsylvania	25	—	2,584,323	53.7	46.3	2,228,131	53.9	46.1
Rhode Island	4	—	208,513	51.8	48.2	194,294	43.8	56.2
South Carolina	8	—	615,539	64.1	35.9	344,459	50.6	49.4
South Dakota	3	—	200,267	63.3	36.7	116,113	65.6	34.4
Tennessee	11	—	990,212	58.2	41.8	711,714	50.2	49.8
Texas	29	—	3,433,428	64.1	35.9	1,949,276	57.2	42.8
Utah	5	—	469,105	75.1	24.9	155,369	78.0	22.0
Vermont	3	—	135,865	58.7	41.3	95,730	53.6	46.4
Virginia	12	—	1,337,078	62.7	37.3	796,250	56.8	43.2
Washington	10	—	1,051,670	56.6	43.4	807,352	57.1	42.9
West Virginia	6	—	405,483	55.3	44.7	328,125	47.6	52.4
Wisconsin	11	—	1,198,584	54.6	45.3	995,740	52.6	47.4
Wyoming	3	—	133,241	71.4	28.6	53,370	69.1	30.9
National Total	525	13	54,450,603	59.17	40.83	37,573,671	55.3	44.7

SOURCE: *New York Times*, 22 December 1984, 10.

Appendix C: The 1988 Presidential Vote

State	Electoral Vote Bush	Electoral Vote Dukakis	Popular Vote Bush	Popular Vote Dukakis	Percentage of 1988 Two-Party Vote Bush	Percentage of 1988 Two-Party Vote Dukakis	Percentage of 1984 Two-Party Vote Reagan	Percentage of 1984 Two-Party Vote Mondale
Alabama	9	—	809,663	547,347	59.7	40.3	61.3	38.7
Alaska	3	—	102,381	62,205	62.2	37.8	69.1	30.9
Arizona	7	—	694,379	447,272	60.8	39.2	67.1	32.9
Arkansas	6	—	463,574	344,991	57.3	42.7	61.2	38.8
California	47	—	4,756,490	4,448,393	51.7	48.3	58.2	41.8
Colorado	8	—	727,633	621,093	54.0	46.0	64.4	35.6
Connecticut	8	—	747,082	674,873	52.5	47.5	61.0	39.0
Delaware	3	—	130,581	99,479	56.8	43.2	60.0	40.0
District of Columbia	—	3	25,732	153,100	14.4	85.6	13.8	86.2
Florida	21	—	2,538,994	1,632,086	60.9	39.1	65.3	34.7
Georgia	12	—	1,070,089	715,635	59.9	40.1	60.2	39.8
Hawaii	—	4	158,625	192,364	45.2	54.8	55.7	44.3
Idaho	4	—	253,467	147,420	63.2	36.8	73.3	26.7
Illinois	24	—	2,298,648	2,180,657	51.3	48.7	56.5	43.5
Indiana	12	—	1,280,292	850,851	60.1	39.9	62.1	37.9
Iowa	—	8	541,540	667,085	44.8	55.2	53.7	46.3
Kansas	7	—	552,659	422,056	56.7	43.3	67.0	33.0
Kentucky	9	—	731,446	579,077	55.8	44.2	60.4	39.6
Louisiana	10	—	880,830	715,612	55.2	44.8	61.4	38.6
Maine	4	—	304,087	240,508	55.9	44.1	61.1	38.9
Maryland	10	—	834,202	793,939	51.2	48.8	52.8	47.2
Massachusetts	—	13	1,184,323	1,387,398	46.1	53.9	51.4	48.6
Michigan	20	—	1,969,435	1,673,496	54.1	45.9	59.5	40.5
Minnesota	—	10	958,199	1,106,974	46.4	53.6	49.9	50.1
Mississippi	7	—	551,745	360,892	60.5	39.5	62.3	37.7
Missouri	11	—	1,081,163	1,004,040	51.9	48.1	60.0	40.0

Montana	4	—	189,598	168,120	53.0	47.0	61.3	38.7
Nebraska	5	—	389,394	254,426	60.5	39.5	71.0	29.0
Nevada	4	—	205,942	132,716	60.8	39.2	67.3	32.7
New Hampshire	4	—	279,770	162,335	63.3	36.7	68.9	31.1
New Jersey	16	—	1,699,634	1,275,063	57.1	42.9	60.5	39.5
New Mexico	5	—	260,792	236,528	52.4	47.6	60.3	39.7
New York	-	36	2,975,276	3,228,304	48.0	52.0	54.0	46.0
North Carolina	13	—	1,232,132	890,034	58.1	41.9	62.0	38.0
North Dakota	3	—	165,517	127,081	56.6	43.4	65.7	34.3
Ohio	23	—	2,411,719	1,934,922	55.5	44.5	59.5	40.5
Oklahoma	8	—	678,244	483,373	58.4	41.6	69.1	30.9
Oregon	-	7	517,731	575,071	47.4	52.6	56.1	43.9
Pennsylvania	25	—	2,291,297	2,183,928	51.2	48.8	53.7	46.3
Rhode Island	-	4	169,730	216,668	43.9	56.1	51.8	48.2
South Carolina	8	—	599,871	367,511	62.0	38.0	64.1	35.9
South Dakota	3	—	165,516	145,632	53.2	46.8	63.3	36.7
Tennessee	11	—	939,434	677,715	58.1	41.9	58.2	41.8
Texas	29	—	3,014,007	2,231,286	56.4	43.6	64.1	35.9
Utah	5	—	426,858	206,853	67.4	32.6	75.1	24.9
Vermont	3	—	123,166	116,419	51.4	48.6	58.7	41.3
Virginia	12	—	1,305,131	860,767	60.2	39.8	62.7	37.3
Washington	-	10	800,182	844,554	48.7	51.3	56.6	43.4
West Virginia	-	6[a]	307,824	339,112	47.6	52.4	55.3	44.7
Wisconsin	-	11	1,043,584	1,122,090	48.2	51.8	54.6	45.3
Wyoming	3	—	106,814	67,077	61.4	38.6	71.4	28.6
National Total	426	112[a]	47,946,422	41,016,429	53.89	46.11	59.17	40.83

SOURCE: *Congressional Quarterly Weekly Report* 46 (12 November 1988): 3245.

a. One elector actually cast a vote for Lloyd Bentsen; the vote is recorded here for the actual Democratic candidate, Dukakis.

Appendix D: The 1992 Presidential Vote

State	Electoral Vote		Popular Vote			Percentage of Three-Party Vote			Percentage of Two-Party Vote	
	Clinton	Bush	Clinton	Bush	Perot	Clinton	Bush	Perot	Clinton	Bush
Alabama	—	9	690,080	804,283	183,109	41.1	47.9	10.9	46.2	53.8
Alaska	—	3	78,294	102,000	73,481	30.9	40.2	29.0	43.4	56.6
Arizona	—	8	543,050	572,086	353,741	37.0	38.9	24.1	48.7	51.3
Arkansas	6	—	505,823	337,324	99,132	53.7	35.8	10.5	60.0	40.0
California	54	—	5,121,325	3,630,575	2,296,006	45.4	32.9	20.8	58.5	41.5
Colorado	8	—	629,681	562,850	366,010	40.4	36.1	23.5	52.8	47.2
Connecticut	8	—	682,318	578,313	348,771	42.4	35.9	21.7	54.1	45.9
Delaware	3	—	126,054	102,313	59,313	43.8	35.6	20.6	55.2	44.8
District of Columbia	3[a]	—	192,619	20,698	9,681	86.4	9.3	4.3	90.3	9.7
Florida	—	25	2,071,651	2,171,781	1,052,481	39.1	41.0	19.9	48.8	51.2
Georgia	13	—	1,008,966	995,252	309,657	43.6	43.0	13.4	50.3	49.7
Hawaii	4[a]	—	179,310	136,822	53,003	48.6	37.1	14.4	56.7	43.3
Idaho	—	4	137,013	202,645	130,395	29.1	43.1	27.7	40.3	59.7
Illinois	22	—	2,453,350	1,734,096	840,515	48.8	34.5	16.7	58.6	41.4
Indiana	—	12	848,420	989,375	455,934	37.0	43.1	19.9	46.2	53.8
Iowa	7[a]	—	586,353	504,891	253,468	43.6	37.5	18.8	53.7	46.3
Kansas	—	6	390,434	449,951	312,358	33.9	39.0	27.1	46.5	53.5
Kentucky	8	—	665,104	617,178	203,944	44.8	41.5	13.7	51.9	48.1
Louisiana	9	—	815,971	733,386	211,478	46.3	41.6	12.0	52.7	47.3
Maine	4	—	263,420	206,504	206,820	38.9	30.5	30.6	56.1	43.9
Maryland	10	—	988,571	707,094	281,414	50.0	35.8	14.2	58.3	41.7
Massachusetts	12[a]	—	1,318,639	805,039	630,731	47.9	29.2	22.9	62.1	37.9
Michigan	18	—	1,871,182	1,554,940	824,813	44.0	36.6	19.4	54.6	45.4
Minnesota	10[a]	—	1,020,997	747,841	562,506	43.8	32.1	24.1	57.7	42.3
Mississippi	—	7	400,258	587,793	85,626	41.1	50.1	8.8	45.1	54.9
Missouri	11	—	1,053,873	811,159	518,741	44.2	34.0	21.8	56.5	43.5

State	Electoral vote (Clinton)	Electoral vote (Bush)	Clinton	Bush	Perot	Clinton %	Bush %	Perot %	Two-party Clinton %	Two-party Bush %
Montana	3	—	154,507	144,207	107,225	38.1	35.5	26.4	51.7	48.3
Nebraska	—	5	216,864	343,678	174,104	29.5	46.8	23.7	38.7	61.3
Nevada	4	—	189,148	175,828	132,580	38.0	35.3	26.6	51.8	48.2
New Hampshire	4	—	209,040	202,484	121,337	39.2	38.0	22.8	50.8	49.2
New Jersey	15	—	1,436,206	1,356,865	521,829	43.3	40.9	15.7	51.4	48.6
New Mexico	5	—	261,617	212,824	91,895	46.2	37.6	16.2	55.1	44.9
New York	33[a]	—	3,444,450	2,346,649	1,090,721	50.1	34.1	15.8	59.5	40.5
North Carolina	—	14	1,114,042	1,134,661	357,864	42.7	43.5	13.7	49.5	50.5
North Dakota	—	3	99,168	136,244	71,084	32.4	44.5	23.2	42.1	57.9
Ohio	21	—	1,984,919	1,894,248	1,036,403	40.4	38.5	21.1	51.2	48.8
Oklahoma	—	8	473,066	592,929	319,878	34.1	42.8	23.1	44.4	55.6
Oregon	7[a]	—	621,314	475,757	354,091	42.8	32.8	24.4	56.6	43.4
Pennsylvania	23	—	2,239,164	1,791,841	902,667	45.4	36.3	18.3	55.5	44.5
Rhode Island	4[a]	—	213,299	131,601	105,045	47.4	29.2	23.3	61.8	38.2
South Carolina	—	8	479,514	577,507	138,872	40.1	48.3	11.6	45.4	54.6
South Dakota	—	3	124,888	136,718	73,295	37.3	40.8	21.9	47.7	52.3
Tennessee	11	—	933,521	841,300	199,968	47.3	42.6	10.1	52.6	47.4
Texas	—	32	2,281,815	2,496,071	1,354,781	37.2	40.7	22.1	47.8	52.2
Utah	—	5	183,429	322,632	203,400	25.9	45.5	28.7	36.2	63.8
Vermont	3	—	133,592	88,122	65,991	46.4	30.6	22.9	60.3	39.7
Virginia	—	13	1,038,650	1,150,517	348,639	40.9	45.3	13.7	47.4	52.6
Washington	11[a]	—	993,037	731,234	541,780	43.8	32.3	23.9	57.6	42.4
West Virginia	5[a]	—	331,001	241,974	108,829	48.5	35.5	16.0	57.8	42.2
Wisconsin	11[a]	—	1,041,066	930,855	544,479	41.4	37.0	21.6	52.8	47.2
Wyoming	—	3	68,160	79,347	51,263	34.3	39.9	25.8	46.2	53.8
National Total	370	168	44,908,233	39,102,282	19,741,048	43.3	37.7	19.0	53.5	46.5

SOURCE: Congressional Quarterly Weekly Report 51 (23 January 1993): 190.

NOTE: The total popular vote officially reported by secretaries of state for the fifty states and the District of Columbia was 104,420,887. The above table omits 0.6 percent of the total, votes that were cast for candidates other than Clinton, Bush, and Perot. Of the total popular vote, Clinton received 43.0 percent, Bush 37.4 percent, and Perot 18.9 percent.

a. States voting Democratic in 1988; total electoral vote=112 under 1980 apportionment.

Appendix E: The 1996 Presidential Vote

State	Electoral Vote		Popular Vote			Percentage of Three-Party Vote			Percentage of Two-Party Vote	
	Clinton	Dole	Clinton	Dole	Perot	Clinton	Dole	Perot	Clinton	Dole
Alabama	—	9	662,165	769,044	92,149	43.5	50.5	6.0	46.3	53.7
Alaska	—	3	80,380	122,746	26,333	35.0	53.5	11.5	39.6	60.4
Arizona	8	—	653,288	622,079	112,072	47.1	44.8	8.1	51.2	48.8
Arkansas	6	—	475,171	325,416	69,884	54.6	37.4	8.0	59.4	40.6
California	54	—	5,119,835	3,828,381	697,847	53.1	39.7	7.2	57.2	42.8
Colorado	—	8	671,152	691,848	99,629	45.9	47.3	6.8	49.2	50.8
Connecticut	8	—	735,740	483,109	139,523	54.2	35.6	10.3	60.4	39.6
Delaware	3	—	140,355	99,062	28,719	52.3	37.0	10.7	58.6	41.4
District of Columbia	3	—	158,220	17,339	3,611	88.3	9.7	2.0	90.1	9.9
Florida	25	—	2,546,870	2,244,536	483,870	48.3	42.5	9.2	53.2	46.8
Georgia	—	13	1,053,849	1,080,843	146,337	46.2	47.4	6.4	49.4	50.6
Hawaii	4	—	205,012	113,943	27,358	59.2	32.9	7.9	64.3	35.7
Idaho	—	4	165,443	256,595	62,518	34.1	53.0	12.9	39.2	60.8
Illinois	22	—	2,341,744	1,587,021	346,408	54.8	37.1	8.1	59.6	40.4
Indiana	—	12	887,424	1,006,693	224,299	41.9	47.5	10.6	46.9	53.1
Iowa	7	—	620,258	492,644	105,159	50.9	40.4	8.6	55.7	44.3
Kansas	—	6	387,659	583,245	92,639	36.5	54.8	8.7	39.9	60.1
Kentucky	8	—	636,614	623,283	120,396	46.1	45.2	8.7	50.5	49.5
Louisiana	9	—	927,887	712,586	123,293	52.6	40.4	7.0	56.6	43.4
Maine	4	—	312,788	186,378	85,970	53.5	31.9	14.7	62.7	37.3
Maryland	10	—	966,207	681,530	115,812	54.8	38.6	6.6	58.6	41.4
Massachusetts	12	—	1,571,509	718,058	227,206	62.4	28.5	9.0	68.6	31.4
Michigan	18	—	1,989,653	1,481,212	336,670	52.3	38.9	8.8	57.3	42.7
Minnesota	10	—	1,120,380	766,395	257,698	52.2	35.7	12.0	59.4	40.6
Mississippi	—	7	394,022	439,838	52,222	44.5	49.6	5.9	47.3	52.7
Missouri	11	—	1,025,935	890,016	217,188	48.1	41.7	10.2	53.5	46.5

State										
Montana	–	3	167,922	179,652	55,229	41.7	44.6	13.7	48.3	51.7
Nebraska	–	5	236,761	363,467	71,278	35.3	54.1	10.6	39.4	60.6
Nevada	4	–	203,974	199,244	43,986	45.6	44.5	9.8	50.6	49.4
New Hampshire	4	–	246,166	196,486	48,387	50.1	40.0	9.9	55.6	44.4
New Jersey	15	–	1,652,361	1,103,099	262,134	54.8	36.6	8.7	60.0	40.0
New Mexico	5	–	273,495	232,751	32,515	50.8	43.2	6.0	54.0	46.0
New York	33	–	3,649,630	1,738,707	503,458	60.7	31.2	8.1	66.0	34.0
North Carolina	–	14	1,107,849	1,225,938	168,059	44.3	49.0	6.7	47.5	52.5
North Dakota	–	3	106,905	125,050	32,515	40.4	47.3	12.3	46.1	53.9
Ohio	21	–	2,148,222	1,859,883	483,207	47.8	41.4	10.8	53.6	46.4
Oklahoma	–	8	488,105	582,315	130,788	40.6	48.5	10.9	45.6	54.4
Oregon	7	–	649,641	538,152	121,221	49.6	41.1	9.3	54.7	45.3
Pennsylvania	23	–	2,215,819	1,801,169	430,984	49.8	40.5	9.7	55.2	44.8
Rhode Island	4	–	233,050	104,683	43,723	61.1	27.4	11.5	69.0	31.0
South Carolina	–	8	506,152	573,339	64,377	44.3	50.1	5.6	46.9	53.1
South Dakota	–	3	139,333	150,543	31,250	43.4	46.9	9.7	48.1	51.9
Tennessee	11	–	909,146	863,530	105,915	48.4	46.0	5.6	51.3	48.7
Texas	–	32	2,459,683	2,736,167	378,537	44.1	49.1	6.8	47.3	52.7
Utah	–	5	221,633	361,911	66,461	34.1	55.7	10.2	38.0	62.0
Vermont	3	–	137,894	80,352	31,024	55.3	32.3	12.4	63.2	36.8
Virginia	–	13	1,091,060	1,138,350	159,861	45.7	47.6	6.7	48.9	51.1
Washington	11	–	1,123,323	840,712	201,003	51.9	38.8	9.3	57.2	42.8
West Virginia	5	–	327,812	233,946	71,639	51.8	36.9	11.3	58.4	41.6
Wisconsin	11	–	1,071,971	845,029	227,339	50.0	39.4	10.6	55.9	44.1
Wyoming	–	3	77,934	105,388	25,928	37.3	50.4	12.4	42.5	57.5
National Total	379	159	47,401,898	39,198,482	8,085,373	50.1	41.4	8.5	54.7	45.3

SOURCE: *Statistics of the Presidential and Congressional Election of November 5, 1996*, at http://clerkweb.house.gov/histrecs/history/elections/1996election.

NOTE: The total national vote was 96,389,818.

Notes

Chapter 1: Introduction

1. "Republicans Like Both Previews and Reruns," *New York Times,* 12 December 1994, E1; Mickey Kaus, *The End of Equality* (New York: Basic Books, 1992).
2. Edward Luttwak, "America's Insecurity Blanket," *Washington Post National Weekly,* 5–11 December 1994, 23.
3. Clifford Orwin makes the democratic case for distrust, within limits, in "Democracy and Distrust: A Lesson from Thucydides," *American Scholar* 53 (1984): 313–25.
4. Bertrand de Jouvenel, *On Power: Its Natural History and Growth* (Indianapolis: Liberty Fund, 1993), 27–28.
5. I quote from "Conversations with Gorbachev," broadcast on PBS's Channel 13, 1 January 1995.
6. Aristotle, *Politics,* 1294b.
7. *The Records of the Federal Convention of 1787,* ed. Max Farrand (New Haven: Yale University Press, 1911), I:51, 135.
8. Following, in this respect, Montesquieu's argument in *The Spirit of the Laws,* book II, ch. 2.
9. *The Federalist,* No. 63; *The Debates in the Several State Conventions, on the Adoption of the Federal Constitution,* ed. Jonathan Elliott (Philadelphia: Lippincott, 1907), II:69, 222.
10. Sidney Verba, "The Voice of the People," *PS* 26 (1993): 678.
11. John Locke, *Second Treatise on Civil Government,* para. 96; see also Herbert McClosky, "The Fallacy of Absolute Majority Rule," *Journal of Politics* 11 (1949): 643.
12. George V. Higgins, *Victories* (New York: Henry Holt, 1990), 298.
13. Paul Kleppner, *Who Voted? The Dynamics of Electoral Turnout, 1870–1980* (New York: Praeger, 1982); John Petrocik, "Voter Turnout and Electoral Preference," in *Elections in America,* ed. Kay Lehman Schlozman (Boston: Allen and Unwin, 1987), 239–60.
14. Alexis de Tocqueville, *Democracy in America* (New York: Knopf, 1945), II:105.
15. Ibid., II:108–9, 116–17; Aristotle, *Politics,* 1252b, 1278b.
16. M.E. Olsen, "Social Participation and Voting Turnout," *American Sociological Review* 37 (1972): 317–33; G.D.H. Cole, *Essays in Social Theory* (London: Macmillan, 1950), 103–4.
17. Christopher Lasch, *The True and Only Heaven* (New York: Norton, 1991), 157, 165–66.
18. Mary Ann Glendon, *Rights Talk* (New York: Free Press, 1991); Benjamin Radcliff, "The Welfare State, Turnout and the Economy," *American Political Science Review* 86 (1992): 444–54.
19. Benjamin Ginsberg and Martin Shefter, *Politics by Other Means* (New York: Basic Books, 1990); James Q. Wilson, "The Newer Deal," *New Republic,* 2 July 1990, 34–36.
20. Walter Dean Burnham, "American Politics in the 1980s," *Dissent* 27 (1980): 155.
21. Gerald M. Pomper, "The Decline of the Party in American Elections," *Political Science Quarterly* 92 (1977): 21–41.
22. Stephen Salmore and Barbara Salmore, *Candidates, Parties and Campaigns* (Washington, D.C.: Congressional Quarterly, 1985); Thomas Byrne Edsall, *The New Politics of Inequality* (New York: Norton, 1984).
23. The signs have been evident for some time. See Jack Dennis, "Trends in Public Support for the American Party System," *British Journal of Political Science* 5 (1975): 187–230.
24. Steven E. Finkel, "Reexamining the 'Minimal Effects' Model in Recent Presidential Campaigns," *Journal of Politics* 55 (1993): 1–21.

25. Hence Jacques Ellul's observation that technique is "inevitably undemocratic." *The Technological Society* (New York: Random House, 1964), 208); see more generally, 208–18.
26. Verba, "Voice of the People," 679. As Ellul writes, "American society is no longer in its youth, when propaganda consisted of one man speaking directly to other men." *Technological Society,* 374.
27. Cole, *Essays in Social Theory,* 90–99; Tip O'Neill (with Gary Hymel), *All Politics Is Local, and Other Rules of the Game* (New York: Random House, 1994).
28. Byron Shafer, "The New Cultural Politics," *PS* 18 (1985): 221–31.
29. L.E. Aylsworth, "The Passing of Alien Suffrage," *American Political Science Review* 25 (1931): 114–16.
30. Michael Barone, *Our Country; the Shaping of America from Roosevelt to Reagan* (New York: Free Press, 1990); William J. Crotty, "The Social Attributes of Party Organizational Activists in a Transitional Political System," *Western Political Quarterly* 20 (1967): 669–81.
31. Robert Dahl, "On Removing Certain Impediments to Democracy in the United States," *Political Science Quarterly* 92 (1977): 1–20.
32. And, of course, economic and class distinctions are complicated and often overlapping. Norbert Wiley, "America's Unique Class Politics: The Interplay of Labor, Credit and Commodity Markets," *American Sociological Review* 32 (1967): 529–41.
33. David Carlin, "It's the Culture, Stupid," *Commonweal,* 23 September 1994, 9–10.
34. Sidney Verba and Gary Orren, *Equality in America* (Cambridge, Mass.: Harvard University Press, 1985), 248–49.
35. The phrase, of course, is Rev. Samuel Borchard's famous description of the Democrats in 1884. Matthew Josephson, *The Politicos* (New York: Harcourt Brace, 1938), 369.
36. John H. Schaar and Wilson C. McWilliams, "Uncle Sam Vanishes," *New University Thought* 1 (1961): 61–68.
37. H.L. Mencken, *Prejudices: A Selection,* ed. James T. Farrell (New York: Vintage, 1958), 47, 61.
38. Daniel Bell observed this separation of the cultural and economic spheres in *The Cultural Contradictions of Capitalism* (New York: Basic Books, 1976).
39. David Carlin, "The Withering of the Working Class," *Commonweal,* 7 October 1994, 11–15; Christopher Lasch, *The Revolt of the Elites and the Betrayal of Democracy* (New York: Norton, 1995).
40. For example, Gunnar Myrdal, *An American Dilemma* (New York: Harper and Bros., 1944), I:3–25.
41. Walter Dean Burnham, "The End of American Party Politics," *Trans-action* 7 (December 1969): 20; see also William G. Carleton, "The Passing of Bughouse Square," *Antioch Review* 20 (1960): 282–93.
42. Maurice Duverger, *Political Parties* (New York: John Wiley, 1963), 215–16.
43. Ibid., 215.
44. In this sense, militants for whom a particular stance on abortion is a political litmus test are only rejecting the *kind* of single-issue politics that divides Republicans and Democrats.
45. William S. Maddox and Stuart A. Lilie, *Beyond Liberal and Conservative* (Washington, D.C.: Cato Institute, 1984).
46. Burnham, "End of American Party Politics," 20.
47. Robert Frost, "Snow," in *The Poetry of Robert Frost* (New York: Modern Library, 1946), 164.

Chapter 2: Presidential Leadership and Changing Parties: The Election of 1980

1. Matthew Josephson, *The Politicos* (New York: Harcourt, Brace, 1938), 287. There are other suggestive similarities between the elections of 1980 and 1880. In 1880, the minority Democrats nominated their closest equivalent of a movie star, a handsome Union general, Winfield Scott Hancock, a hero of Gettysburg famed for his copious and

wide-ranging profanity. General Hancock's economics were also as weirdly imaginative as Ronald Reagan's: he once described the tariff as a "local question." E.E. Robinson, *The Evolution of Political Parties* (New York: Harcourt, Brace, 1924), 198–99.

2. This wonderful description of Reagan was coined by Mike Royko, "Maybe It's Better to Know Nothing," *Newark Star-Ledger*, 8 November 1980.

3. *I understand the extent to which Reagan's election reflected a distrust of government. Still, the most important "meaning" of 1980 grew out of the Reagan presidency, especially given Reagan's gift of understanding and working an audience, combined with a disposition to back away from anything too painful or militant in the conservative agenda, a caution apparently encouraged by Mrs. Reagan. And finally, Reagan, unlike Carter, enjoyed a striking run of good luck at least until the Iran-contra affair.* –Author note, 1995.

4. Irwin Ross, *The Loneliest Campaign* (New York: New American Library, 1969), 35–57.

5. I have tried to make my list inclusive: I count Coolidge, Cox, Davis, Goldwater, Harding, Landon, McKinley, Nixon, and Parker, although Professor Harry Jaffa is engaged in the attempt to rehabilitate Coolidge, and others on this list — like Landon and Goldwater — are men of parts by our contemporary standards.

6. Plato, *Republic*, bk. I, 347 B-D.

7. Austin Ranney, "The Representativeness of Primary Electorates," *Midwest Journal of Political Science* 12 (1968): 224–38.

8. James Ceaser, "America's Primaries: Part of the Problem or Part of the Solution?" *Los Angeles Times*, 8 June 1980.

9. Walter Nicgorski, "The New Federalism and Direct Popular Election," *Review of Politics* 34 (1972): 3–15.

10. Henry Jones Ford, "The Direct Primary," *North American Review* 190 (1909): 1–14.

11. Louis Hartz, *The Liberal Tradition in America* (New York: Harcourt, Brace, 1955).

12. Mancur Olson, *The Logic of Collective Action* (Cambridge, Mass.: Harvard University Press, 1965).

13. I have vivid memories of McGovern supporters explaining to devout Catholics that opposition to abortion was not, after all, in their "real" interest.

14. Otto Kirchheimer, "The Party in Mass Society," *World Politics* 10 (1958): 289–94; see also John L. Sullivan and Robert O'Connor, "Electoral Choice and Popular Control of Public Policy," *American Political Science Review* 66 (1972): 1256–68.

15. The quotation is from Roosevelt's acceptance speech, 27 June 1936: *The Public Papers and Addresses of Franklin D. Roosevelt* (New York: Random House, 1938), 5:235.

16. William V. Shannon, "Liberalism, Old and New," *New York Times*, 2 October 1976, 25.

17. Adrienne Koch and William Peden, eds., *The Life and Selected Writings of Thomas Jefferson* (New York: Modern Library, 1944), 404.

18. Otto Eckstein, "The Economics of the Sixties," *Public Interest* 19 (Spring 1970): 86–97.

19. Ross, *Loneliest Campaign*, 176–80.

20. Josephson, *The Politicos*, 287.

21. David Burner, *The Politics of Provincialism: The Democratic Party in Transition, 1918–1932* (New York: Knopf, 1967); see also Arthur N. Holcombe, *The New Party Politics* (New York: Norton, 1933).

22. Samuel Lubell, *The Revolt of the Moderates* (New York: Harper & Row, 1956).

23. Daniel P. Moynihan, "Bosses and Reformers," *Commentary* 31 (June 1961): 461–70.

24. An extraordinary amount of this is anticipated in V.O. Key, "The Future of the Democratic Party," *Virginia Quarterly* 28 (1952): 161–75; see also Donald Matthews and James Prothro, *Negroes and the New Southern Politics* (New York: Harcourt Brace Jovanovich, 1966).

25. Shannon, "Liberalism, Old and New."

26. Steven V. Roberts, "The Year of the Hostage," *New York Times Magazine*, 2 November 1980, 26ff.

27. Richard K. Betts, "From Vietnam to Yemen," *New York Times*, 25 March 1979.

28. Reagan also voted for Truman, apparently; John Connally, of course, voted Democratic as late as 1968, but he, evidently, is still regarded as a turncoat.

29. Ross, *Loneliest Campaign*, 42.

30. Alvin Toffler, "Law and Order," *Encounter* 41 (July 1973): 19.

31. I find it illustrative that in our tax code, *six months* is a "long term" for the purpose of assessing capital gains. (*Since I wrote this, reforms have changed the holding period to one year, but this does not weaken the basic point.* –Author note, 1995.)

32. Scott Greer, *The Emerging City* (New York: Free Press, 1962).

33. Herbert Hendin, *The Age of Sensation* (New York: Norton, 1975); see also Christopher Lasch, *The Culture of Narcissism* (New York: Norton, 1979).

34. Jeane J. Kirkpatrick, "Why We Don't Become Republicans," *Commonsense*, Fall 1979, cited in the *New York Times*, 23 December 1980, A13; see also J. Hitchcock, "The Uses of Tradition," *Review of Politics* 35 (1973): 3–16.

Chapter 3: Old Virtues, New Magic: The Election of 1984

1. *New York Times*, 4 November 1984. E5.

2. For example, about 70 percent of Americans were convinced, despite the president's protestations, that taxes would have to be raised.

3. Hedrick Smith, "Political Memo," *New York Times*, 7 December 1984, B18.

4. Alexis de Tocqueville, *Democracy in America* (New York: Schocken, 1961), 1:33, 364.

5. *The Public Papers and Addresses of Franklin D. Roosevelt* (New York: Random House, 1983), 2:11.

6. Dennis Hale and Marc Landy, "Are Critical Elections Extinct?" *Boston College Biweekly* 5 (15 November 1984): 8.

7. I find it suggestive that James Monroe, running in 1820 as the architect of the Era of Good Feeling, won a victory even more one-sided than Reagan's, and his triumph resulted in the death of the old party system and the rise of mass political parties.

8. Even after the election, the administration balanced its sharp cuts in domestic welfare programs — including Medicare — with a surprisingly liberal plan for tax reform.

9. Tom Wicker, "The Other Fritz," *New York Times*, 3 February 1984, A29.

10. On abortion, after all, Mondale was arguing that "you can't legislate morality."

11. Hale and Landy, "Are Critical Elections Extinct?"

12. Tom Wicker, "After 1984, What?" *New York Times*, 23 November 1984, A35.

13. Theodore J. Lowi, *The End of Liberalism* (New York: Norton, 1969).

14. For example, see Paul F. Lazarsfeld et al., *The People's Choice* (New York: Columbia University Press, 1944).

15. *New York Times*, 8 November 1984, A19.

16. James Reston, "Insiders and Outsiders," *New York Times*, 19 August 1984, E19.

17. Walter Robinson, "Accessibility and Excessibility," *Boston Globe*, 14 October 1984, A17ff; James Reston, "Reagan Beats the Press," *New York Times*, 4 November 1984, E25.

18. Television reporters, despite their array of technological supports, are often embarrassingly bad at covering politics: During an interview intended to introduce Gary Hart to the voters, for example, Roger Mudd seemed fixated on the stylistic question whether Hart was imitating Kennedy. See John Corry, "TV: Coverage of Hart," *New York Times*, 16 March 1984, 24.

19. David Burnham, "Experts Fear Computers' Use Imperils Government History," *New York Times*, 16 August 1984, 1ff.

20. We are, after all, on the political eve of TV's second generation — children raised by parents who themselves grew up in the era of television.

21. By contrast, when Roosevelt spoke of "inheriting a mess" in 1933, the Republicans had held office for 24 of the 32 preceding years; in the 32 years before Reagan took office, Republicans and Democrats had each held office for 16.

22. Michael Rogin's Gauss lecture, "Reagan, the Movie," at Princeton University in 1984 develops this theme in a matchless way. See also Gwinn Owens, "Reagan's Confusion of Fact and Fantasy Raises Doubts about Future Competency," *New Brunswick Home News*, 26 March 1984, 7.

23. William V. Shannon, "The Actor Comes Out in the President," *Easton Express*, 8 June 1984, A4; see the similar criticism in the *Wall Street Journal*, 16 February 1984, 62.

24. Philip Rieff, "Aesthetic Functions in Modem Politics," *World Politics* 5 (1953): 78–502; this protectiveness extends, with better reason, to the president's staff. Given Reagan's disinterest in policy analysis or administrative detail, his staff — by insulating the president and controlling the information he gets — has a more than usual ability to maneuver Reagan, provided they respect his traditional beliefs, since Reagan is unlikely to seek additional information on his own. David Broder, "Shielding Reagan," *Boston Globe,* 14 October 1984, 23.

25. "Mr. Reagan's Civil Religion," *Commonweal* 111 (21 September 1984): 483–85; despite his evangelical support, Reagan's own theological comments are likely to be remarkably latitudinarian: "Everyone can make his own interpretation of the Bible," Reagan observed, "and many individuals have been making different interpretations for a long time." Cited in Leo P. Ribuffo, *The Old Christian Right* (Philadelphia: Temple University Press, 1983), 268.

26. Richard Reeves, "The Ideological Election," *New York Times Magazine,* 19 February 1984, 26ff.

27. This assertion of Paine's is part of an argument that is radically hostile to the teachings of revealed religion; that Reagan uses it so often is an indication of his own civil religion.

28. *New York Times,* 11 November 1984, 30.

29. Ashby Bladen, "The Acid Test," *Forbes* 134 (17 December 1984): 245; *New York Times,* 2 February 1984, B9, and 5 February 1984, 1ff.

30. Bladen, "Acid Test"; in fact, taking into account the stabilization of oil prices, there has been little decline in inflation under Reagan; see Robert Levine's letter to the *New York Times,* 17 September 1984, 18.

31. William Serrin, "White Men Discover It's a Shrinking Market," *New York Times,* 9 December 1984, E2.

32. "New Ideas," *New York Times,* 11 November 1984, E20.

33. See, for example, James Reichley, *The Art of Government* (New York: Fund for the Republic, 1959); or Everett C. Ladd, *Where Have All the Voters Gone? The Fracturing of Political Parties* (New York: Norton, 1978).

34. Gerald M. Pomper, "The Decline of the Party in American Elections," *Political Science Quarterly* 92 (1977): 21–41.

35. *New York Times,* 25 November 1984, E2.

36. *New York Times,* 8 November 1984, A19.

37. The Teamsters Union did endorse Reagan, following its usual Republican habits, but the support probably embarrassed the president, since it was suggested that the Teamsters expected in return a less-than-zealous prosecution of their president, Jackie Presser.

38. *New York Times,* 18 December 1984, B14.

39. David Rosenbaum, "Blacks in Poll Prefer Mondale to Jackson as Nominee," *New York Times,* 10 July 1984, 1ff.

40. Incidentally, the pattern is almost reversed for vice-presidential candidates. During the same period, the Democrats chose four southerners (Barkley, Sparkman, Kefauver, and Johnson) and three Catholics (Muskie, Shriver, and Ferraro); only Barkley and Johnson were on winning tickets. By contrast, both northern Protestants nominated by the Democrats (Humphrey and Mondale) were elected, even though Mondale was defeated in 1980.

41. Terry Eastland and William J. Bennett, *Counting by Race: Equality from the Founding Fathers to Bakke and Weber* (New York: Basic Books, 1979).

42. It surfaced first in 1972, because of McGovern's support for "free choice," and it became inescapable given the Supreme Court's decision in 1973 that abortion during the first trimester of pregnancy involves private rights protected by the Constitution (*Roe v. Wade,* 410 U.S. 113, 1973).

43. The Protestant right grumbles, from time to time, but for the moment it is content with a kind of ecumenism that concentrates fire on the main "secular humanist" enemy. Ribuffo, *Old Christian Right,* 267–68.

44. For example, see the long debate on the "End of Catholicism," centering on Thomas Sheehan's critique of the "liberal consensus" in Catholic theology. *Commonweal* 111 (21 September 1984): 490–502.

45. Only 8 percent of Catholics cited abortion as a reason for their vote in 1984. *New York Times,* 25 November 1984, E2.

46. Ferraro helped make it clear that opposition to busing *need* not involve racism (although obviously it often does), since she strongly supports the integration of neighborhoods.

47. Leonard Silk, "The Bishops' Letter and U.S. Goals," *New York Times,* 14 November 1984, D2.

48. Paul Steidl-Meier, "A Reformist Document," *Commonweal* 111 (30 November 1984): 650.

49. J. Brian Benestad, *The Pursuit of a Just Social Order* (Washington, D.C.: Ethics and Public Policy Center, 1982).

50. Theodore White, "New Powers, New Politics," *New York Times Magazine,* 5 February 1984, 32, 34; Michael Novak, *The Rise of the Unmeltable Ethnics* (New York: Macmillan, 1971).

51. That Hispanics, a group defined by language, are at least a partial exception to the rule almost certainly underlines the distinction between favored and disfavored groups.

52. William V. Shannon, "Liberalism, Old and New," *New York Times,* 2 October 1976, 25.

53. According to Curtis Gans of the Committee for the Study of the American Electorate, the Republicans "are going to be a competitive party in the South, and may be the dominant party in the next six years." *New York Times,* 11 November 1984, 53. For the long-term trend in this direction, see Bruce Campbell, "Patterns of Change in the Partisan Loyalties of Native Southerners, 1955–72," *Journal of Politics* 39 (1977): 730–61.

54. In choosing Ferraro as a running mate, of course, Mondale passed over the available southern candidates, and his choice of a woman was not well received in southern circles.

55. Benton Johnson, "Ascetic Protestantism and Political Preference," *Public Opinion Quarterly* 26 (1962): 35–46.

56. As Leo Ribuffo observes, however, Carter "barely qualified as an evangelical." *Old Christian Right,* 262–63.

57. "Mr. Reagan's Civil Religion," 484; William G. McLoughlin, "Faith," *American Quarterly* 35 (1983): 101–15.

58. Adam Clymer, "Contradictory Lessons of the 1982 Election," *New York Times,* 4 November 1982, 1, 24.

59. *New York Times,* 11 November 1984, 30.

60. David Carlin, "The Abortion Debate: Rules for Liberals," *Commonweal* 111 (21 September 1984): 486–87.

61. Daniel Bell, *The Cultural Contradictions of Capitalism* (New York: Basic Books, 1976).

62. Sonia Orwell and Ian Angus, eds., *The Collected Essays, Journalism, and Letters of George Orwell* (New York: Harcourt, Brace, 1968), 2:15.

63. Bernice Buresh, "Students, Conservative, Fearful," *New York Times,* 4 November 1984, E25.

64. Serrin, "White Men Discover It's a Shrinking Market."

65. *Firefighters v. Stotts,* 104 S.Ct. 2576 (1984).

66. *New York Times,* 25 November 1984, E2.

67. White, "New Powers, New Politics," 34.

68. Kuttner is quoted from James Cook, "Ends and Means," *Forbes* 134 (17 December 1984): 140; see Kuttner's own *The Economic Illusion* (Boston: Houghton Mifflin, 1984).

69. For example, see Harry C. Boyte, *The Backyard Revolution: Understanding the New Citizen Movement* (Philadelphia: Temple University Press, 1980), on the neighborhoods movement.

70. Daniel Yankelovich, *New Rules: Searching for Fulfillment in a World Turned Upside Down* (New York: Random House, 1981), 251; the exact figure is 47 percent, up from 32 percent in 1973.

71. Sidney Verba and Norman Nie, *Participation in America* (New York: Harper & Row, 1972), 49.

Chapter 4: Enchantment's Ending: The Election of 1988

1. Harold W. Stanley, William T. Bianco, and Richard Niemi, "Partisanship and Group Support Over Time," *American Political Science Review* 80 (1986): 969–76; E.J. Dionne, " 'Solid South' Again, but Republican," *New York Times,* 13 November 1988, 32; John Herbers, "A Few but Sturdy Threads Tie New South to the Old," *New York Times,* 6 March 1988, E 1.

2. Paul Abramson, "Measuring the Southern Contribution to the Democratic Coalition," *American Political Science Review* 81 (1987): 569.

3. The phrase is from E.J. Dionne, "Political Memo," *New York Times,* 20 October 1988, A1.

4. *New York Times,* 12 May 1987, 16.

5. "On My Mind," *New York Times,* 4 November 1988, A35.

6. Ernst Kantorowicz, *The King's Two Bodies* (Princeton, N.J.: Princeton University Press, 1957).

7. Doubly so, since the proximate cause of disaster in Twain's story is a stockmarket crunch engineered by Sir Lancelot.

8. Lena Williams, "It Was a Year When Civility Really Took It on the Chin," *New York Times,* 18 December 1988, 1ff.

9. R.W. Apple recalled Cleveland's experience in relation to the Hart fiasco (*New York Times,* 8 May 1987, 1ff), and Charles Paul Freund invoked it in comparison to the campaign (*Washington Post National Weekly,* 7–13 November 1988, 29–30).

10. Matthew Josephson, *The Politicos* (New York: Harcourt, Brace, 1938), 46; Allan Nevins, *Grover Cleveland: A Study in Courage* (New York: Dodd, Mead, 1932), 428ff; and Allan Nevins, ed., *The Letters of Grover Cleveland* (Boston: Houghton Mifflin, 1933), 183–84, 188–89.

11. Alexis de Tocqueville, *Democracy in America* (New York: Schocken Books, 1961), 1:204–15; Sally Foreman Griffith, *Home Town News: William Allen White and the Emporia Gazette* (New York: Oxford University Press, 1988).

12. Josephson, *Politicos,* 423–24, 427.

13. Jeffrey R. Abramson, F. Christopher Arterton, and Gary R. Orren, *The Electronic Commonwealth* (New York: Basic Books, 1988), 11–13; Joseph Schlesinger, "The New American Party System," *American Political Science Review* 79 (1985): 1152–69.

14. Laura L. Vertz, John P. Feress, and James L. Gibson, "Nationalization of the Electorate in the United States," *American Political Science Review* 81 (1987): 961–66; William J. Crotty, *Political Reform and the American Experiment* (New York: Crowell, 1977); Committee on Political Parties of the American Political Science Association, *Toward a More Responsible Two-Party System* (New York: Rinehart, 1950).

15. *Providence Journal,* 10 November 1988, A11.

16. Todd Gitlin, "The Candidate Factory," *Boston Review* 13 (August 1988): 6. Implicitly, critics acknowledged the point when they faulted Dukakis's campaign for being "too thin," too centralized, and too little inclined to reach out to local party leaders — and overreliant on "experts." See *New York Times,* 12 November 1988, 8; and Michael Barone, "Those Dukakis Ads Just Don't Work," *Washington Post National Weekly,* 17–23 October 1988, 29.

17. James David Barber, "How to Pick Our Presidents," *New York Times,* 8 March 1987, E23, observed that within broad limits, "the man makes the office."

18. Since James G. Blaine, Cleveland's opponent, combined private rectitude with public sleaziness, Moorfield Storey argued that "we should elect Mr. Cleveland to the public office he is so admirably qualified to fill, and relegate Mr. Blaine to the private life he is so eminently fitted to adorn." Mark DeWolfe Howe, *Portrait of an Independent* (Boston: Houghton Mifflin, 1932), 151.

19. Michael Arlen, "The Candidates Deserve Each Other," *New York Times,* 28 September 1988, A27; it is doubtful that JFK — and possibly even Franklin Roosevelt or Dwight Eisenhower — would have met the media's moral test for the presidency.

20. W. Russell Neuman, *The Paradox of Mass Politics: Knowledge and Opinion in the American Electorate* (Cambridge, Mass.: Harvard University Press, 1986).

21. Paul Corcoran, "The Limits of Democratic Theory," in *Democratic Theory and Practice,* ed. Graeme Duncan (New York: Cambridge University Press, 1983), 19; *The Nature of*

Politics: Selected Essays of Bertrand de Jouvenel, ed. Dennis Hale and Marc K. Landy (New York: Schocken Books, 1987), 44–54.

22. Richard Sennett, *The Fall of Public Man* (New York: Knopf, 1977), 283. Of course, many Americans do talk back to the television set — my father-in-law was particularly eloquent — in a response that is probably healthy but certainly futile.

23. Abramson, Arterton, and Orren, *Electronic Commonwealth,* 15, 46–49; Todd Gitlin, *Inside Prime Time* (New York: Pantheon, 1985), 325–35.

24. Abramson, Arterton, and Orren, *Electronic Commonwealth,* 13.

25. Mark Hertsgaard, *On Bended Knee: The Press and the Reagan Presidency* (New York: Farrar, Straus and Giroux, 1988).

26. Kathleen Hall Jamieson, "Is the Truth Now Irrelevant in Presidential Campaigns?" *Washington Post National Weekly,* 7–13 November 1988, 28.

27. Gitlin, "Candidate Factory," 23.

28. Eleanor Randolph, "Now There Are Two 'Stealth Candidates,'" *Washington Post National Weekly,* 26 September–2 October 1988, 14.

29. James North, "While the Soviets Debated, We Poured on the Pabulum," *Washington Post National Weekly,* 5–11 September 1988, 25.

30. Eugene J. Alpert, "The Media and the Message," *Political Science Teacher* 1 (Summer 1988): 13; John Chancellor, "Putting Zip, Juice Interest into Campaigns," *New York Times,* 29 November 1988, A25.

31. Abramson, Arterton, and Orren, *Electronic Commonwealth,* 177; Gitlin, *Inside Prime Time,* 330, 332; Daniel Boorstin, *The Americans: The Democratic Experience* (New York: Random House, 1973), 393.

32. Barbara Lippert, "Ronald Reagan and Michael Jackson Together at Last," *Washington Post National Weekly,* 5–11 September 1988, 24; Robert Brustein, "Can Bush as Bush Steal the Show?" *New York Times,* 21 August 1988, E25.

33. Gitlin, *Inside Prime Time,* 248.

34. T.W. Adorno, "Television and the Problem of Mass Culture," in *Mass Culture,* ed. Bernard Rosenberg and David Manning White (New York: Free Press, 1957), 435.

35. Aristotle, *Politics,* 1253a, 9–18.

36. Marc Landy and I made a similar argument in "On Political Edification, Eloquence and Memory," *PS* 17 (1984): 203–10.

37. Dorothy B. James, "Television and the Syntax of Presidential Leadership," *Presidential Studies Quarterly* 18 (1988): 737–39.

38. Gitlin, "Candidate Factory," 7. Hoping to encourage more substantive discussion, Michael Woo, a Democratic member of the Los Angeles City Council, sensibly suggested legislation requiring political ads on television to be purchased in longer blocks of time. *New York Times,* 13 November 1988, E3.

39. *New York Times,* 14 October 1988, A14.

40. Tocqueville, *Democracy in America,* 1:293.

41. Edwin O'Connor, *The Last Hurrah* (Boston: Little, Brown, 1956), 70; cf. Frank Kent, *The Great Game of Politics* (New York: Doubleday Doran, 1935).

42. Martin P. Wattenberg, "The 1988 and 1960 Elections Compared: What a Difference Candidate-Centered Politics Makes," paper presented at the annual meeting of the American Political Science Association, Washington, D.C., 1–4 September 1988.

43. Byron Shafer, "Scholarship on Presidential Selection in the United States," *American Political Science Review* 82 (1988): 962.

44. *New York Times,* 4 April 1988, A21.

45. Dukakis and his staff may have mistaken for positive support what was only antipathy to Jackson, especially since the voters who rejected Jackson as "too liberal" would obviously be vulnerable to later Republican appeals. Scot Lehigh, "Michael Dukakis: The Unmaking of a President," *Phoenix's The NewPaper,* 10 November 1988, 4; *New York Times,* 27 April 1988, A24.

46. Philip Weiss, "The Cultural Contradictions of the GOP," *Harpers* 276 (January 1988): 4–58. In Iowa, Robertson did better than Dole among younger voters and three times better than Bush.

47. The phrase is from Richard Morin, "Jackson's White Support Is the 'Peugeot Proletariat,'" *Washington Post National Weekly,* 2–8 May 1988, 37.

48. Since Jackson's nomination was not a real possibility, his candidacy meant — and probably will mean — that black voters have only a negative influence on the Democratic nominee. Juan Williams, "How Jackson Is Jeopardizing the Influence of Blacks," *Washington Post National Weekly*, 15 June 1987, 23.

49. The distinction derives from Max Weber, "Politics as a Vocation," *From Max Weber: Essays in Sociology*, ed. Hans Gerth and C. Wright Mills (New York: Oxford University Press, 1946), 77–128; on the contemporary aspects, see Thomas Byrne Edsall, *The New Politics of Inequality* (New York: Norton, 1984).

50. James Lengle, "Democratic Party Reforms: The Past as Prologue to the 1988 Campaign," *Journal of Law and Politics* 4 (1987): 233–73; David Broder and Paul Taylor, "The Democrats' Problem," *Washington Post National Weekly*, 14–20 November 1988, 12.

51. *New York Times*, 12 November 1988, 8.

52. David Broder, "For Dukakis, the Glass Is Half Full," *Washington Post National Weekly*, 2–8 May 1988, 4; and "An Uncertain Electorate Is Tilting Democratic," *Washington Post National Weekly*, 4–10 July 1988, 12.

53. Morris P. Fiorina, *Retrospective Voting in American National Elections* (New Haven: Yale University Press, 1981).

54. John Garvey, "Age of Distraction," *Commonweal* 114 (25 September 1987): 40.

55. Michael Wallace, "Reagan and History," *Tikkun* 2, no. 1 (1987): 13–18; Seymour Martin Lipset, "Americans Sneer at Liberalism, Why?" *New York Times*, 28 October 1988, A35.

56. *Washington Post*, 29 October 1988, A17; Paul Taylor, "Bush Has Dukakis Trapped in a Time Warp," *Washington Post National Weekly*, 10–16 October 1988, 13.

57. Scot Lehigh, "Michael Dukakis: The Unmaking of a President," *Phoenix's The NewPaper*, 10 November 1988, 6.

58. David Broder, "What Dukakis Should Have Said," *Washington Post National Weekly*, 19–25 September 1988, 4; Edward Walsh, "An Immigrant's Kid for the Immigrants," *Washington Post National Weekly*, 6–12 June 1988, 7.

59. E.J. Dionne, "Political Memo," *New York Times*, 20 October 1988, A1.

60. On the second debate, see *New York Times*, 12 November 1988, A1ff.

61. Steven D. Stark, "The Mandate in the Gray Flannel Suit," *Washington Post National Weekly*, 6–12 June 1988, 24–25; Leo Strauss, *Natural Right and History* (Chicago: University of Chicago Press, 1953), 35–80.

62. Daniel Bell, *The End of Ideology: On the Exhaustion of Political Ideas in the Fifties* (Glencoe, Ill.: Free Press, 1960).

63. Theodore J. Lowi, *The End of Liberalism: Ideology, Policy and the Origins of Public Authority* (New York: Norton, 1969).

64. Bruce Miroff, *Pragmatic Illusions: The Presidential Politics of John F. Kennedy* (New York: McKay, 1976); Robert Gaines, "Cursing the Darkness," *Phoenix's The NewPaper*, 10 November 1988, 1ff.

65. George Will, "A National Embarrassment," *Washington Post National Weekly*, 3–9 October 1988, 33; James Skillen, *Public Justice Report* 12 (October 1988): 6.

66. Robert Kuttner, *The Life of the Party: Democratic Prospects in 1988 and Beyond* (New York: Viking, 1987), 13. The classic statement of modern American liberalism is John Dewey, *The Public and Its Problems* (New York: Holt, 1927).

67. By almost 2 to 1 (60 to 33 percent), Americans responding to a poll late in 1987 rejected any cut in government services. *New York Times*, 1 December 1987, B24.

68. Michael Robinson, "Can Values Save George Bush?" *Public Opinion* 11 (July/August 1988): 13, 59–60.

69. On George Bush's early statement of his views, see Robert Zwier, "George Bush," *Public Justice Report* 11 (January 1988): 4. On 1 December 1987, the *New York Times* reported that an identical percentage of Republicans and Democrats (37 percent) favored the existing system of abortion rights, while 40 percent of Republicans *and* 43 percent of Democrats favored limiting abortion to cases of rape, incest, and protecting the life of the mother (p. B24). Abortion divides both parties, but it is more polarizing to Democrats who, on both sides of the issue, appear to feel more strongly than Republicans. See Lewis Bolce, "Abortion and Presidential Elections," *Presidential Studies Quarterly* 18 (1988): 815–27. Of course, Bush's position is an administrative nightmare: Would a

woman be entitled to an abortion merely by claiming rape or incest? If she is required to substantiate the charge, what would the standard of proof be? And could a decision be reached within the first trimester, or even the period of gestation?

70. Michael Kammen, *People of Paradox* (New York: Knopf, 1972).

71. John Kenneth Galbraith, "Coolidge, Carter, Bush, Reagan," *New York Times,* 12 December 1988, A16.

72. Edward Corwin, *The President: Office and Powers* (New York: New York University Press, 1957), 300–304.

73. *The Federalist,* No. 70.

74. Kurt Vonnegut, *Player Piano* (New York: Dell, 1952), 118–19.

75. Robert Kuttner, *The Life of the Party: Democratic Prospects in 1988 and Beyond* (New York: Viking, 1987), 15; in what follows, I am indebted to Kuttner, *Life of the Party,* 205–47.

76. E.J. Dionne, "Political Memo," *New York Times,* 29 September 1988, A1. On Democratic divisions, see Bolce, "Abortion and Presidential Elections."

77. Amitai Etzioni, "The Party, Like Reagan's Era, Is Over," *New York Times,* 16 February 1987, 27; Michael Lerner, "Neo-Compassionism," *Tikkun* 2 (November/December 1987): 12.

78. Benjamin Friedman, *Day of Reckoning: The Consequences of American Economic Policy under Reagan* (New York: Random House, 1988); Marie Natoli, "Campaign '88," *Presidential Studies Quarterly* 18 (1988): 714.

79. John Berry, "The U.S. Trade Deficit Won't Vanish Overnight," *Washington Post National Weekly,* 11–17 January 1988, 20.

80. Jeffrey Garten, "How Bonn, Tokyo Slyly Help Bush," *New York Times,* 21 July 1988, A25.

81. Paul Kennedy, *The Rise and Fall of Great Powers* (New York: Random House, 1987); Lester Thurow, "A Briefing for the Next President," *New York Times,* 21 August 1988, F2.

82. George Berkeley, "On the Prospect of Planting Arts and Learning in America" (1752). Berkeley would be as disturbed as most Americans, since he prophesied that America's rise would "close the drama."

83. Tom Wicker, "Always with Us," *New York Times,* 19 November 1987, 27.

84. Frank Levy, *Dollars and Dreams* (New York: Russell Sage Foundation, 1987); Paul Blustein, "The Great Jobs Debate," *Washington Post National Weekly,* 5–11 September 1988, 20–21.

85. "A Modell of Christian Charity," in *Puritan Political Ideas,* ed. Edmund Morgan (Indianapolis: Bobbs-Merrill, 1965), 90.

86. *Washington Post National Weekly,* 15–21 August 1988, 10.

87. A.A. Berle and Gardiner C. Means, *The Modern Corporation and Private Property* (New York: Macmillan, 1934).

88. The vulnerability of managers is not much comfort to ordinary stockholders, although corporate raiders sometimes present themselves as allies of investors, as Gordon Gekko did in the movie *Wall Street.* Even when stockholders make profits, "golden parachutes" (payments to displaced managers) and "greenmail" (payments by management to raiders) indicate the shareholders' basic disadvantage.

89. James Glassman, "The Monster That's Eating Wall Street," *Washington Post National Weekly,* 18–24 January 1988, 23; Etzioni, "The Party, Like Reagan's Era."

90. The phrase "conservative permissiveness" is from Kevin Phillips, "The Reagan Revolution Is Over and the GOP Should Be Grateful," *Washington Post National Weekly,* 17 August 1987, 23. On the general point, see Daniel Goleman, "How Is America?" *New York Times,* 25 December 1988, E12; and Daniel P. Moynihan, "Half the Nation's Children Born without a Fair Chance," *New York Times,* 25 September 1988, E25.

91. *New York Times,* 18 October 1988, A29.

92. Lewis Lapham, "Supply-Side Ethics," *Harpers* 270 (May 1985): 11.

93. Herbert London, "What TV Drama Is Teaching Our Children," *New York Times,* 23 August 1987, H23ff.

94. *New York Times,* 22 November 1987, 37; Allan Bloom, *The Closing of the American Mind* (New York: Simon and Schuster, 1987).
95. Frederic Jameson, "On Raymond Chandler," *Southern Review* 6 (1970): 624–50. In Vonnegut's *Player Piano,* workers displaced by technology do not long for a world without machines, but one in which they are needed to tend and repair machines.
96. Bennett Berger, "Disenchanting the Concept of Community," *Society* 25 (September/October 1988): 50–52; Michael J. Himes and Kenneth R. Himes, "The Myth of Self-Interest," *Commonweal* 115 (23 September 1988): 493–98.
97. Tocqueville, *Democracy in America,* 1:33.
98. Ibid., 2:118–20; Robert Bellah et al., *Habits of the Heart* (Berkeley: University of California Press, 1985).
99. Walt Harrington, "Has Truth Gone Out of Style?" *Washington Post National Weekly,* 4–10 January 1988, 6–7.
100. Plato, *Republic,* 358 D.
101. Christopher Lasch, "Traditional Values, Left, Right and Wrong," *Harpers* 273 (September 1986): 13–16.
102. Russell Baker, "Talk So Big, Do So Nothing," *New York Times,* 29 March 1986, A27.
103. Steven V. Roberts, "Reagan's Social Issues: Gone but Not Forgotten," *New York Times,* 11 September 1988, E4.
104. For what follows, I am indebted to Stanley C. Brubaker, "Can Liberals Punish?" *American Political Science Review* 82 (1988): 821–36; see also Michael Sandel, *Liberalism and the Limits of Justice* (Cambridge, England: Cambridge University Press, 1982), 89–91.
105. Thomas Pangle, *The Spirit of Modern Republicanism* (Chicago: University of Chicago Press, 1988); for a modern example, although one that nominally rejects individualism, see David Truman, *The Governmental Process* (New York: Knopf, 1951), 50–51.
106. Such incentives evidently work in the long term, if at all.
107. Brubaker, "Can Liberals Punish?" 831.
108. "In a good state," Rousseau wrote, "there are few punishments, not because pardons are frequent but because criminals are few.... When pardons are plentiful, it is a sure sign that crimes will soon have no need of them, and everyone can see where that leads." Jean-Jacques Rousseau, *Social Contract,* bk. 2, chap. 5.
109. *Bush had his moments, not only in foreign policy, but also in recanting his foolish pledge never to raise taxes (even though, under pressure from the right, Bush later apologized for this departure from ideological orthodoxy). As most Americans saw, however, Bush had no particular goals for America beyond a cautious desire to keep the ship afloat.* –Author note, 1995.
110. Robert Samuelson, "End of the Carter Era," *Newsweek,* 14 November 1988, 59.
111. Kuttner, *Life of the Party,* 210; Bruce Babbitt, "The Democrats' Long Road Back," *New York Times,* 15 November 1988, A31.
112. Mark Shields, "If the Democrats Are to Win in '88," *Washington Post National Weekly,* 11–17 January 1988, 28; A.M. Rosenthal, "On My Mind," *New York Times,* 4 November 1988, A35.
113. *New York Times,* 1 December 1987, B24.
114. E.J. Dionne, "Reopening an Old Wound," *New York Times,* 23 August 1988, A1ff; Fox Butterfield, "Disparity in College Courses on Vietnam," *New York Times,* 27 April 1988, B11.
115. Anthony Kohlenberger, "Jack O'Connell: The Grass-roots Politician," *California Journal* 19 (November 1988): 478.
116. And only ruling principles give the party a claim on those who dissent from its social positions, particularly its stance on abortion. See David Carlin's fine "It's My Party," *Commonweal* 115 (7 October 1988): 521–22.
117. Anthony Lewis, "The Dirty Little Secret," *New York Times,* 20 October 1988, A27.
118. Harry McPherson, "How Race Destroyed the Democrats' Coalition," *New York Times,* 28 October 1988, A31; Edward G. Carmines and James A. Stimson, *Issue Evolution: The Racial Transformation of American Politics* (Princeton, N.J.: Princeton University Press, 1988).

119. *In the aftermath of 1994, the assault on affirmative action, now more aggressive and less apologetic, has even begun to attract Democratic support.* – Author note, 1995.
120. See my essay, "What Will Jackson Do?" *Commonweal* 115 (23 September 1988): 488.
121. Aristotle, *Politics*, 1274b32–1275b24; Robert Dahl, *Dilemmas of Pluralist Democracy* (New Haven: Yale University Press, 1982).

Chapter 5: Thinking about Tomorrow Worriedly: The Election of 1992

1. A century earlier, prophetically, Henry Adams saw the American people "wandering in a wilderness more sandy than ... Sinai," and in 1893, the Columbian Exposition seemingly "asked ... for the first time ... whether the American people knew where they were driving." Henry Adams, *The Education of Henry Adams*, ed. Ernest Samuels (Boston: Houghton Mifflin, 1974) 329, 343. But few Americans, back then, shared the vision.
2. Leslie Gelb, "1932 and 1992," *New York Times,* 7 February 1992, A29; R.W. Apple Jr., "Close Three-Way Race Holds Opportunities for Clinton," *New York Times,* 23 June 1992, A18. Some voters compared their excitement with that of the first Roosevelt election, as they told Michael Winerip, "Fever Pitch: Democracy at Work," *New York Times,* 1 November 1992, E49.
3. "George Herbert Hoover Bush," *The Economist,* 31 October 1992, 30.
4. David Broder, "Clinton's No Kennedy Either," *Washington Post National Weekly,* 12–18 October 1992, 4; Steven Greenhouse, "Clinton's Economic Plan Has a Roosevelt Tone," *New York Times,* 9 July 1992, 30.
5. David McCullough, *Truman* (New York: Simon and Schuster, 1992), 660–61, 668.
6. Russell Baker, "All Joy Departed," *New York Times,* 13 October 1992, A23.
7. R.W. Apple Jr., "The Economy's Casualty," *New York Times,* 4 November 1992, A1.
8. *San Francisco Chronicle,* 20 August 1992, B3.
9. For the hope, see Robert Kuttner, *The Life of the Party: Democratic Prospects in 1988 and Beyond* (New York: Viking, 1987); by contrast, cultural cleavages were dominant in 1988. Joel Lieske, "Cultural Issues and Images in the 1988 Presidential Campaign," *PS* 24 (1991): 180–87.
10. Robert D. Hershey Jr., "The Politics of Declining Incomes," *New York Times,* 9 March 1992, D6.
11. Jim Hoagland, "Bush: First of Many to Fall," *Washington Post National Weekly,* 12–18 October 1992, 29.
12. Michael S. Lewis-Beck, *Economics and Elections* (Ann Arbor: University of Michigan Press, 1988); Michael MacKuen, Robert S. Erickson, and James A. Stimson, "Peasants or Bankers: The American Electorate and the U.S. Economy," *American Political Science Review* 86 (1992): 597–611; Donald Kinder and D. Roderick Kiewiet, "Economic Grievances and Political Behavior: The Role of Personal Discontents and Collective Judgments in Congressional Voting," *American Journal of Political Science* 23 (1979): 495–527.
13. Hobart Rowen, "Misdiagnosing the Recession," *Washington Post National Weekly,* 27 January–12 February 1992, 5.
14. David Broder, "The Uneasy Electorate," *Washington Post National Weekly,* 22–28 July 1991, 4; Leonard Silk, "The Many Faces of the Electorate," *New York Times,* 10 April 1992, D2.
15. *Notes on Virginia,* Letter to John Jay, 31 August 1785, and Letter to John Adams, 28 October 1813, all in Adrienne Koch and William Peden, eds., *The Life and Selected Writings of Jefferson* (New York: Modern Library, 1944), 280, 377, 633.
16. William Schmidt, "Hard Work Can't Stop Hard Times," *New York Times,* 25 November 1990, 1ff. For the best days of industrial labor, see E.E. LeMasters, *Blue Collar Aristocrats* (Madison: University of Wisconsin Press, 1975).
17. Frank Levy, *Dollars and Dreams* (New York: Russell Sage Foundation, 1987); Juliet Shor, *The Overworked American* (New York: Basic Books, 1991); Jodie T. Allen, "It's Morning in America, All Right," *Washington Post National Weekly,* 4–10 November 1991, 23.
18. Paul Starr, "The New Politics of Health Care," *Harper's,* October 1991, 22–30.

19. *New York Times,* 22 February 1992, L9. See also Sylvia Nasar, "The 1980s: A Very Good Time for the Very Rich," *New York Times,* 5 March 1992, 1ff.

20. Sylvia Nasar, "Fed Gives New Evidence of '80's Gains by Richest," *New York Times,* 21 April 1992, 1ff; Charles Murray, "The Shape of Things to Come," *National Review,* 8 July 1991, 29–30.

21. As, to some extent, Mickey Kaus does in *The End of Equality* (New York: Basic Books, 1992).

22. Robert Samuelson, "White Collar Blues," *Washington Post National Weekly,* 6–12 January 1992, 29.

23. Hobart Rowen, "Misdiagnosing the Recession," *Washington Post National Weekly,* 27 January–12 February 1992, 5; Anne Swardson, "The Swelling Ranks of the Underemployed," *Washington Post National Weekly,* 17–23 February 1992, 20; Peter Passell, "Clinton's Luck ... Or Albatross?" *New York Times,* 13 August 1992, D2. It is a sign of the times that, by October 1991, more Americans, by a margin of over half a million, worked for government than in manufacturing. When Reagan took office, manufacturing led by 25 percent. Floyd Norris, "The Jobs Are in Government, Not Industry," *New York Times,* 6 September 1992, F1.

24. Carl Rowan, "GOP Hasn't Been Kind to 'Family Values,'" *Newark Star-Ledger,* 7 August 1992, 20; Steven Nock and P.W. Kingston, "Time with Children: The Impact of Couples' Work-Time Commitments," *Social Forces* 67 (1988): 59–85.

25. Urie Bronfenbrenner, "Contexts of Child Rearing," *American Psychologist* 34 (1979): 844–50; 74 percent of Americans, in one finding, consider that parents should have the greatest impact on their children's values, but a substantial plurality think that the media exert that influence. American Enterprise Public Opinion and Demographic Report, in *Public Perspective* 3 (September/October 1992): 86.

26. Gerald M. Pomper, ed., *The Election of 1988* (Chatham, N.J.: Chatham House, 1989), 194–95; Mickey Kaus, *The End of Equality* (New York: Basic Books, 1992), 55–57; James Q. Wilson, "Crime, Race and Values," *Society,* December 1992, 90–93.

27. Robert Reich, "The Secession of the Successful," *New York Times Magazine,* 20 January 1991, 17ff; the term *autoanesthesia* is from Joseph Lyford's *The Airtight Cage* (New York: Harper, 1966).

28. Bush used the image of untroubled sleep so often that reporters began referring to the theme as "bedtime in America," parodying Reagan's "morning in America" slogan.

29. Norman J. Ornstein, "Foreign Policy in the 1992 Elections," *Foreign Affairs* 71 (Summer 1992): 3, 7; Sidney Blumenthal saw that 1988 was the "last campaign of the Cold War": *Pledging Allegiance* (New York: HarperCollins, 1990).

30. Leslie Gelb, "No National Interest," *New York Times,* 18 October 1992, E15; and "Bush Gets Tough on Iraq," *New York Times,* 23 August 1992, E15.

31. Richard Morin, "How Quickly They Regret," *Washington Post National Weekly,* 20–26 January 1992, 37.

32. Jeffrey Frank, "Buy American or Bye, American," *Washington Post National Weekly,* 21–27 September 1992, 25; Lawrence Harrison, "Huddled Masses, Unskilled Labor," *Washington Post National Weekly,* 20–26 January 1992, 25.

33. Kevin Phillips, "The Old Boys' Club of the West Is Getting Left in the Dust," *Washington Post National Weekly,* 13–19 July 1992, 23; Hobart Rowen, "A Little Help from His Friends," *Washington Post National* Weekly, 20–26 April 1992, 5; Benjamin Ginsberg and Martin Shefter describe "alliances with foreign governments" as one of the new modes of politics, in *Politics by Other Means: The Declining Importance of Elections in America* (New York: Basic Books, 1990), 11.

34. Leslie Gelb, "Three Whine Mice," *New York Times,* 13 January 1992, A15.

35. Ibid.; on Clinton, see William Safire, "Bush-Clinton Debate," *New York Times,* 2 April 1992, A23.

36. Pomper, *Election of 1988,* 189–90.

37. That the phrase hurt is indicated by Bush's effort to counter it by referring to "trickle-down" government.

38. Similarly, while Michael Novak rejects "socialist" versions of health insurance, he argued for a national plan based on tax credits. "Dead but Fair," *Forbes,* 16 March 1992, 112–13.

39. Steven Pearlstein, "First, Let's Kill All the Economists," *Washington Post National Weekly,* 30 November–5 December 1992, 31, cites Paul Krugman, "for people in their fifties, the cutting edge of economics was to show how markets were perfect. For people in their thirties, the cutting edge is now showing how markets are imperfect." See also Leonard Silk, "Is Liberalism Back in the Saddle?" *New York Times,* 17 April 1992, D2.

40. Frank Levy and Richard Michel, *The Economic Future of American Families* (Washington, D.C.: Urban Institute, 1991); on the failure of the equivalence theorem, see Leonard Silk, "The Crucial Issue Politicians Ignore," *New York Times,* 24 April 1992, D2.

41. Hobart Rowen, "Productivity Not the Problem," *Washington Post National Weekly,* 30 November–5 December 1992, 5.

42. According to the American Enterprise Public Opinion and Demographic Report, 68 percent said candidates should talk about family values; 53 percent said government should concern itself. *Public Perspective* 3 (September/October 1992): 85.

43. For example, see Daniel P. Moynihan, "A Landmark for Families," *New York Times,* 16 November 1992, A13.

44. Peter Steinfels, "A Political Movement Blends Its Ideas from Left and Right," *New York Times,* 24 May 1991, E6; "in providing for the poor," *Commonweal* (24 February 1992, 5) editorialized, "we must make reasonable demands on them — for work, schooling and, yes, sexual responsibility." See also Christopher Jencks, *Rethinking Social Policy: Race, Poverty, and the Underclass* (Cambridge, Mass.: Harvard University Press, 1992).

45. Joel Garreau, "It's a Mall World After All," *Washington Post National Weekly,* 10–16 August 1992, 25.

46. Aristotle, *Ethics,* trans. J.A.K. Thompson (Harmondsworth, England: Penguin, 1956), book 2, chap. 1, pp. 55–56.

47. G.K. Chesterton noted that "what is unique is not America, but what is called Americanisation." *What I Saw in America* (New York: Dodd, Mead, 1922), 14.

48. James Davison Hunter, *Culture Wars: The Struggle to Define America* (New York: Basic Books, 1991).

49. Tom Wicker, "An Alienated Public," *New York Times,* 13 October 1991, E15.

50. Humphrey Taylor, "The American Angst of 1992," *Public Perspective* 3 (July/August 1992): 3, table 1.

51. Rohde is cited by Dan Balz, "America the Morning After," *Washington Post National Weekly,* 21–27 October 1991, 13–14.

52. Jeffrey Schmalz, "Words on Bush's Lips in '88 Now Stick in Voters' Craw," *New York Times,* 14 June 1992, 1.

53. Martin P. Wattenberg, *The Decline of American Political Parties, 1952–1988* (Cambridge, Mass.: Harvard University Press, 1990).

54. Richard Zeiger, "Few Citizens Make Decisions for Everyone," *California Journal* 21 (November 1990): 517, 519; the belief in universal corruption is cited by Leslie Gelb, "Throw the Bums Out," *New York Times,* 23 October 1991, A23.

55. Garry Wills, "Ross Perot and the Immaculate Election," *Washington Post National Weekly,* 1–7 June 1992, 23; see also William Safire, "Protesting Too Much," *New York Times,* 6 April 1992, A19.

56. Richard Morin and E.J. Dionne Jr., "Turning Down the Party Invitation," *Washington Post National Weekly,* 13–19 July 1992, 9; much the same position is espoused by Theodore Lowi, "The Party Crasher," *New York Times Magazine,* 23 August 1992, 28ff.

57. Anthony Lewis, "Time for a Change," *New York Times,* 9 April 1992, A25.

58. Russell Baker, "Potomac Breakdown," *New York Times,* 12 October 1991, 29; Lewis, "Time for a Change."

59. I am not persuaded by the notion that divided government is "accidental." See James Sundquist, "Needed: A Political Theory for the New Era of Coalition Government in the U.S.," *Political Science Quarterly* 103 (1988): 633–34. The more purposive model implied by Morris Fiorina in *Divided Government* (New York: Macmillan, 1992), 128–29, is more compelling, especially since divided government need not result in "gridlock" and did not do so under Nixon. See also David Mayhew, *Divided We Govern* (New Haven: Yale University Press, 1991).

60. David Rosenbaum, "The Paralysis of No-Pain Politics," *New York Times*, 19 April 1992, E1; Roberto Suro, "Viewing Chaos in the Capital, Americans Express Outrage," *New York Times*, 19 November 1990, 1ff; Adam Clymer, "Citing Rise in Frustration, Dozens of Lawmakers Quit," *New York Times*, 5 April 1992, 1ff. On the Balanced Budget Amendment, see David Broder, "A Congressional Balancing Act," *Washington Post National Weekly*, 25–31 May 1992, 4.

61. James Q. Wilson, "The Newer Deal," *New Republic*, 2 July 1990, 34; Daniel Yankelovich, *Coming to Public Judgment* (Syracuse, N.Y.: Syracuse University Press, 1991), 4.

62. Jeffrey Schmalz, "Americans Sign Up in Record Numbers to Cast a Ballot," *New York Times*, 19 October 1992, 1ff; compare Paul R. Abramson and John H. Aldrich, "The Decline of Electoral Participation in America," *American Political Science Review* 76 (1982): 502–21.

63. Gerald Pomper and Loretta Sernekos, "Bake Sales and Voting," *Society*, July/August 1991, 10–16. Tocqueville argued that Americans were driven into politics by necessity but held there by the habits and pleasures of community life. See *Democracy in America* (New York: Schocken, 1961), 2:127.

64. Dan Balz, "They're Angry but Not Apathetic," *Washington Post National Weekly*, 26 October–1 November 1992, 13.

65. Tocqueville, *Democracy in America*, 1:210–11; 2:137.

66. Ibid., 2:134–37.

67. Bill Moyers, "The Old News and the New Civil War," *New York Times*, 22 March 1992, E15.

68. Russell Baker, "Hear America Listening," *New York Times*, 2 November 1991, 23.

69. Wicker, "An Alienated Public."

70. Thomas Rosenstiel, "Networks Rethink Political Coverage," *Berkshire Eagle*, 17 July 1991, C6; Anthony Lewis, "Hair on their Chests," *New York Times*, 19 April 1992, E11; "Old News Deconstructed," *The Economist*, 31 October 1992, 23.

71. *New York Times*, 11 July 1992, L7.

72. Harvey Mansfield refers to a "tendency toward the left." See *America's Constitutional Soul* (Baltimore: Johns Hopkins University Press, 1991), 167. By contrast, Deborah Tannen refers to the news media as manipulated by "mostly Republican" admakers in a review of Kathleen Hall Jamieson, *Dirty Politics* (New York: Oxford University Press, 1992). "Lies, Damned Lies and Political Ads," *Washington Post National Weekly*, 21–27 September 1992, 35.

73. Todd Gitlin, "On Being Sound-Bitten," *Boston Review*, December 1991, 17.

74. Mansfield, *America's Constitutional Soul*, 166–68. In an admittedly extreme example in 1990, Madonna, wrapped in an American flag, urged young Americans to vote on the principle that "freedom of speech is as good as sex," thus identifying public words with private passions and justifying the former in terms of the latter. *New York Times*, 20 October 1990, 7.

75. Russell Baker, "You'd Hate It There," *New York Times*, 7 December 1991, 23; Roger Masters, Sigfried Frey, and Gary Bente, "Dominance and Attention: Images of Leaders in German, French and American TV News," *Polity* 23 (1991): 393.

76. John Tierney, "Now, Journalists Renege on Election Promises," *New York Times*, 31 January 1992, A12; newspaper coverage of TV ads similarly focused on strategy. Randall Rothenberg, "Newspapers Watch What People Watch in the TV Campaign," *New York Times*, 4 November 1990, E5.

77. Maureen Dowd, "Populist Media Forums and the Campaign of '92," *New York Times*, 3 November 1992, 14; Howard Kurtz, "The Year the Candidates Took to the Airwaves," *Washington Post National Weekly*, 2–8 November 1992, 14.

78. Elizabeth Kolbert, "Heard by Few, Clinton Speech Shows Candidates' Quandary," *New York Times*, 9 April 1992, A21.

79. Elizabeth Kolbert, "Perot Takes Issue While Clinton Takes on Issues," *New York Times*, 12 June 1992, A14.

80. Joe S. Foote, *Television Access and Political Power* (New York: Praeger, 1990).

81. Hume is cited by Richard Berke, "Campaign '92," *New York Times*, 26 June 1992, A13;

Masters et al., "Dominance and Attention"; Jan Hoffman, "Larry King: Kingmaker to the Pols," *New York Times*, 28 June 1992, H27.

82. Gerald Marzorati, "From Tocqueville to Perotville," *New York Times*, 28 June 1992, E17.

83. David Broder, "Tabloid Election," *Washington Post National Weekly*, 3–9 February 1992, 4. The importance of local media in 1992 is a somewhat more hopeful sign. See Phyllis Kaniss, "A Victory for Local News," *New York Times*, 5 December 1992, 19.

84. And politically, the truth matters. Intellectual champions of the view that reality is "constructed" and "plural" did not apply their teaching to the verdict constructed by the jury that tried the officers who arrested and beat Rodney King. "Postmodernists," Todd Gitlin writes, "enjoy skating on the surface, but they, we, are still probing for bedrock truth." Gitlin, "On Being Sound-Bitten," 17. On the King verdict, see Jeffrey Frank, "When Truth Becomes Image, History Becomes Myth," *Washington Post National Weekly*, 11–17 May 1992, 24.

85. Michael Paul Rogin, "JFK: The Movie," *American Historical Review* 97 (1992): 502, 505. Sidney Blumenthal saw many of the same themes in Jerry Brown's campaign. "He's a New Age Demagogue," *New York Times*, 5 April 1992, E17.

86. Caryl Rivers, "It's Tough to Tell a Hawk from a Lonesome Dove," *New York Times*, 10 February 1991, H29ff. We need to remember the spectacle of the vice-president of the United States in national dialogue with fictional TV characters. See Russell Baker, "To Cloud Men's Minds," *New York Times*, 23 May 1992, Y15.

87. Rogin, "JFK," 503; Lloyd Grove, "Looking for President Perfect," *Washington Post National Weekly*, 6–12 April 1992, 6–7.

88. Steven Holmes, "Perot-Bush 'Dirty Tricks' Feud Persists," *New York Times*, 27 October 1992, A1ff; on Perot's dealings with Hanoi, see *New York Times*, 4 June 1992, 1.

89. Gwen Ifill, "Perot's Popularity Sends Clinton into Frustration," *New York Times*, 25 May 1992, 8; see also Elizabeth Kolbert's report on Perot's spending, *New York Times*, 28 October 1992, A1.

90. Walter Goodman, "Perot Leaves a Field of Broken Rules," *New York Times*, 10 October 1992, 46.

91. Maureen Dowd, "Once Again, Questions of Character," *New York Times*, 28 June 1992, E1.

92. David Broder, "A Knight in Shining Armor," *Washington Post National Weekly*, 4–10 May 1992, 4; Peter Milius, "Ross Perot's Fuzz," *Washington Post National Weekly*, 11–17 May 1992, 29.

93. John Mintz and David Von Drehle, "The Day Perot Pulled the Plug," *Washington Post National Weekly*, 27 July–2 August 1992, 9.

94. Perot's style should be compared to Richard Rosenstone's observations in "Historical Fact/Historical Film," *American Historical Review* 97 (1992): 507.

95. Dan Balz and E.J. Dionne Jr., "In a Quirky Year, Perot Could Be a Loose Cannon," *Washington Post National Weekly*, 4–10 May 1992, 8.

96. Wills, "Ross Perot and the Immaculate Election"; Michael Kelly, "Perot's Vision: Consensus by Computer," *New York Times*, 6 June 1922, 1ff; Richard Cohen, "Deconstructing Perot," *Washington Post National Weekly*, 18–24 May 1992, 28.

97. Michael Schrage, "Perot: A Man of Revolution, Not Evolution," *Washington Post*, 1 May 1992, B3; Steven Greenhouse, "Hardly Laissez-Faire," *New York Times*, 27 June 1992, L9.

98. Kevin Sack, "Why Perot Thrived in Fertile Kansas," *New York Times*, 6 November 1992, A20.

99. Lawrence Goodwyn, *Democratic Promise* (New York: Oxford University Press, 1976); the St. Louis Conference, early in 1892, seated delegates of twenty-two separate organizations. John Hicks, *The Populist Revolt* (Minneapolis: University of Minnesota Press, 1931), 225.

100. Matthew Josephson, a bit disdainful of the Populists as a party of "peasant proprietors," noted that "principles and platform" were central to them. *The Politicos* (New York: Harcourt, Brace, 1938), 502–3.

101. Hicks, *Populist Revolt*, 234.

102. George Will, "Ross Perot: America's Rohrschach Test," *Washington Post National Weekly*, 8–14 June 1992, 29. Perot's third-party candidacy thus violated Lowi's crucial "proviso" that such a party be built "from bottom up." Lowi, "The Party Crasher," *New York Times Magazine*, 23 August 1992, 33.

103. Russell Baker, "Stressed All Over," *New York Times*, 6 June 1992, A23; R.W. Apple Jr., "The Voters' Message," *New York Times*, 8 April 1992. Even Edward Kearny and Robert Heineman, who predicted a centrist third party, overestimated the attachment of voters to the primaries. "Scenario for a Centrist Revolt: Third Party Prospects in a Time of Ideological Polarization," *Presidential Studies Quarterly* 22 (1992): 114.

104. It sometimes seemed that Democrats would be better off with a generic "Brand X" candidate. Robin Toner, "Bad News for Bush as Poll Shows National Gloom," *New York Times*, 28 January 1992, A1ff.

105. Cuomo certainly received plenty of advice akin to Leslie Gelb's counsel to wait for 1996, using the time to cope with his "inner demons." "To Cuomo or Not to Cuomo," *New York Times*, 27 November 1991, A21. Since the Democratic nomination is not likely to be doubtful in 1996, it might be a noncontroversial time to institutionalize Terry Sanford's proposal for a preprimary convention of superdelegates to screen candidates. See Walter Mondale's fine critique of primaries, "Primaries Are No Test of Character," *New York Times*, 26 February 1992, A23.

106. Thomas Byrne Edsall, "Those Crucial Voters Not Yet Heard From," *Washington Post National Weekly*, 30 March–5 April 1992, 12; my comments on the Buchanan vote derive from *New York Times* exit polls (e.g., 5 March 1992, A22).

107. *New York Times*, 5 March 1992, A22, for Clinton's vote on Super Tuesday. In New York, Tsongas — no longer an active candidate — had an edge among white Christians. Clinton depended on his margin among blacks and Jews. *New York Times*, 9 April 1992, A20.

108. With both parties, this is an old tradition. See Herbert Croly, "Democratic Factions and Insurgent Republicans," *North American Review* 191 (May 1910): 626–35.

109. Thomas Byrne Edsall with Mary D. Edsall, *Chain Reaction: The Impact of Race, Rights and Taxes on American Politics* (New York: Norton, 1992); Ronald P. Formisano, *Boston Against Busing* (Chapel Hill: University of North Carolina Press, 1991), 232–33.

110. The comments of Robert Huckfeldt and Carol Weitzel Kohfeld are apposite. See *Race and the Decline of Class in American Politics* (Champaign: University of Illinois Press, 1989), ix, 188.

111. David Broder, "Jackson's Decline, Brown's Ascent," *Washington Post National Weekly*, 20–26 July 1992, 4.

112. Ronald Brownstein, "New Studies of U.S. Tensions Put Focus on Class, Not Race," *Berkshire Eagle*, 28 July 1991, A3; William Julius Wilson, *The Truly Disadvantaged* (Chicago: University of Chicago Press, 1987).

113. Lena Williams, "In a 90s' Quest for Black Identity, Intense Doubts and Disagreement," *New York Times*, 30 November 1991, 1ff.

114. Lena Williams, "Growing Black Debate on Racism: When Is It Real, When an Excuse," *New York Times*, 5 April 1992, 1ff. "To join the public household of this great nation," Orlando Patterson wrote after the election, "is to share responsibility for its fortunes and for one's failings." "Our History vs. Clinton's Covenant," *New York Times*, 13 November 1992, A29.

115. William Julius Wilson, "The Right Message," *New York Times*, 17 March 1992, A25.

116. It helped, of course, that Bush's record on the politics of race showed a combination of indifference and backsliding, while Perot was clearly impossible after his early gaffes. Ruth Marcus, "The Shifting Sands of George Bush's Civil Rights Positions," *Washington Post National Weekly*, 24–30 August 1992, 8–9.

117. Orlando Patterson, "Our History vs. Clinton's Covenant," *New York Times*, 13 November 1992.

118. William Schneider, "The Political Legacy of the Reagan Years," in *The Reagan Legacy*, ed. Sidney Blumenthal and Thomas Byrne Edsall (New York: Pantheon, 1988), 12. At that, Republican divisions are probably less severe than those among Democrats. Corwin Smidt and James Penning, "A Party Divided?" *Polity* 23 (1990): 138.

119. John J. Farmer, "Republicans Sound Like the Ideologues Now," *Newark Star-Ledger,* 13 August 1992, 24; Garry Wills, "George Bush: Prisoner of the Crazies," *New York Times,* 16 August 1992, E17.
120. *New York Times,* 5 November 1992, B9.
121. Andrew Rosenthal, "The Politics of Morality," *New York Times,* 22 May 1992, A19; on the Republican campaign, see Robin Toner, "How Bush Lost Five Chances to Save the Day," *New York Times,* 11 October 1992, E1ff.
122. Harvey Mansfield, *America's Constitutional Soul* (Baltimore: Johns Hopkins University Press, 1991),69.
123. David Rosenbaum, "Missing from Politics: The Blueprints for the Future," *New York Times,* 2 February 1992, E1; Blumenthal, *Pledging Allegiance,* 49–76.
124. "President Noodle," *New York Times,* 5 March 1992, A26; George Will, "Serious People Flinch," *Washington Post National Weekly,* 31 August–6 September 1992, 29.
125. Mary McGrory, "You Say Potato and I Say It Takes Only 35 Percent to Win," *Washington Post National Weekly,* 29 June–5 July 1992, 25; Kevin Phillips, "GOP Crackup," *New York Times,* 4 June 1992, A23.
126. John Green and James Guth, "The Christian Right in the Republican Party," *Journal of Politics* 50 (1988): 150–65.
127. David Maraniss, "Clinton's Journey of the Spirit," *Washington Post National Weekly,* 13–19 July 1992, 10–11.
128. The figures are 23 percent and 18 percent respectively. *New York Times,* 5 November 1992, B9.
129. Garry Wills, "The Hostage," *New York Review of Books,* 13 August 1992, 21–27.
130. Alan Geyer identifies Bush with "political docetism," a creed of vague, disembodied values. See *Christianity and Crisis,* 21 September 1992, 291; David Broder, "Value Added Politics," *Washington Post National Weekly,* 1–7 June 1992, 4.
131. Thomas Byrne Edsall, "The GOP May Be Losing Its Realignment Linchpin," *Washington Post National Weekly,* 21–27 September 1992, 15; Mary Jordan, "More Freshmen Lean to Left," *Washington Post National Weekly,* 20–26 January 1992, 37.
132. Clinton drew 44 percent of voters aged 18–29. Dukakis had attracted 47 percent. *New York Times,* 5 November 1992, B9; Barbara Vobejda, "Family Value Voting," *Washington Post National Weekly,* 30 November–5 December 1992, 36.
133. Peter Cellupica, "The Political Dawn Arrives for Gays," *New York Times,* 7 November 1992, 21; David Broder argues that homophobia among Republicans and from Perot, by guaranteeing that Jackson's gay financial backers had no alternative, helped encourage Clinton to criticize Sister Souljah. Broder, "Jackson's Decline, Brown's Ascent."
134. Harvey Schantz, "The Erosion of Sectionalism in American Elections," *Polity* 24 (1992): 355–77.
135. Robin Toner, "Clinton's Southern Roots Trip Him in New York," *New York Times,* 1 April 1992, A20.
136. Bush helped by calling Arkansas "the lowest of the low" in the third debate, which to sensitive ears, sounded like regional and class contempt. *New York Times,* 1 November 1992, A1.
137. Meredith Nicholson, *The Valley of Democracy* (New York: Scribners, 1918).
138. Even in Mississippi, Clinton carried all the counties that touch the river except Warren and DeSoto, if county-by-county maps are accurate.
139. Mary Ann Glendon, *Rights Talk: The Impoverishment of Political Discourse* (New York: Basic Books, 1991).
140. The Democrats' internal conflict is well presented by David Carlin, "Blame the Message," *Commonweal,* 8 May 1992, 9–10; and Margaret O'Brien Steinfels, "Safe, Legal and Rare," *Commonweal,* 20 November 1992, 4–5.
141. This critique of liberalism was the message of Ben Wattenberg's PBS special on the Democrats. (See Walter Goodman's review, *New York Times,* 16 October 1992, B16.) Clinton's record provides some support for his critics: David Maraniss, "Clinton's Arkansas Legacy," *Washington Post National Weekly,* 26 October–1 November 1992, 7.
142. Baker, "To Cloud Men's Minds."
143. Gwen Ifill, "Clinton Sees Bush Engaging in Empty Talk on Families," *New York Times,* 22 May 1992, A18.

144. For a realistic "family agenda," see Timothy Bates, "Paying for Values: The Real Needs of Real Families," *Commonweal,* 9 October 1992, 6–7.

145. E.J. Dionne Jr., "Bogart in '92: The Fundamental Things Apply," *Washington Post National Weekly,* 16–22 December 1991, 25. Ironically, Dionne's own defense of the moral center in *Why Americans Hate Politics* (Simon and Schuster, 1991) has been criticized by David O'Brien as "too easy and too conciliatory." *American Political Science Review* 86 (1992): 800.

146. Thomas Byrne Edsall, "Nibbling Rivalry: Democrats Are One Big, Scrappy Family," *Washington Post National Weekly,* 16–22 November 1992, 23.

147. Walter Goodman, "The Convention Images: Plenty for Both Sides," *New York Times,* 18 July 1992, 49.

148. David Rosenbaum, "No Painless Way Out for the Next President," *New York Times,* 4 October 1992, E1.

149. Tocqueville, *Democracy in America,* 1:217–18; 2:124.

150. Moyers, "Old News and the New Civil War."

151. Raising the too-present danger, Albert Borgmann observes that the public will be reduced to sullen consumers on one hand and hyperactive careerists on the other. *Crossing the Postmodern Divide* (Chicago: University of Chicago Press, 1992).

Chapter 6: Uncertainties at Midcrossing: The Election of 1996

1. Garry Wills, "A Mandate to Get Along," *New York Times,* 7 November 1996, A33.

2. Frank Rich, "Blowing in the Wind," *New York Times,* 20 November 1994, E15.

3. Peter Baker, "An All-Time High for Ballot Box No-Shows," *Washington Post National Weekly,* 11–17 November 1996, 11.

4. Robin Toner, "In This Race, It's the Center against the Middle," *New York Times,* 17 March 1996, E3.

5. Albert O. Hirschman, *The Rhetoric of Reaction: Perversity, Futility, Jeopardy* (Cambridge, Mass.: Harvard University Press, 1991); Thomas Byrne Edsall, "The GOP Gains Ground as Trust in Government Erodes," *Washington Post National Weekly,* 12–18 February 1996, 12. This analysis follows Tocqueville's discussion of individualism, *Democracy in America* (New York: Knopf, 1980), 2:99.

6. Peter L. Berger, *The Sacred Canopy: Elements of a Sociological Theory of Religion* (Garden City, N.Y.: Doubleday, 1967), 93–101.

7. Jean Bethke Elshtain, *Democracy on Trial* (New York: Basic Books, 1994).

8. William Graham Sumner, *What Social Classes Owe to Each Other* (1883) (Caldwell, Idaho: Caxton, 1978), 10. Of course, the "all" in Sumner's saying refers to orthodox social scientists, as opposed to promoters of "social quackery," 101.

9. Stephen Skowronek, "The Risks of 'Third-Way' Politics," *Society* 33 (September/October 1996): 32–36. With Cleveland, however, this policy had a hard, principled edge: in 1887, vetoing a bill to provide seed corn to devastated Texas farmers, Cleveland declared that "though the people should support the government, the government should not support the people." Veto Message, 16 February 1887, cited in Matthew Josephson, *The Politicos* (New York: Harcourt Brace, 1938), 391.

10. In fact, in his three presidential campaigns, Bryan never carried an industrial state.

11. William Jennings Bryan, "Speech Concluding Debate On the Chicago Platform," in *Late Nineteenth Century American Liberalism,* ed. Louis Filler (Indianapolis: Bobbs Merrill, 1967), 61; in place of the later "trickle-down," Bryan referred to the idea that elite prosperity will "leak through on those below."

12. As Louis W. Koenig observed, the transformation of the Democrats, and the party system, was confirmed by Bryan's tireless work, over the next two decades, in party caucuses and conventions. *Bryan: A Political Biography* (New York: Putnam's, 1971).

13. Henry Allen, "In a Manner of Speaking," *Washington Post National Weekly,* 10–16 June 1996, 11.

14. With the exception of Indiana and North Dakota, Clinton carried every state that went for McKinley in 1896.

15. David Broder, "Hanging Together," *Washington Post National Weekly*, 2–8 September 1996, 4.

16. R.W. Apple, "Economy Helps Again," *New York Times*, 6 November 1996, A1.

17. In February Dole told a New Hampshire audience that he hadn't expected jobs and trade to be important issues (Howell Raines, "Struggle in the Snow," *New York Times*, 20 February 1996, A18), a comment as startling as his mid-campaign praise for the no-hitter pitched by Hideo Nomo of the *Brooklyn* Dodgers.

18. Greenstein's comment is taken from the *New York Times*, 10 November 1994, B5. On the economy in 1994, see Peter Passell, "Why Isn't a Better Economy Helping Clinton's Popularity?" *New York Times*, 3 November 1994, D2.

19. Clay Chandler and Richard Morin, "Two Sides of the Coin," *Washington Post National Weekly*, 10 November 1996, 9.

20. Harvey C. Mansfield Jr., "Change and Bill Clinton," *TLS*, 13 November 1992, 14–15; Robert E. Lane, *The Market Experience* (New York: Cambridge University Press, 1991).

21. Louis Uchitelle, "The Rise of the Losing Class," *New York Times*, 20 November 1994, E1. On postwar American optimism, see James Patterson, *Great Expectations: The United States, 1945–1974* (New York: Oxford University Press, 1996).

22. Richard Morin, "A Nation Split Down the Middle," *Washington Post National Weekly*, 24–30 July 1995, 37; Richard Morin and Mario Brossard, "A Gamble that Isn't Paying Off," *Washington Post National Weekly*, 3–9 June 1996, 37.

23. Louis Uchitelle, "It's a Slow Growth Economy, Stupid," *New York Times*, 17 March 1996, E1.

24. *New York Times*, 3 August 1996, 8.

25. The *New York Times'* series, "The Downsizing of America," began on 3 March 1996. On the general point, see Edwin Luttwak, "America's Insecurity Blanket," *Washington Post National Weekly*, 5–12 December 1994, 23.

26. *New York Times*, 19 August 1996, D2.

27. Louis Uchitelle, "A New Era of Ups and Downs," *New York Times*, 15 August 1996, 1; Hobart Rowen, "Our Own Worst Enemy," *Washington Post National Weekly*, 26 September–2 October 1994, 10; the 1996 improvement is reported in the *New York Times*, 5 October 1996, A1.

28. E.J. Dionne Jr., *They Only Look Dead: Why Progressives Will Dominate the Next Political Era* (New York: Simon and Schuster, 1996); Louis Uchitelle, "A Top Economist Switches His View on Productivity," *New York Times*, 8 May 1996, D2; William Julius Wilson, *When Work Disappears: The World of the New Urban Poor* (New York: Knopf, 1996).

29. Richard Morin and John M. Berry, "Economic Anxieties," *Washington Post National Weekly*, 4–10 November 1996, 6–7; Kerth Bradsher, "Gap in Wealth in U.S. Called Widest in West," *New York Times*, 17 April 1995, A1; Steven A. Holmes, "Income Disparity between Poorest and Richest Rises," *New York Times*, 20 June 1996, A1.

30. Russell Baker, "Let's Get Sore," *New York Times*, 18 November 1995, 21.

31. Peter Passell, "Economic Scene," *New York Times*, 29 March 1996, D2; Kerth Bradsher, "America's Opportunity Gap," *New York Times*, 4 June 1995, E4; Chandler and Morin, "Two Sides of the Coin."

32. Benjamin Schwartz, "American Inequality: Its History and Scary Future," *New York Times*, 19 December 1995, A25.

33. Robert H. Frank and Philip J. Cook, *The Winner-Take-All Society* (New York: Martin Kessler/Free Press, 1995); see also Derek C. Bok, *The Cost of Talent: How Executives and Professionals Are Paid and How it Affects America*, New York: Free Press, 1993.

34. Jacques Ellul, *The Technological Society* (New York: Random House, 1964), 208–18; Steve Lohr, "Reluctant Conscripts in the March of Technology," *New York Times*, 17 September 1995, E16; technological change also creates a mystique around new, high performance products, which come to be valued beyond their utility. Robert Post, *High Performance* (Baltimore: Johns Hopkins University Press, 1996).

35. Daniel Bell, *The Cultural Contradictions of Capitalism* (New York: Basic Books, 1984); Joshua Meyerowitz, *No Sense of Place* (New York: Oxford University Press, 1985). For a very concrete example, see Sara Rimer, "A Hometown Feels Less Like Home," *New York Times*, 6 March 1996, A1.

36. Robert Putnam, "The Strange Disappearance of Civic America," *American Prospect* 24 (Winter 1996): 34–48; Henry Allen, "Ha! So Much for Loyalty," *Washington Post National Weekly,* 4–10 March 1996, 11; Tara L. White and Elaine Washington, "Youth: Changing Beliefs and Behavior," in *The State of the Americans: This Generation and the Next,* ed. Urie Bronfenbrenner (New York: Free Press, 1996), 1–28.

37. Evan McKenzie, *Privatopia: Homeowner Associations and the Rise of Residential Private Government* (New Haven: Yale University Press, 1994).

38. Lester Thurow, "Companies Merge: Families Break Up," *New York Times,* 3 September 1995, E11.

39. Todd Gitlin, *The Twilight of Common Dreams: Why America Is Wracked by Culture Wars* (New York: Metropolitan, 1995); Frank Rich, "Jenny Jones' Victory," *New York Times,* 23 March 1995, A25.

40. Robert Putnam, "Tuning In, Tuning Out: the Strange Disappearance of Social Capital in America," *PS* 28 (1995) 671; Steve Scott, "Defining Family Values," *California Journal* 27 (August 1996): 8–12.

41. E.J. Dionne Jr., "Dole v. Hollywood," *Washington Post National Weekly,* 12–18 June 1996, 29.

42. Robert Kuttner, "Free Market, Bad Medicine," *Washington Post National Weekly,* 29 July–4 August 1996, 5; and "The Case for Regulation," *Washington Post National Weekly,* 18–24 December 1995, 5.

43. Luttwak, "America's Insecurity Blanket"; Robert Reich, "Drowning in the Second Wave," *New York Times,* 2 April 1995, E15.

44. James Davison Hunter, *Culture Wars: the Struggle to Define America* (New York: Basic Books, 1991); Theodore J. Lowi, *The End of the Republican Era* (Norman: University of Oklahoma Press, 1995).

45. E.J. Dionne Jr., "A Matter of Respect," *Washington Post National Weekly,* 4–10 September 1995, 24; Eric M. Uslaner, *The Decline of Comity in Congress* (Ann Arbor: University of Michigan Press, 1994).

46. Richard Flacks, "Reflections on Strategy in a Dark Time," *Boston Review,* December/ January 1996, 25; Michael Sandel, "America's Search for a New Public Philosophy," *Atlantic,* March 1996, 57, 72.

47. *New York Times,* 10 August 1992, A9.

48. Thomas L. Friedman, "Rethinking Foreign Affairs," *New York Times,* 7 February 1992, A7.

49. Thomas W. Lippman and Ann Devroy, "Matching Policy to Rhetoric," *Washington Post National Weekly,* 18–24 September 1995, 6–7.

50. R.W. Apple, "What's Bad for Hussein Seems Good for Clinton," *New York Times,* 5 September 1996, A11.

51. William Kristol and Robert Kagan, "The New Isolationist?" *New York Times,* 14 October 1996, A17.

52. Roger Cohen, "Global Forces Batter Politics," *New York Times,* 17 November 1996, E1.

53. Cohen, "Global Forces Batter Politics."

54. Jurgen Habermas, *The Structural Transformation of the Public Sphere: An Inquiry into a Category of Bourgeois Society,* trans. Thomas Burger (Cambridge, Mass.: M.I.T. Press, 1991).

55. E.H. Carr, *The Soviet Impact on the Western World* (New York: Macmillan, 1949).

56. Alexei Bayer, "Beneficial Capitalism, R.I.P.," *New York Times,* 16 June 1996, F13.

57. Adolf Berle, *The Twentieth Century Capitalist Revolution* (New York: Harcourt Brace, 1954); Karl Marx and Friedrich Engels, *The Communist Manifesto,* trans. Samuel Moore (Baltimore: Penguin, 1967).

58. Peter Passell, "Life's Hard? Blame the Market," *New York Times,* 8 May 1994, E3; Steve Lohr, "Big Business in Turmoil," *New York Times,* 28 January 1993, A1; A.H. Rosenthal, "American Class Struggle," *New York Times,* 21 March 1995, A21; Flacks, "Reflections on Strategy," 26.

59. Louis Uchitelle, "Rise of the Losing Class."

60. Apple, "Economy Helps Again."

61. Russell Baker, "Yellow Peril's Return," *New York Times,* 7 December 1996, 23.

62. Thomas L. Friedman, "Buchanan for President," *New York Times,* 24 December 1995, E9.

63. Marc B. Haefele, "California Shipwreck," *Boston Review,* April/May 1995, 26–27.

64. Robert Pear, "Citizenship Proposal Faces Obstacle in Constitution," *New York Times,* 7 August 1996, A13.

65. Ronald Steel, "Internationalism Reconsidered," *Washington Post National Weekly,* 12–18 June 1995, 23.

66. *Works of the Rt. Hon. Edmund Burke* (Boston: Little, Brown, 1884), 3:359.

67. Michael Paul Rogin, "JFK: The Movie," *American Historical Review* 97 (1992): 502–5; Peter Applebome, "An Unlikely Legacy of the '60s: The Violent Right," *New York Times,* 7 May 1995, 1.

68. *Newsweek,* 8 July 1996, 50.

69. Frank McConnell, "Expecting Visitors?" *Commonweal,* 22 November 1996, 21–22; David Ansen, "Earth, You Have a Problem: Kaboooom!" *Newsweek,* 8 July 1996, 51.

70. Paul Berman, "Clinton Does Battle with Chicago '68," *New York Times,* 25 August 1996, E13; E.J. Dionne Jr., "Why the 60's Still Won't Go Away," *San Francisco Chronicle,* 27 August 1996, A19; Carol Muske Dukes, "When 'The System' Worked," *New York Times,* 30 May 1995, A17.

71. Although the Centennial Park bombing during the Olympics remains unexplained, the idea that it was connected to rightist fears of World Order is more plausible than most. *New York Times,* 28 July 1996, E12.

72. Dukes, "When 'The System' Worked."

73. *New York Times,* 9 May 1995, A18, and 11 May 1995, A1; Fox Butterfield, "Terror in Oklahoma: the Gun Lobby," *New York Times,* 8 May 1995, A17.

74. Todd Purdom, "Shifting Debate to the Political Climate, Clinton Condemns 'Promoters of Paranoia,'" *New York Times,* 25 April 1995, A19; "Combustible Rhetoric," *New York Times,* 27 April 1995, A24.

75. Dan Morgan, "A Revolution Derailed," *Washington Post National Weekly,* 28 October–3 November 1996, 21.

76. Ibid.

77. Richard Morin, "Not So Fast on Those Budget Cuts," *Washington Post National Weekly,* 22–28 May 1995, 37.

78. Ibid.

79. Ann Devroy and Ruth Marcus, "The Clutch Seems to Be Slipping," *Washington Post National Weekly,* 14–20 June 1993,12; Richard Morin, "A Not-So-Bad Midterm Grade," *Washington Post National Weekly,* 20–26 February 1995, 37.

80. R.W. Apple, "The Selling of a Used President Gets Easier," *New York Times,* 2 April 1995, E1.

81. Richard Morin, "The Message from the Voters: Less Is More," *Washington Post National Weekly,* 21–27 November 1994, 8.

82. *New York Times,* 4 September 1995, 8.

83. Baker is quoted in Richard Berke, "Epic Realignments Often Aren't," *New York Times,* 1 January 1995, E3; E.J. Dionne Jr., "A Shift, Not a Mandate," *Washington Post National Weekly,* 28 November–4 December 1994, 28.

84. Adam Clymer, "Politics and the Dead Arts of Compromise," *New York Times,* 22 October 1995, E1.

85. The description of Gingrich comes from an admirer, Jeffrey Eisenach, explaining the Speaker's opposition to a proposed antismut rule for the Internet, which Dole favored. (Edmund L. Andrews, "Gingrich Opposes Smut Rule for Internet," *New York Times,* 22 June 1995, A20). On the direction of Republican policy, see David Broder, "Is Gingrich a Democratic Mole?" *Washington Post National Weekly,* 3–9 April 1995, 4; and Robin Toner, "Coming Home from the Revolution," *New York Times,* 10 November 1996, E1.

86. Russell Baker, "Time for the Pain," *New York Times,* 13 May 1995, 19.

87. David Broder, "So Much for Fairness," *Washington Post National Weekly,* 2–8 October 1995, 4; Robert J. Samuelson, "And Principles," *Washington Post National Weekly,* 2–8 October 1995, 5; E.J. Dionne Jr., "Moynihan's Complaint," *Washington Post*

National Weekly, 7–13 August 1995, 28. For O'Connor's comments, see *New York Times*, 5 March 1995, 24.

88. Richard Morin, "Fed Up with Welfare," *Washington Post National Weekly*, 29 April–5 May 1996, 37; Richard L. Berke, "Poll Finds Public Doubts Key Parts of GOP Agenda," *New York Times*, 28 February 1995, A21.

89. Adam Clymer, "A Big Risk for GOP," *New York Times*, 11 November 1995, 10; in a remarkably unfortunate image, one Republican operative, Bill McIntruff, called Clinton a "hostage" to "terrorist" Republicans. Katharine Q. Seelye, "Wouldn't Mother Have Been Proud?" *New York Times*, 18 June 1995, E5.

90. Kuttner, "Case for Regulation"; Richard Morin, "A Shutdown with Few Winners, Many Losers," *Washington Post National Weekly*, 20–26 November 1995, 37.

91. Helen Dewar and Eric Pianin, "Choosing Pragmatism Over Partisanship," *Washington Post National Weekly*, 12–18 August 1996, 12.

92. E.J. Dionne Jr., "A Shift, Not a Mandate;" Alfred Tuchfarber and Eric Rademacher, "The Republican Tidal Wave of 1994," *PS* 28 (1995) 689–96. Notably, there was no increase in the percentage of voters calling themselves Republicans. (Richard Berke, "Asked to Place Blame, Americans in Surveys Chose, All of the Above," *New York Times*, 10 November 1994, B1.)

93. John Hart, "President Clinton and the Politics of Symbolism," *Political Science Quarterly* 110 (1995): 398; Adam Clymer, "Americans Have High Hopes for Clinton, Poll Finds," *New York Times*, 19 January 1993, A13; Robert DiClerico, "Assessing Context and Character," *Society*, September/October 1996, 29–31.

94. Adam Clymer, "The Hidden Antagonist of Clinton's Health Care Plan," *New York Times*, 19 June 1994, E1; David Broder, "A Presidential Seal of Disapproval," *Washington Post National Weekly*, 12–18 September 1994, 14; Charles O. Jones, "The Separated System," *Society*, September/October 1994, 18–24.

95. Howard Kurtz, "Over Easy on the Opposition," *Washington Post National Weekly*, 12–18 September 1994, 24.

96. Steven D. Stark, "Populist Revolt," *Providence Phoenix*, 11 November 1994, 12; Richard Morin, "Message from the Voters."

97. E.J. Dionne Jr., *They Only Look Dead;* William Raspberry detected a mandate to "fix" a government that wasn't working. "It Doesn't Work," *Washington Post National Weekly*, 28 November–4 December 1994, 28.

98. Stephen Skowronek, "Risks of 'Third-Way' Politics," 32–36; E.J. Dionne Jr., "Clinton Swipes the GOP's Lyrics," *Washington Post National Weekly*, 29 July–6 August 1996, 22.

99. Walter Dean Burnham, "The 1996 Elections: Drift or Mandate?" *American Prospect*, July/August 1996, 43–49; Dionne, "Clinton Swipes the GOP's Lyrics."

100. Byron E. Shafer and William J.M. Claggett, *The Two Majorities: The Issue Context of Modern American Politics* (Baltimore: Johns Hopkins University Press, 1995).

101. Juan Williams, " 'Morning in America': The Sequel," *Washington Post National Weekly*, 20–26 November 1995, 23.

102. Mickey Kaus, "The Revival of Liberalism," *New York Times*, 9 August 1996, A27; Richard L. Berke, "Fulfilling a 1992 Promise, Capturing a 1996 Issue," *New York Times*, 1 August 1996, A25.

103. *New York Times*, 19 August 1996, B7.

104. Russell Baker, "The Charisma Chasm," *New York Times*, 23 April 1996, A23; Garry Wills, "One Sings, the Other Doesn't," *New York Times*, 14 May 1996, A23; *New York Times*, 11 March 1996, A16.

105. Adam Nagourney, "Dole Meets a Setback," *New York Times*, 18 April 1996, A1.

106. R.W. Apple, "Going 'Outside': Bold, May be Perilous," *New York Times*, 16 May 1996, A1; Morin and Brossard, "A Gamble that Isn't Paying Off—Yet"; Eric Schmitt, "GOP Seems Ready to Drop Political Fight," *New York Times*, 18 September 1996, B6.

107. Richard Cohen, "Not as Low as Yeltsin—Yet," *Washington Post National Weekly*, 17–23 June 1996, 28; Blane Harden, "The Changing Value of Bob Dole's 'Word,'" *Washington Post National Weekly*, 4–10, November 1996, 12. Dole's resistance to fiscal demagoguery had led Harvey Mansfield to make him the example of "responsible

conservatism." *America's Constitutional Soul* (Baltimore: Johns Hopkins University Press, 1991), 79–80.

108. On Dole's "bridge" image, see Russell Baker, "Surely He Is Spoofing," *New York Times,* 20 August 1996, A19.

109. Hobart Rowen, "The Job Ahead," *Washington Post National Weekly,* 6–12 December 1993, 5; Elizabeth Kolbert and Adam Clymer, "The Politics of Layoffs: In Search of a Message," *New York Times,* 8 March 1996, A1; Richard Goodwin, "Has Anybody Seen the Democratic Party?" *New York Times Magazine,* 25 August 1996, 33–36.

110. Louis Uchitelle, "President's Theme: Layoffs Fall and Wages Rise," *New York Times,* 27 July 1996, 8; *New York Times,* 5 March 1996, A19.

111. David Sanger, "Dole's Tax Message Heard, Not Heeded in Midwest City," *New York Times,* 18 September 1996, A1; Kolbert and Clymer, "Politics of Layoffs," A22.

112. Bradsher, "America's Opportunity Gap."

113. Helen Dewar and David Broder, "Giving Democrats a Cents of Unity," *Washington Post National Weekly,* 29 April–5 May 1996, 14.

114. Alan Blinder, "The Republican Riverboat Gamble," *New York Times,* 20 August 1996, A19; David Sanger, "Dole's Tax Message;" Steven Weisman, "The Return of Voodoo Politics," *New York Times,* 23 August 1996, A26.

115. Rudy Teixeira, "A Democratic Revival," *Boston Review,* October/November 1995, 36.

116. Goodwin, "Has Anybody Seen the Democratic Party?"; Joel Garreau, "Candidates Take Note," *Washington Post National Weekly,* 10–16 August 1992, 25.

117. Kevin Phillips, "The Voters Are Already Tapping Their Feet," *Washington Post National Weekly,* 21–27 November 1994, 23.

118. Alison Mitchell, "Clinton, in Midwest, Takes Page from Reagan's 'Morning in America,' " *New York Times,* 18 September 1996, A18; Todd Purdom, "Advisers See Bright Side in Criticism of First Lady," *New York Times,* 25 August 1996, 1.

119. David Maraniss, "Bill Clinton, Born to Run," *Washington Post National Weekly,* 20–26 June 1992, 6–7.

120. Richard Ford, "The Master of Ambiguity," *New York Times,* 17 October 1996, A17.

121. Richard Cohen, "Character Issue Fatigue," *Washington Post National Weekly,* 4–10 November 1996, 28.

122. See my essay, "Losing—the Hard Way," *In These Times,* 10 June 1996, 22ff.

123. Harvey C. Mansfield Jr., *Machiavelli's Virtue* (Chicago: University of Chicago Press, 1996).

124. Dan Balz and David Broder, "The Clinton Republicans," *Washington Post National Weekly,* 14–20 October 1996, 11.

125. *The Federalist,* No. 63.

126. Herbert J. Storing, ed., *The Complete Anti-Federalist* (Chicago: University of Chicago Press, 1981), 2:111, 6:158.

127. Lowi, *End of the Republican Era;* Steven J. Rosenstone and John Mark Hansen, *Mobilization, Participation and Democracy in America* (New York: Macmillan, 1993), 218.

128. Kenneth N. Weine, "Campaigns without Human Faces," *Washington Post National Weekly,* 4–10 November 1996, 24; the privileged status of "soft money," of course, makes matters worse. Elizabeth Drew, "The 'Reform' That Corrupted The System," *Washington Post National Weekly,* 11–17 November 1996, 34.

129. Dan Balz, "In Control of His Own Fate," *Washington Post National Weekly,* 25–31 December 1995, 14; David Broder, "Not in Front of the Voters," *Washington Post National Weekly,* 14–20 October 1996, 10; *New York Times,* 6 March 1996, A1.

130. Henry E. Brady, Sidney Verba, and Kay Lehman Schlozman, "Beyond SES: A Resource Model of Political Participation," *American Political Science Review* 89 (1995): 271–94; James L. Hyland, *Democratic Theory: The Philosophical Foundations* (Manchester: Manchester University Press, 1995), 254, 264; Michael Wines, "Bradley's Exit Is Not Just the Democrats' Problem," *New York Times,* 20 August 1995, E1.

131. Thomas Byrne Edsall, *The New Politics of Inequality* (New York:Norton, 1984); Darrell M. West and Richard Francis, "Electronic Advocacy: Interest Groups and Public Policy Making," *PS* 29 (1996): 25–29; David Samuels, "Presidential Shrimp," *Harpers,* March 1996, 47.

132. 424 U.S. 1 (1976).

133. Drew, "The 'Reform' That Corrupted the System."

134. Cass R. Sunstein, *Democracy and the Problem of Free Speech* (New York: Free Press, 1993); John Rawls, *Political Liberalism* (Cambridge, Mass.: Harvard University Press, 1993), 362–63.

135. Bill Bradley, "Congress Won't Act. Will You?" *New York Times,* 11 November 1996, A15.

136. Putnam, "Tuning In, Tuning Out," 677–81; Samuel Popkin, *The Reasoning Voter* (Chicago: University of Chicago Press, 1991), 226–31.

137. Walter Ong, *Orality and Literacy: The Technologizing of the Word* (London: Methuen, 1982).

138. Walter Goodman, "What's Bad for Politics Is Good for Television," *New York Times,* 27 November 1994, 33.

139. Michael Beschloss, "Let's Have Conventions with Cliffhangers," *New York Times,* 11 August 1996, E13; James Bennet, "GOP Readies a Made-for-TV Convention," *New York Times,* 8 August 1996, A1.

140. R.W. Apple, "Fleeing the Ghost of 1992," *New York Times,* 13 August 1996, A1.

141. Frank Rich, "San Diego Unplugged," *New York Times,* 17 August 1996, 19; Richard Sandomir, "With So Little to Report, There's Little to Watch," *New York Times,* 16 August 1996, A28; Christopher Reeve's appearance at the Democratic convention inspired a mild dissent from the rule. E.J. Dionne Jr., "Non-Pols Deliver the Message," *San Francisco Chronicle,* 28 August 1996, A19.

142. Thomas Patterson, "Bad News, Period," *PS* 29 (1996): 17–20.

143. Thomas Patterson, *Out of Order* (New York: Knopf, 1993); Richard Morin, "Keeping Watch on the Pollsters," *Washington Post National Weekly,* 18–24 November 1996, 37.

144. Richard Morin, "Tuned Out, Turned Off," *Washington Post National Weekly,* 5–11 February 1996, 6–8.

145. Dukes, "When 'The System' Worked"; Bill Moyers, "Old News and the New Civil War," *New York Times,* 22 March 1992, E15; Robert Entman, *Democracy without Citizens: The Media and the Decay of American Democracy* (New York: Oxford University Press, 1989).

146. *New York Times,* 13 March 1996, B7.

147. *New York Times,* 10 November 1994, B4.

148. Burnham, "1996 Elections," 45, 49; Lowi, *End of the Republican Era;* David Broder, "Is the Party Over?" *Washington Post National Weekly,* 19–25 August 1996, 21–22.

149. E.J. Dionne Jr., *Why Americans Hate Politics* (New York: Simon and Schuster, 1991).

150. Robert J. Samuelson, "Mixed Messages," *Washington Post National Weekly,* 19–25 August 1996, 5; David Rosenbaum, "Republicans Like Both Previews and Reruns," *New York Times,* 11 November 1994, E1.

151. Lisa Schiffren points out the shortcomings of a post-Reagan GOP, but without acknowledging how difficult it would be to replace Reagan himself. "Nixon's GOP Will Always Be a Loser," *New York Times,* 9 November 1996, 23.

152. For example, see *New York Times,* 19 December 1995, A20.

153. *New York Times,* 13 August 1996, A16, and 15 August 1996, A1.

154. Advocates of abortion rights, the *Times* reported, were notably "subdued" in voting to sustain Clinton's veto. *New York Times,* 27 September 1996, A20. On late-campaign relations between Dole and social conservatives, see Gustav Niebuhr, "Dole Gets Christian Coalition's Trust and Prodding," *New York Times,* 16 September 1996, A1.

155. Dan Balz, "For the Republicans, Was It Half Empty or Half Full?" *Washington Post National Weekly,* 18–24 November 1996, 11; the Iowa state platform is reported in the Rutgers *Daily Targum,* 8 October 1996, 7. On the concept of "subnational realignment," see Peter F. Nardulli, "The Concept of Critical Realignment, Electoral Behavior and Political Change," *American Political Science Review* 89 (1995): 10–22.

156. David Broder, "Power to Both Parties," *Washington Post National Weekly,* 11–17 November 1996, 7–9.

157. Thomas Byrne Edsall, "But the Democrats Don't Seem to Get It Either," *Washington Post National Weekly,*18–24 November 1996, 11.

158. Tuchfarber and Rademacher, "Republican Tidal Wave of 1994."

159. James Bennet, "Liberal Use of 'Extremist' Is the Winning Strategy," *New York Times,* 7 November 1996, B1. In the 6 October presidential debate, President Clinton stopped just short of directly disclaiming liberalism — he disdained "labels" — but he clearly thought the term no advantage, as in his comment, regarding reductions in Medicare, "calling it conservative won't make it right." *New York Times,* 7 October 1996, B10.

160. William G. Mayer, *The Divided Democrats* (Boulder, Colo.: Westview, 1996); Thomas Byrne Edsall, "The Revolt of the Discontented," *Washington Post National Weekly,* 21–27 November 1994, 28; Joseph M. Schwartz, *The Permanence of the Political: A Democratic Critique of the Radical Impulse to Transcend Politics* (Princeton: Princeton University Press, 1995).

161. Thomas Byrne Edsall and Dan Balz, "United They Stand — For Now," *Washington Post National Weekly,* 2–8 September 1996, 10–11.

162. For example, see Mickey Kaus, *The End of Equality* (New York: Basic Books, 1992).

163. Mansfield, "Change and Bill Clinton."

164. Dionne, *They Only Look Dead.* This persuasion is anything but monolithic. For two very different voices, see Michael Lind, *Up from Conservatism* (New York: Free Press, 1996), and Joshua Cohen and Joel Rogers, "After Liberalism?" *Boston Review,* April/May 1995, 20–23.

165. Michael Kazin, "The Workers' Party?" *New York Times,* 19 October 1995, A21; Goodwin, "Has Anybody Seen the Democratic Party?"; Robert Kuttner, "Will Clinton Pay His Union Dues?" *Washington Post National Weekly,* 18–24 November 1996, 5.

166. Edsall and Balz, "United They Stand — For Now," 11; E.J. Dionne Jr., "Work, Kids and Families," *Washington Post National Weekly,* 30 September–6 October 1996, 29.

167. William Raspberry, "Less Heat, More Light," *Washington Post National Weekly,* 22–28 May 1995, 29; Wilson, *When Work Disappears;* Sam Roberts, "The Greening of America's Black Middle Class," *New York Times,* 18 June 1995, E1; Jennifer Hochschild, *Facing Up To The American Dream: Race, Class and the Soul of a Nation* (Princeton: Princeton University Press, 1995).

168. Kevin Sack, "Victory of 5 Redistricted Blacks Recasts Gerrymandering Dispute," *New York Times,* 23 November 1996, 1; Charles Cameron, David Epstein, and Sharyn O'Halloran, "Do Majority-Minority Districts Maximize Substantive Black Representation in Congress?" *American Political Science Review* 90 (1996): 794–812.

169. Mickey Kaus, "Revival of Liberalism"; Peter Passell, "Economic Scene," *New York Times,* 8 August 1996, D2; E.J. Dionne Jr., "In the Wake of a Bogus Bill," *Washington Post National Weekly,* 12–18 August 1996, 26.

170. Dionne, *They Only Look Dead.* Dionne is not alone; witness Michael Lind's reference to a "new nationalism," with its echoes of TR, in *The Next American Nation: The Nationalism and the Fourth American Revolution* (New York: Free Press, 1995).

171. Eldon J. Eisenach, *The Lost Promise of Progressivism* (Lawrence: University Press of Kansas, 1994).

172. See Philip Selznick's review of Rawls' *Political Liberalism in Society,* September/October 1994, 93; Hadley Arkes, *First Things: An Inquiry Into the First Principles of Morals and Justice* (Princeton: Princeton University Press, 1986).

173. As Todd Gitlin observes, "postmodern" theory actually illustrates this principle, since it characteristically "privileges" accounts from the victim's point of view, claims universality for the doctrine that all theories are only "standpoints," and hopes to *overcome* the cultural identities it often treats as impenetrable monads. ("Where We're Coming From: Blinded Identities," *The Good Society* 6 (1996): 24–27; see also Ronald Beiner, *What's The Matter With Liberalism* (Berkeley: University of California Press, 1992).

174. Sandel, "Search for a New Public Philosophy," 70.

Chapter 7: Beyond Disappointment? Exhaustion and Hope in the Elections of 1998

1. William Bennett, *The Death of Outrage: Bill Clinton and the Assault on American Ideals* (New York: Free Press, 1998).

2. Helen Dewar, "Doesn't Anybody Want to Be a Senator?" *Washington Post National Weekly,* 13 April, 1998, 13–14.
3. Maureen Dowd, "Pulp Nonfiction," *New York Times,* 13 September 1998, WK21.
4. This includes me: see my "Fallout from the Clinton Capers," *Commonweal,* 9 October 1998, 11–12.
5. Richard L. Berke, "Playing it Safe, Republicans Offer Silence," *New York Times,* 13 September 1998, 1.
6. Raymond Struther, "The Southern Surprise," *New York Times,* 5 November 1998, A29; this is especially notable given earlier signs of discontent with the Democrats among African-American voters. Terry Neal and Thomas B. Edsall, "The Summer of Black Democrats' Discontent," *Washington Post National Weekly,* 10 August 1998, 10. On Clinton and African Americans, see Don Wycliff, "One of Ours," *Commonweal,* 26 February 1999, 14–15.
7. Alan Wolfe, *One Nation After All* (New York: Viking, 1998). Richard Morin and David Broder, "Worried About Morals But Reluctant to Judge," *Washington Post National Weekly,* 21 September 1998, 10–11.
8. Gustav Niebuhr and Richard Berke, "Unity Is Elusive as Religious Right Ponders 2000 Vote," *New York Times,* 7 March 1999, 1.
9. Richard Morin, "Conventional Wisdom Got It Wrong Again," *Washington Post National Weekly,* 5 May 1997, 34.
10. Keith Bradsher, "At Town Meeting, Republicans Begin to Reshape Image," *New York Times,* 16 February 1999, A1.
11. *New York Times,* 5 November 1998, B4.
12. Ibid.; Steven R. Weisman, "A Democratic 'Ground War' Slips by the Radar," *New York Times,* 16 November 1998, A20.
13. E.J. Dionne Jr., "Bill's Other Problem," *Commonweal,* 20 June 1997, 8; Alison Mitchell, "Clinton's Way Isn't His Party's," *New York Times,* 23 November 1997, WK3; Robert Kuttner, "Collateral Damage of the Clinton Mess," *Berkshire Eagle,* 13 September 1998, A9.
14. John R. Zaller, "Monica Lewinsky's Contribution to Political Science," *PS* 31 (1998): 182–89.
15. *The Federalist,* No. 70; John Locke, *Second Treatise on Civil Government,* chap. XIV; see also Harvey C. Mansfield Jr., *Taming the Prince: the Ambivalence of Modern Executive Power* (New York: Free Press, 1989).
16. Alan Wolfe, "Oh, Those Beltway Innocents," *New York Times,* 30 August 1998, WK13.
17. Michael Sandel, *Democracy's Discontent: America in Search of a Political Philosophy* (Cambridge, Mass.: Harvard University Press, 1996), 12.
18. W. Lance Bennett, "The Uncivic Culture: Communications, Identity and the Rise of Lifestyle Politics," *PS* 31 (1998): 757; Mary Ann Glendon, *Rights Talk: The Impoverishment of Political Discourse* (New York: Basic Books, 1991).
19. Bennett, "Uncivic Culture," 745, 747; Benjamin Ginsberg and Martin Shefter, *Politics By Other Means* (New York: Basic Books, 1990).
20. *Newsweek,* 20 August 1998; John Harris, "What Clinton's Problems Have Cost Us," *Washington Post National Weekly,* 10 August 1998, 21.
21. Arthur Schlesinger Jr., *The Imperial Presidency* (Boston: Houghton Mifflin, 1973).
22. Dan Balz, "A Hard Line that May Trip GOP," *Washington Post National Weekly,* 1 February 1999, 12; Thomas B. Edsall, "Just the Tip of the Iceberg," *Washington Post National Weekly,* 15 February 1999, 12.
23. Edward Luttwak, *Turbo-Capitalism: Winners and Losers in the Global Economy* (New York: HarperCollins, 1999).
24. Robert Putnam, "Bowling Alone: America's Declining Social Capital," *Journal of Democracy* 6 (1995): 65–78; Samuel Bowles and Herbert Gintis, "Is Equality Passé?" *Boston Review,* December 1998–January 1999, 7–8.
25. The *Washington Post National Weekly* paired articles under the title, "The New Bleeding Hearts of American Politics," E.J. Dionne Jr. writing "The Prospect Is Enough to Make a Liberal's Day," and David Brooks, of the conservative *Weekly Standard,* referring to a "Decade of Higher Things" in an essay titled, " 'Compassionate' Conservatives:

Can They Reinvent the Right?" 24 February 1997, 22–23. On Marx, see Paul Lewis, "Marx's Stock Rises on a 150-Year Tip," *New York Times,* 27 June 1998, B9.

26. Louis Uchitelle, "The Middle Class: Winning in Politics, Losing in Life," *New York Times,* 19 July 1998, WK1; William Finnegan, "Prosperous Times, Except for the Young," *New York Times,* 12 June 1998, A21.

27. Todd S. Purdom, "Suburban 'Sprawl' Takes Its Place on the Political Landscape," *New York Times,* 6 February 1999, A1.

28. Kristin Downey Grimsley, "Leaner and Definitely Meaner," *Washington Post National Weekly,* 20–27 July 1998, 21.

29. Barry Bluestone and Stephen Rose, "Overworked and Underemployed," *American Prospect,* March/April 1997, 59, 60, 67.

30. Theodore J. Lowi, "Think Globally, Lose Locally," *Boston Review,* April/May 1998, 10; Bennett, "Uncivic Culture," 751.

31. David Broder and Dan Balz, "Who Wins?" *Washington Post National Weekly,* 15 February 1999, 7.

32. Bennett, "Uncivic Culture," 758.

33. Ronald Inglehart, *Modernization and Postmodernization* (Princeton: Princeton University Press, 1997), 295–323.

34. Kathleen Sullivan, "Madison Got It Backward," *New York Times,* 16 February 1999, A19.

35. G.K. Chesterton, *What I Saw in America* (New York: Dodd, Mead, 1922), 16.

36. Alan Wolfe, "America Flunks Civics," *New York Times,* 25 December 1998, A33.

Index

About the Author

WILSON CAREY MCWILLIAMS was born in California and grew up talking politics; his father was Carey McWilliams, the premier analyst of California politics and the long-time editor of *The Nation*.

He attended the University of California, Berkeley, where he received his Ph.D. in political science. He has taught at Oberlin College and Brooklyn College and, since 1970, has been professor of political science at Rutgers University, specializing in American politics and political thought, as well as religion and politics.

His writings include *The Idea of Fraternity in America,* which won the National Historical Society prize in 1973; in addition, he is a frequent contributor to *Commonweal* and other journals of opinion.

He has served as secretary and vice-president of the American Political Science Association and received the John Witherspoon Award for distinguished service to the humanities.